Wiki Writing

DIGITaLCULTUreBOOKS
is an imprint of the University of Michigan Press and
the Scholarly Publishing Office of the University of Michigan Library
dedicated to publishing innovative and accessible work exploring new media
and its impact on society, culture, and scholarly communication.

WIKI WRITING

Collaborative Learning in the College Classroom

Edited by Robert E. Cummings and Matt Barton

THE UNIVERSITY OF MICHIGAN PRESS AND
THE UNIVERSITY OF MICHIGAN LIBRARY • ANN ARBOR

Published in the United States of America by
The University of Michigan Press and
The University of Michigan Library
Manufactured in the United States of America
⊗ Printed on acid-free paper

2011   2010   2009   2008   4   3   2   1

A CIP catalog record for this book is available from the British Library.

Library of Congress Cataloging-in-Publication Data

Wiki writing : collaborative learning in the college classroom /
edited by Robert E. Cummings and Matt Barton.
       p.   cm.
   Includes bibliographical references and index.
   ISBN-13: 978-0-472-11671-3 (cloth : alk. paper)
   ISBN-10: 0-472-11671-1 (cloth : alk. paper)
     1. English language—Rhetoric—Study and teaching (Higher)
2. Academic writing—Study and teaching (Higher)   3. Internet
publishing.   4. User-generated content.   I. Cummings, Robert E.,
1967–   II. Barton, Matt.
PE1404.W533   2008
808′.0420711—dc22   2008032084

for ECS —R E C

for Elizabeth Barton —M D B

Preface

*W*iki *Writing: Collaborative Learning in the College Classroom* is, as the title suggests, an exploration by teachers in higher education of the online writing spaces called wikis. How do wikis change student writing and collaboration? The answer lies in the way they structurally invite collaboration and yet tolerate dissension. Wikis are not blogs or Web spaces where one user writes and all others read. Similarly, wikis are not forums or messaging boards where users post multiple statements in a hierarchical chain. Because wikis allow all readers to write (typically—there are important exceptions), but write the same document, they provide a unique Web space where differing opinions are expressed, explored, and, yes, sometimes eviscerated, but gradually moved toward consensus. If wikis do not foster complete consensus, they facilitate a defined disagreement. But as these spaces create communities of inquiry around topics, they facilitate a gradual move toward a more singular comprehension of the state of knowledge for that community topic. The content on wikis will differ greatly from one community to the next. But it is the underlying commonality of that shared site space, the wiki itself, that moves users from complete divergence of opinion toward often greater understanding through dialogue.

Wikis—and specifically the clashes surrounding that most famous wiki, Wikipedia—have evoked what some might term "intellectual lawlessness." As wikis emphasize diversity of expression on a massive scale, creativity and originality erupt in spaces beyond official endorsement or review. Similarly, fraud, character assassination, hoax, and simple hyperbole thrive in this uneven landscape. For a Web that seemed to promise so much in terms of diversity of points of view in the late 1990s, too much territory has been worn bare with familiar paths. Wikis represent a proximal negotiation between community and individual on the Web: a way for the individual (one) to work in dialogue with a community of inquiry (one) dedicated to a particular topic or mode of inquiry.

Wikis are often simplistically described as Web sites that anyone can edit and seem to many people to represent nothing but textual chaos. As Robert E. Cummings explores more fully in his introductory essay to this volume, there is a difference to appreciate between wikis generally and Wikipedia singularly. But a glance through that most famous wiki, Wikipedia, would reveal tens of thousands of entries that are well written, lavishly researched, and probably more up-to-date than any printed encyclopedia. Whenever Wikipedia is mentioned in the popular press, however, it is almost always in conjunction with some abuse of the system or scandal, such as when a politician or CEO is discovered to be creating or "spinning" his or her own pages.

Meanwhile, flocks of zealots settle down on controversial pages and exercise brute force in an effort to keep "their" pages biased in their favor. Concerned scholars, scientists, and educators make "corrections" to pages that are later overturned, while other contributions are rejected for being "original research." Shouldn't there be some kind of system in place to privilege contributions from "experts"?

Many of the most successful wiki communities emulate an encyclopedia format. One of the better-known examples of these is Wikitravel, an "open source travel guide." As of this writing, users have contributed 16,313 "destination guides" and articles of interest to world travelers. Another well-populated wiki community is Memory Alpha, a wiki dedicated to all things *Star Trek*. That project currently boasts 25,953 articles. We also find businesses turning to wikis to collaborate with customers in building help sites and guides for their products or services. Companies that have jumped on the wiki bandwagon include Amazon, eBay, Intel, and Symantec.

Amazon's project is called Amapedia, which encourages users to write about their favorite products. The articles typically describe the product in question, list similar items, and place the item in a network of related content (such as larger categories or genres). The Amapedia is integrated with Amazon's product database, so an article titled "Real-Time Strategy Games" may include dozens (if not hundreds) of links to other such games sold at Amazon. The idea seems to be that customers will buy more products if they are better informed.

eBay uses wikis to help its customers understand online auctions. A good example is a page called For Buyers: Protecting Yourself Against Fraud. The page appears to be authored by individuals who have firsthand experience with criminal activity on the popular online auction site. The Intel Software Network wiki is intended for users who want to share their hands-on knowledge about Intel's products with other professionals. Symantec uses wikis internally to help its employees "track ideas and collaborate." A company named QAD, which provides enterprise software to large manufacturing companies, uses wikis to facilitate the sales proposal process. QAD's customers work with the company to collaborate on proposals, speeding up the process "from up to a month to just days" and providing much more satisfying service.

Wikis have also attracted the interest of many professional educators all over the world. These educators not only are motivated to analyze wikis from a theoretical perspective but also want to understand how and why their students should invest in them. What can writing in a wiki teach students about the composition process? What kind of rhetoric is needed to successfully enter and actively participate in a wiki community? What are the different stages of collaboration, and how do they foster course outcomes? And, on a more pragmatic level, what kind of wiki-related writing assignments will truly benefit students? If wikis are good for anything in a writing classroom, it is their ability to open up issues that may have seemed hopelessly abstract before. Postmodern theory has, for example, been waxing on for decades about how we should question our Romantic notions of authors and authority. Wikis demonstrate the problem quite concretely by conflating the roles of author and audience. Likewise, what were once puzzling and baffling discussions about the role of expertise in knowledge production, such as how much we should privilege expert or "official" knowledge over "the wisdom of crowds," are now vivid and concrete, immediately accessible. Some dream of daily newspapers published as citizen wikis; there is even an effort to build virtual universities in wikis, and plenty of professors have worked together to create free college "wikitexts." Even if these projects ultimately fail, the social, cultural, and technological milieu that led to their existence is a rich and fertile ground for scholars. Far more than some new "hip" technology, the wiki phenomenon promises to provide fundamental and important insights into the nature of knowledge production itself.

Thus while the essays in this collection explore the wiki phenomenon from a variety of perspectives, this collection is mainly concerned with helping students, teachers, administrators, and other stakeholders in higher education understand the potential for wikis in the college classroom. The essays are grouped into three main sections, based on how their authors have envisioned their audiences: Wikis and the Scholarship of Teaching and Learning; Wikis in Composition and Communication Classrooms; and, most generally, Wikis and the Higher Education Classroom. In all cases, the writers explore approaches to using wikis in the classroom that reveal their strengths and weaknesses, not only conveying to readers how wikis might apply to their college classroom but also gesturing toward the potential of these platforms.

In the introductory essay, coeditor Robert E. Cummings provides a brief historical introduction for readers who might want more background on wikis. Much of the essay traces the cultural history of Wikipedia, but the main theme is epistemology and concerns the extent to which wikis have permanently shifted how we create and evaluate knowledge. Cummings develops this epistemological narrative by tracing the evolution of popular awareness of wikis, as it is reflected primarily in a series of controversies about Wikipedia, including the various charges of inaccuracy by editors of print encyclopedias, the *Nature* study comparing Wikipedia's accuracy to other online journals, and Stephen Colbert's satire of Wikipedia's impact on popular culture. Cummings concludes by noting that, while the impact of wikis seems to be widely appreciated, their long-term effects on productivity, knowledge creation, and authority are in need of serious and sustained study. Cummings's introduction is followed by a cluster of four collaboratively authored essays focused on wikis and the scholarship of teaching and learning.

Mark Phillipson of the Columbia Center for New Media Teaching and Learning (CCNMTL) gives readers a very useful taxonomy of the different wikis in "Wikis in the Classroom: A Taxonomy." Phillipson surveys a broad number of wiki projects and provides an intellectual template to help readers assess what these varied sites can accomplish. He reminds us that, although Wikipedia is likely the first wiki that springs to mind when thinking about their potential classroom use, it is not necessarily the most apt. The truly collaborative nature of this software tool becomes most apparent when a wiki is designed specifically for the course in question. Surveying many different college-level classroom wikis, Phillipson identifies a series of wiki genres—the resource wiki, the presentation wiki, the gateway wiki, the simulation wiki, and the illuminated wiki—and, by describing the key qualities and processes of each, provides readers with a useful entry point for understanding the wide variety of wikis available today.

One exemplary project featured in Phillipson's wiki tour is the Social Justice Movements wiki at Columbia University, which was developed in the course of Robin D. G. Kelley. In "Wiki Justice, Social Ergonomics, and Ethical Collaborations," Jonah Bossewitch, John Frankfurt, and Alexander Sherman, also of CCNMTL, explain how they developed this wiki to transform a traditional teaching space into a unique and active community. Kelley's undergraduate course Black Movements in the U.S. provides a rich collaborative platform for students who desire to collaborate on social justice projects but heretofore lacked the tools for doing so. Going one step further, the team also entertains the question, What is the point of a wiki?—looking to other landmark collaborative efforts in intellectual history, such as Diderot's *Encyclopédie* and the *Oxford English Dictionary*, as analytic tools. This essay completes the circle between a technology design team and teacher with a statement by Kelley on teaching with the wiki.

Meanwhile, across the country, another team of academic researchers at the Stanford Center for Innovations in Learning (SCIL) and Stanford's Center for Teaching and Learning (CTL) was also exploring the questions of how best to apply wikis in the classroom. In "Building Learning Communities with Wikis," Dan Gilbert, Helen L. Chen, and Jeremy Sabol collaborate to explore and document the different stages in which learning communities evolve as a result of their deployment of wiki technology in the classroom. The highest form of engagement they identify, learning communities, proves to be an elusive but rewarding level of interaction, and the essay lays out strategies for moving students from one stage of engagement to the next by using a novel yet insightful diagram inspired by the children's board game "Chutes and Ladders." The SCIL team's essay brings a wealth of teaching knowledge to bear on wikis, detailing the strengths and weaknesses of differing software platforms in multiple undergraduate classes.

In "Success through Simplicity: On Developmental Writing and Communities of Inquiry," two communications professors, John W. Maxwell and Michael Felczak, both of Simon Fraser University, recount their experience of teaching large undergraduate courses using wikis. They too focus on the concept of establishing communities of inquiry among students. For their part, they find wikis to live up to Ward Cunningham's call for "the simplest thing that would work."

"Disrupting Intellectual Property: Collaboration and Resistance in Wikis" shifts our focus toward the practices of composition and rhetoric. Authors Stephanie Vie and Jennifer deWinter are teachers of writing, and their examination of wiki writing is well grounded in theories of collaborative authoring (including the work of Kenneth Bruffee) and explores materialist questions of textual property and ownership. Wikis certainly do challenge the traditional notion of the author in question, and Vie and deWinter clarify this challenge by exploring the currency of intellectual property in the university setting. They write that as teachers "we advocate research and teaching practices that highlight multivocality such as citing sources, building upon prior knowledge in the field, and echoing the familiar terms of a discourse community." At the same time, Vie and deWinter point out that, while collaboration is a familiar concept, sites of practice are rare and the value of wikis consists in their ability to provide such a site.

Continuing in the composition classroom, in "Agency and Accountability: The Paradoxes of Wiki Discourse," D. A. Caeton writes of his experience teaching writing with Wikipedia. Caeton is certainly not the only teacher in this collection to focus on this topic. What makes Caeton's experience unique, however, is the lens of his student Emina, who migrated to California from Bosnia. Caeton's essay details how the impassioned exchanges of this student on Wikipedia over the definition of "Bosniak" led her to both a fuller and more personal understanding of theories of rhetoric than he could have ever planned for as an instructor.

The next essay also focuses on the student experience with wikis but in the communication classroom. David Elfving and Ericka Menchen-Trevino explore the learner perspective in "One Wiki, Two Classrooms." The authors recount the experience of communication graduate students at the University of Illinois-Chicago who decided to collaborate to attack the mountain of reading that they had been assigned in two graduate seminars. The wiki proved a great tool for one class but was not well used in another. The authors tell us why and in so doing discover some of the barometers of a healthy wiki community.

Will Lakeman's "Content and Commentary: Parallel Structures of Organization and Interaction on Wikis" investigates the question of how wikis allow authors to shape and access content effectively. In many ways, Lakeman's essay picks up where the work of the wiki creator, Ward Cunningham, leaves off. Cunningham created the wiki to enable electronic mailing list writers to store and access older content. Lakeman's theoretically grounded essay explores how wikis can facilitate this access, as well as what happens to our theoretical understanding of authorship in the process. Lakeman encourages us to view content on wiki discussion pages and wiki pages themselves not as diametrically opposed to each other but rather as parallel forms of interaction.

The last essay in the section dedicated to the use of wikis in the composition and communication classroom imports the computer programming concept of refactoring to better map and explain the necessary work flow of wiki documents to uninitiated students. In "Above and Below the Double Line: Refactoring and That Old-Time Revision," Michael C. Morgan blends coding practice with composition theory to reinforce the importance of revision for student writing and, naturally, to explain how wikis can facilitate such a process. Exploring the inevitable overlap of the coding community and the writing community that wikis portend, Morgan writes, "Refactoring is a kind of revision, but where composition and rhetoric types tend to see revision changing and developing meaning, refactoring attempts to preserve meaning. . . . Refactoring is synthesis."

The next essay begins the third section of the collection, which focuses on the effect of wikis on the higher education classroom. In "Is There a Wiki in This Class? Wikibooks and the Future of Higher Education," coeditor Matt Barton is concerned with two main tasks. First, he describes what kind of class assignments work well for wikis (and which ones do not), and, second, he discusses the value that good wiki assignments bring to the university and beyond. His main contention is that wikis have a strong civic or service-learning potential that tends to get overlooked (and compromised) by well-meaning instructors improperly integrating wikis into their classroom. Barton is not apologetic about advancing his agenda: he believes in the civic values and virtues of wikis and encourages teachers to allow those concerns to trump any misgivings about "security" and "ownership" when introducing wikis to students.

In examining the challenges of incorporating wikis in the classroom,

Thomas J. Nelson pays special attention to how their collaborative nature reveals to students a truer, more complex understanding of the nature of knowledge production. In "Writing in the Wikishop: Constructing Knowledge in the Electronic Classroom," Nelson posits that some of the typical problems teachers face in incorporating collaborative work into the classroom—particularly the difficult issue of assessing collaborative work—can serve as learning opportunities about how we make meaning collectively.

"Wiki Lore and Politics in the Classroom" is contributed by Cathlena Martin and Lisa Dusenberry, both of the University of Florida. These teachers frame their essay by examining questions salient to all teachers who might consider the adoption of a wiki in the classroom: "Does a wiki truly provide a common, collaborative space where students can be creative and address the theoretical concerns of a college classroom? How do students accept and use their public, online writing space? Do wikis provide the same type of online voice as blogs? Is using a wiki for compositional writing seen by students as a subversive or marginal writing space? Does the writing medium of a wiki place an informal, creative bent on academic writing for a college class? Is a wiki only appropriate in a class dealing with popular media?" To find an answer, these teachers begin by exploring the analogy comparing a University of Florida community graffiti wall to the electronic space of a wiki. They record and examine students' perceptions of a wiki, enumerate specific wiki writing assignments, and examine how students handled potentially divisive collaborative editing issues. And since they worked with wikis in different courses, the authors also examine where, in a curricular sense, wikis make the most pedagogical sense.

In "GlossaTechnologia: Anatomy of a Wiki-Based Annotated Bibliography," author Ben McCorkle recounts his aims, goals, and experiences in conceiving a new wiki project. McCorkle envisions the wiki as the ultimate electronic tool for the bibliography, combining the ability to correlate the opinions of multiple readers in an ever-present, ever-updated metabook. McCorkle gives an honest account of his attempts to establish GlossaTechnologia, detailing both its successes and failures.

Our last offering is, in many ways, our most refreshing voice and the vision of our greatest pragmatist. Bob Whipple's "An (Old) First-Timer's Learning Curve: Curiosity, Trial, Resistance, and Accommodation" is very much a teacher's missive to fellow teachers. Whipple's voice is lighthearted but provides a very practical guide for teachers who might want to employ wikis in their classrooms for the first time.

While this collection seeks to provide readers with a comprehensive overview of the emerging phenomenon of wikis and how to engage with them, it also represents a very self-conscious effort. All authors who write about technology—especially those who write books about technology—remain acutely aware that their subject is evolving even as they write. Nevertheless, the essays in this collection remain convinced of several principles. First, though we recognize that the wiki platform has been accused of destroying authorial integrity and textual authority, we believe that the advent of this technology in fact provides a valuable service by inviting us to understand how these concepts are fundamentally connected. Too often, authorial reputation has been misappropriated by the medium—book, periodical, or paper—rather than by the reputation of the author or even the worth of the text itself. By collapsing the distinction between author and audience in new and concrete ways, wikis provide the opportunity to reassess the value not of author and authority but of our application thereof.

As the conflicts surrounding Wikipedia have shown, the arrival of wikis has revealed perhaps another lazy habit of mind. Whenever a new concept arrives, we must metaphorically map an existing concept onto a new phenomenon; in the case of Wikipedia, we continue to look for The World Book but are surprised when it violates that template. Until we have enough practice of seeing the wiki for what it is and applying the tool based on its known strengths and weaknesses, false controversies will continue to flare up. This volume hopes to usher along that process of seeing the wiki for what it is—and for what it is not.

Acknowledgments

We would like to thank Mark Phillipson, Jonah Bossewitch, John Frankfurt, Alexander Sherman, Robin D. G. Kelley, Stephanie Vie, Jennifer deWinter, Dan Gilbert, Helen L. Chen, Jeremy Sabol, Will Lakeman, D. A. Caeton, David Elfving, Ericka Menchen-Trevino, Cathlena Martin, Lisa Dusenberry, Bob Whipple, Michael C. Morgan, John W. Maxwell, Michael Felczak, Thomas J. Nelson, and Ben McCorkle for their excellent contributions to this volume. We would also like to thank our editor, Alison MacKeen, and her assistant, Christy Byks-Jazayeri, for shepherding us through this process and refusing to quit on us, even after we steadily—without faltering—blew through innumerable deadlines. We give thanks as well to two anonymous reviewers from the computers and writing community who crafted honest and critical feedback that greatly strengthened this collection.

Robert E. Cummings thanks Christy Desmet, Nelson Hilton, Ron Balthazor, Charlie Lowe, and Steve Ramsay, as well as the entire computers and writing community for their perpetual interest in this topic and the dedication to expand it into its fullest iteration. He also gives special thanks to Cindy Selfe for yielding immediate guidance at a critical juncture for this project.

Matt Barton would like to thank Joseph Moxley of the University of South Florida, who first introduced him to wikis and all that computers have to offer the teaching of composition.

Contents

What Was a Wiki, and Why Do I Care?
A Short and Usable History of Wikis

The meeting occurred on October 7, 2006. On a Milledgeville, Georgia, campus, the new leader of the university system of the ninth largest state in the nation met with a potentially fractious body, Georgia's chapter of the American Association of University Professors (AAUP).[1] This educators' union has a reputation for confronting administrators, and while the new chancellor had been on an eight-month tour of the state's thirty-five campuses, he was only then addressing the thorny issues advanced by this academic crowd.

The toughest issue on the agenda was labeled as "shared governance." But, in reality, the power shift at hand was typical of the now familiar conflict between traditional hierarchical power structures and flatter, more cooperative power structures popularized by Manuel Castells.[2] The new chancellor had a business background, which would seem to identify him squarely with a hierarchical power structure. Yet these university professors had, over time, improved their position of power sharing by increasing both their access to and their responsibility for decision making on the state's campuses. The teachers in that room clearly felt that students, parents, teachers, and taxpayers benefited from a university system that sought input from all ranks before making decisions on planning and budgeting. But the chancellor's stance sounded more like a power entrenchment in his office rather than power sharing among the faculty as a whole.

> I recognize that in higher education, there exists a very well-established culture of shared governance, and you of course recognize I did not grow up within that culture. . . . I do believe in that well-worn adage that when every one is responsible no one is responsible.[3]

While the chancellor amicably characterized responsible leadership as attentive to broad input, he clearly envisioned a hierarchical power structure for the state's body of creating and disseminating original knowledge.[4] If anyone in the audience found these remarks anachronistic or ill-informed, no such response was indicated in the AAUP newsletter that reported on the chancellor's speech. Before the advent of the wiki, or, more specifically, Wikipedia, these comments, and this meeting, would have been routine.

But Wikipedia has made it clear that the business of knowledge creation has been irrevocably altered. Before Wikipedia, the act of creating and disseminating reliable knowledge was entrusted largely to those holding advanced degrees and offering statements that were vetted by the same crowd. Wikipedia has clearly demonstrated, however, that knowledge can be created and disseminated by people who may or may not be credentialed, who contribute as little or as much as they like, who do not need to wait for approval or other works, and who are motivated by something more elusive than cash. No, the statements in Wikipedia are not always reliable. But as the *Nature* study has shown, they cannot simply be dismissed as unreliable either.[5] Wikipedia has fundamentally and finally altered epistemology itself—our commonly held ideas about knowledge. For the academy at large, the significance of Wikipedia is roughly equivalent to that which the Heisenberg uncertainty principle had in the sciences in the 1920s—stating what is not possible rather than what is. It is no longer possible to plan, tax, and budget for universities as if their model of knowledge creation is the only epistemological path. No matter how improbable it might seem that a Web page that anyone can edit would lead to valuable knowledge, Wikipedia makes clear that there is now another model for knowledge creation. And it also recasts the comments of the diplomatic chancellor in a supremely ironic light: here is the leader of a massive state system for knowledge creation stating that "when every one is responsible no one is responsible," while he, and certainly everyone in that audience, has probably relied upon a knowledge acquisition path—from Google to Wikipedia—for which everyone is responsible and no one is responsible at once.

But bureaucratic inertia in the face of a tectonic knowledge shift is not the focus of this essay. Rather, this introduction hopes to show nonbelievers, the uninitiated, and wiki followers alike that the simple act of allowing a Web page to be edited by a reader—which is really all that a wiki does—has created a global transition to networked epistemology that affects most anyone who is concerned with knowledge acquisition, whether it is defined broadly, as the search for teleological ends, or narrowly, as the search for Chinese takeout. I want to introduce this collection, then, by providing interested readers a brief history of the wiki and a bit of thought on what it portends for knowledge creation and acquisition.

Wiki, or Wikipedia?

Your author *(approaching an acquisitions editor at a book fair)*: Hi. I'm wondering if I can share a manuscript proposal with you.
Well-meaning acquisitions editor: Sure. What's the book about?
Your author: Wikis!
Well-meaning acquisitions editor: Oh. We don't do books on the occult. But if you want, I can give you some ideas on where to look.
Your author: The occult? No. Wait—I didn't say "Wiccans," I said "Wikis."
Well-meaning acquisitions editor: What's a "wikis"?
Your author: No, "wiki"—singular. Well, it's a Web page. Which anyone can edit. Usually, but not all the time. I mean, it's an electronic mailing list with memory. It's really a collaborative Web space where the mechanics of epistemology and the politics of knowledge creation can be revealed and explored.
Puzzled acquisitions editor:
(silence)
Your author: You ever heard of Wikipedia?
Well-meaning acquisitions editor: Oh! Wikis!

Understanding the history of the wiki is inextricably bound up with Wikipedia. This is simply due to the fact that it is clearly the largest wiki with the greatest cultural impact. In fact, probably only a handful of users beyond the initial group of programmers who created the first wiki had their first encounter with a wiki *other* than Wikipedia.

But there are significant problems with conflation of all wikis with Wikipedia generally. As we explore the short history of wikis, it is important to examine three key ways in which Wikipedia differs from other wikis. First, Wikipedia is an online encyclopedia (or at least it claims the encyclopedia as a model—it diverges from those expectations in some significant ways). Other wikis may or may not adopt the model of an encyclopedia for deciding what should or should not be posted.

Second, Wikipedia started as an open wiki, meaning that anyone who visited the Web page could edit the content. As time passed, it limited its access, but it remains substantially open. And third, and most important, Wikipedia should be acknowledged as much a knowledge creation methodology as a wiki. Plenty of people rely on Wikipedia for timely and knowledgeable references to millions of topics; others eschew it for its lack of editorial control. Other wikis, with a more clearly defined topic, might behave much differently once reaching the number of articles Wikipedia has achieved—or once becoming a large database. But once a wiki grows as large as Wikipedia, it assumes multiple roles. Thus Wikipedia is not only a reference source, but it is the acknowledged site on the Web for claiming an interpretation of knowledge, as well as a place for controlling public image on an important figure. Both of these functions are substantial and substantially beyond the scope of a traditional encyclopedia.

As we go forward exploring wiki history, it is critical to always understand ways in which other wikis might differ from Wikipedia. But that important exception does not diminish the fact that in order to understand the historical impact of wikis on our culture, and the potential impact on the future, one must begin by reviewing the vanguard of wikis in popular consciousness, Wikipedia.

Origins

The wiki had a coming out party, a debutant ball in large, popular, old media outlets, in the fall of 2004. Multiple mainstream publications including *Time*, *Business Week*, *Newsweek*, and *PC Magazine* introduced this "new" technology to their readers with articles bearing titles such as "What's a Wiki?" "It's Like a Blog, But It's a Wiki," and "Something Wiki This Way Comes."[6] For most writers, the story was Wikipedia. After all, the idea of an online encyclopedia that anyone could edit was quite a novelty. Initial reviews compared the wiki to the blog and generally listed it as the official "next big thing on the Internet" (only to be replaced by Web 2.0 months later). But the more technical analyses acknowledged that there was a difference between a "wiki" and "Wikipedia" and focused on the platform that permitted collaborative authoring, tracing its roots to the software programmer Ward Cunningham rather than focusing strictly on Jimmy Wales and Wikipedia.

The technical definition of a wiki is, surprisingly, the easiest to understand. A wiki is a Web page that users can modify. The earliest known wiki, the WikiWikiWeb project, was envisioned essentially as a software development tool. On May 1, 1995, Ward Cunningham posted a note to the "Patterns" electronic mailing list. Patterns is an e-mail list of software developers gathered under the moniker "the Hillside Group" to "build on Erich Gamma's foundation work studying object-oriented patterns, to use patterns in a generative way in the sense that Christopher Alexander uses patterns for urban planning and building architecture."[7]

Cunningham had developed a database to collect the contributions of the e-mail list members. He had noticed that the content of the electronic mailing list tended to get buried, and therefore the most recent post might be underinformed about posts that came before it. The way around this problem was to collect ideas in a database and then edit those ideas rather than begin anew with each e-mail list posting. Cunningham's post states, "The plan is to have interested parties write web pages about the People, Projects and Patterns that have changed the way they program. Short stories that hint at patterns are welcome too." As to the rhetorical expectations, Cunningham added, "The writing style is casual, like email or netnews, but doesn't have to be so repetitive since the things being discussed don't disappear. Think of it as a moderated list where anyone can be moderator and everything is archived. It's not quite a chat, still, conversation is possible."[8] Torn down to its basic terms, then, the wiki is a software piece that combines the contemporaneous focus of an electronic mailing list with the data storage capabilities of a database. It's an e-mail list with a memory.

But it is equally important to remember the context of the wiki's origin—as a tool for software development. Discussions on an electronic mailing list in an applied sciences community would operate under fundamentally different rhetorical constraints than an open-source encyclopedia such as Wikipedia. As it was originally conceived, readers of the first wiki would share a common goal of producing a verifiable product, a working piece of software. Therefore, both its audience and its writers would have a shared lexicon; shared worldview; and, most important, shared means of verifying truth—the software product. The end goal of a wiki conversation could be confirmed or discredited by the results of a software project. Either the resulting software worked as intended, or it didn't. This is not to say that all discussions on Cunningham's wiki were either practical or even related to software development. Surely many conversations were open-ended or even off-topic. But the important fact remains that these software developers formed a rhetorical discourse community—or a community that defines meaning through the context of shared values—and provided themselves with a means of verifying or discrediting the contents of the wiki.

Compare that situation with the controversy surrounding Wikipedia. Wikipedia works because of the massive scale of the Internet; there are simply so many users that articles can be destroyed and reconstructed overnight because enough readers on any given topic are invested in the discussion. These readers/contributors can be the "wikizens," or frequent contributors to Wikipedia who share a set of protocols for contributions, or casual visitors. Thus this rhetorical discourse community is radically different from the Patterns group that created the wiki precisely because the Wikipedia community has no shared assumptions on defining and verifying truth. Viewed from a mechanical perspective, then, trouble comes when the perpetually posted content of the wiki, or its e-mail list behavior, is measured against its own database. The basis of many critics' complaints with Wikipedia lies in the fact that they view the project against the ideal of a singular, verifiable truth, while Wikipedia envisions itself as a project wide enough to host competing truths.

Nupedia to Wikipedia

Although Cunningham developed the first wiki in 1995, it was not until 2000 that an erstwhile options trader named Jimmy Wales began a project entitled Nupedia. Nupedia was to have been an Internet encyclopedia that followed the traditional model of peer review to create encyclopedia articles. It lasted from March 2000 until September 2003, completing only twenty-four articles.[9] Wales then reversed course and created the completely open Wikipedia, placing it on wiki software and allowing anyone to edit articles.

The well-documented growth of the encyclopedia has been phenomenal. During its first year of operation articles were created at the rate of fifteen hundred per month, jump-started in part due to references on the popular Web site Slashdot.org.[10] The encyclopedia quickly expanded to include articles in other languages. Near the time of composing this essay, the English language version contained 1.5 million articles.[11] The basic ideas of how Wikipedia operates, and how it has grown, while novel, are fairly well documented. What is significant in the shift from Nupedia to Wikipedia is its epistemological impact: the move represented not only a change in software platforms but, more important, a change in terms of knowledge development. Ideas in this online encyclopedia were no longer to be peer-reviewed by authorized sources. The jobs of topic selection, content development, review for relevance, and review for accuracy now fell to anyone who would take up the task. The trade-off was obvious: knowledge could be produced rapidly, with much greater responsiveness, with much greater agility, and eventually with a much more comprehensive focus. But could this knowledge be trusted?

The most compelling way to measure the cultural influence of wikis may be through the history of Wikipedia conflicts about knowledge production. I suggest in what follows that there are five major stages in the cultural history of Wikipedia: the Robert McHenry article, the *Nature* study, the Seigenthaler incident, Colbert's truthiness, and the advent of Wikia. Each stage evidences a new aspect in the central question over Wikipedia: namely, can its knowledge be trusted?

The Robert McHenry Article

In 2004 Robert McHenry, former editor in chief of *Encyclopedia Britannica*, brought forth the most infamous and apt criticism against wikis to date. In "The Faith-Based Encyclopedia," McHenry defines Wikipedia as a Web site where

> Anyone, irrespective of expertise in or even familiarity with the topic, can submit an article and it will be published. . . . Anyone, irrespective of expertise in or even familiarity with the topic, can edit that article, and the

modifications will stand until further modified. Then comes the entirely
faith-based step: . . . some unspecified quasi-Darwinian process will as-
sure that those writings and editings by contributors of greatest expertise will survive; articles will eventually reach a steady state that corre-
sponds to the highest degree of accuracy.[12]

With McHenry's heavily nuanced language, a reader entirely unfamiliar with
the idea of a wiki would get the impression that Wikipedia is a Web site mired
in some underdeveloped nineteenth-century ontological conflict between
Darwinian science and religious fundamentalism, a sort of online Scopes
Monkey Trial anachronistically returning scholarship to a crisis of intentionality. Repeated phrases such as "irrespective of expertise" leave no doubt in
readers' minds that McHenry values comments from credentialed authors
over the insights of those without demonstrated and accepted authority. This
is not to say that McHenry fails to appreciate the striking sweep of the
changes to scholarship and reference tools both achieved and foreshadowed
by the exponential growth of Wikipedia, perhaps the most successful Web
site ever launched in terms of potential impact on the pursuit of knowledge.
Perhaps as the former editor of Encyclopedia Britannica, the exemplary print-
based, peer-edited reference containing eighty-five thousand articles,
McHenry is all too aware of the impact of Wikipedia's then-estimated three
hundred thousand or more English articles.

Similarly, it is hardly surprising that McHenry's comments carry a great
deal of merit. In summarizing Wikipedia as he does, he opens up several av-
enues of conflict. If we push aside the question of whether Wikipedia seeks
to compete with the print-based model of reference (Nupedia might be a
more accurate comparison), we can thank McHenry for pointing up the key
question of revision in evaluating wiki content.

McHenry offers persuasive evidence that Wikipedia articles are poorly revised. Rather than arguing that each successive edit adds to the worth of the
article, McHenry finds that the successive edits contain all the hallmarks of
poor writing—they obfuscate accurate statements, harden the prose like ar-
terial sclerosis, and generally retrograde them from a previously more useful
state. Though McHenry does not offer this specific comparison, his statements lead wiki readers to conclude that writing, as a product of multiple authors, takes a legislative turn: as a product of compromise between multiple

parties and competing perspectives, conclusions trend conservative as style worsens.

But beyond issues of style, McHenry argues that one simply cannot trust the accuracy of content if no one person is assigned responsibility for verifying it. He concludes his article with the following infamously derogatory remark on this point:

> The user who visits Wikipedia to learn about some subject, to confirm some matter of fact, is rather in the position of a visitor to a public restroom. It may be obviously dirty, so that he knows to exercise great care, or it may seem fairly clean, so that he may be lulled into a false sense of security. What he certainly does not know is who has used the facilities before him.[13]

Perhaps a more amicable analogy for Wikipedia is not a public restroom but a public street. What really makes a project like Wikipedia work is that undeniable and apparently universal impulse to simply share knowledge when one is asked for directions by a complete stranger. When placed in these circumstances, almost no one seems able to resist sharing the information; few of us can turn down the role of momentary expert. Equally pervasive, and yet unknown before the Nupedia project transferred itself to a wiki, is the idea that a Web site could perpetuate this proposition across a worldwide electronic network to project the knowledge of a collective consciousness. That is to say, until Wikipedia came along, no one could envision innumerable, perpetual "stranger needing directions" conversations in cyberspace yielding comprehensive and reliable knowledge.

But whether the act of creating knowledge through a public commons is altruistic or simply naive, McHenry framed a key question: Just how accurate is Wikipedia?

The *Nature* Study

In late 2005, the editors of the science journal *Nature* set out to answer this question. They decided to compare, through blind review, articles from Wikipedia to Encyclopedia Britannica Online.

In the study, entries were chosen from the websites of Wikipedia and Encyclopaedia Britannica on a broad range of scientific disciplines and sent to a relevant expert for peer review. Each reviewer examined the entry on a single subject from the two encyclopaedias; they were not told which article came from which encyclopaedia. A total of 42 usable reviews were returned out of 50 sent out, and were then examined by *Nature*'s news team. Only eight serious errors, such as misinterpretations of important concepts, were detected in the pairs of articles reviewed, four from each encyclopaedia. But reviewers also found many factual errors, omissions or misleading statements: 162 and 123 in Wikipedia and Britannica, respectively.[14]

Rather than settling the question, however, the *Nature* study occasioned a vitriolic backlash from *Encyclopedia Britannica*, which found fault with the study for several reasons. As a result, some of the anonymous reviewers employed for the study surrendered anonymity and jumped into the fray to defend their work. In the end, the polarizing study seemed mainly to further entrench those who already held opinions on the viability of Wikipedia as a useful resource. The central assertion of the article—that while Encyclopedia Britannica Online remains more accurate than Wikipedia the difference is negligible—had been challenged but not disproved.

Later, Wales himself would make news with comments about the reliability and accuracy of Wikipedia. While speaking at a college conference in June 2006 called "The Hyperlinked Society,"

> Wales said that he gets about 10 e-mail messages a week from students who complain that Wikipedia has gotten them into academic hot water. "They say, 'Please help me. I got an F on my paper because I cited Wikipedia'" and the information turned out to be wrong, he says. But he said he has no sympathy for their plight, noting that he thinks to himself: "For God['s] sake, you're in college; don't cite the encyclopedia."[15]

These comments were prematurely heralded by Wikipedia detractors as an admission of its inaccuracies. But in fact, Wales's comments had more to do with the idea that college-level scholarship should reflect deeper thinking and research skills than an encyclopedia than a wholesale retraction of the worth of Wikipedia.

The Seigenthaler Controversy

Implicit in Wales's statement is the idea that at least some of the knowledge on Wikipedia cannot be trusted. The *Nature* study states that Wikipedia's level of inaccuracy is simply comparable to other online encyclopedias. But is it possible that the inaccuracies in Wikipedia can be of a greater magnitude than the errors in peer-reviewed counterparts? This seemed to be the case in November 2005, when John Seigenthaler, a retired journalist and former administrative assistant to Robert Kennedy, wrote an editorial for his former employer, *USA Today*.[16] In his editorial Seigenthaler detailed his experience of Wikipedia as irresponsible host of character assassination. A Wikipedia entry in his name contained several insulting inaccuracies. Once notified of this, Seigenthaler contacted "executives at three websites," including the Wikipedia copy sites Answers.com and Reference.com, who removed the inaccurate statements. Seigenthaler also contacted Jimmy Wales, who, while sympathetic to Seigenthaler's plight, could do little to identify the author of the false information. Almost two weeks later, the culprit would turn out to be a manger of a Nashville, Tennessee, courier company who confessed to planting the story as a joke.[17]

Seigenthaler's criticisms of Wikipedia were considered and, given his position as victim, carried considerable weight. In his initial editorial, Seigenthaler wrote, "I am interested in letting many people know that Wikipedia is a flawed and irresponsible research tool."[18] After pointing out that, unlike traditional publishers, Internet publishers were protected from lawsuits of libel and slander, Seigenthaler went on to note that, even though Wales claimed that Wikipedia contributors "correct mistakes within minutes," false information about him had remained on the Web site for roughly four months. Though the response of many Wikipedians to finding false postings might be "Well, clean it up and move on," Seigenthaler's case points up more than one flaw in Wikipedia as a knowledge production system.

The *Nature* study showed Wikipedia as generally accurate or at least not substantially less accurate than online encyclopedias produced under the traditional print paradigm. True, if Seigenthaler's false biography had been posted on Encyclopedia Britannica Online, while he might not have had legal recourse, there would have been a clear author and editor to hold accountable. Wikipedia could not provide this. Instead, Wikipedia relies on those invested in a knowledge community on a volunteer basis to provide edits, and the failure of that system is aptly noted in Seigenthaler's case since one Wikipedian looked at the article after its first post and merely corrected a misspelling, leaving the false content in place. In essence, all that the Wikipedia model could offer Seigenthaler is the opportunity to join this knowledge community and continually monitor his own biography on Wikipedia. Hardly a workable solution.

In response to the Seigenthaler controversy, Wikipedia did implement several new policies. At first, it appeared that Wikipedia would only allow registered users to make edits, though this was later implemented only in the case of selected articles. The Wikimedia Foundation also introduced a new policy for biographies of living persons. Most important, however, was the foundation's decision to create a new level of oversight, consisting of seventeen appointed users. These users have the ability to "permanently delete page revisions containing personal information, copyright violations, or libelous content."[19]

The Seigenthaler incident is important for understanding the cultural influence of wikis and Wikipedia on several levels. In some ways, it represented a clash of generations; Seigenthaler, though certainly an experienced and accomplished journalist, attacked not only Wikipedia but the entire concept of the online knowledge creation when he wrote, "we live in a universe of new media with phenomenal opportunities for worldwide communications and research—but populated by volunteer vandals with poison-pen intellects."[20] But just as important, it also occasioned reluctant changes in Wikipedia's own knowledge creation policies, some of which, such as user registration, could have been justified and implemented long before any damage was done to a bystander. At the resolution of the incident, it was clear to all involved that wiki-based knowledge production was here to stay; both sides seemed weary of a world where the credibility of information was impossible to verify, for once false knowledge was released, the damage was difficult to undo. Seigenthaler phrased it this way: "When I was a child, my mother lectured me on the evils of 'gossip.' She held a feather pillow and said, 'If I tear this open, the feathers will fly to the four winds, and I could never get them back in the pillow. That's how it is when you spread mean things about people.' For me, that pillow is a metaphor for Wikipedia."[21]

This raises the following question: If Wikipedia is able to propagate false information and enough users believe it, what happens to truth?

Truthiness

This peculiarly postmodern state of affairs is best illustrated by the work of Stephen Colbert, through his television show *The Colbert Report*. In his initial episode, Colbert lampooned Wikipedia for "truthiness"—or relying on a truth established through consensus opinion rather than verified facts.[22] But Colbert's perspective is much more sanguine than a straight read of his material would convey. His humor acknowledges that the contemporary landscape of knowledge production over Internet networks prohibits a return to a simpler media culture, where we received our news mainly through a chain of professional journalists. Some six months later, *The Colbert Report* would cause another Wikipedia controversy with the term "wikiality."[23] During the WORD segment, Colbert mocked the idea that truth is merely a product of consensus by editing Wikipedia articles during the show in order to make them support his statements; as he stated, "Together, we can create a reality that we can all agree on—the reality we just agreed on." He continued to develop the now infamous false statement in a Wikipedia article alleging that there are more elephants in Africa today than there were ten years ago. Stating that "What we're doing is bringing Democracy to knowledge" (with the subtext on the screen reading "Definitions will greet us as liberators"), Colbert asked his audience to create entries in Wikipedia reflecting a trebling in their numbers. In fact, many viewers did just this, leading Wikipedia to lock the article and many to wonder whether Colbert's audience understood his satire.

Colbert's episodes on national television not only document the scope of Wikipedia's particular cultural impact but also indicate a fundamental and general shift in epistemology. The controversies surrounding the use of wikis in contemporary knowledge production were so familiar that they could be satirized on national television. Together with the Seigenthaler incident, "truthiness" even made some aspects of traditional knowledge production seem appealing again.

Wikia and Beyond

What is the next step for wikis and Wikipedia? Writing for *Entrepreneurs* magazine, Adam Lashinsky interviewed Gil Penchina to explain Jimmy Wales's latest project, Wikia. Penchina, formerly of eBay, joined Wikia in order to help Wales build a site that will capture much of the rhetorical heat Wikipedia spins off in the process of creating knowledge. Lashinsky writes:

> Whereas Wikipedia aspires to be a neutral reference tool, Wikia's business plan is to capitalize on opinion. It aims to have articles and discussion groups on any subject under the sun. And while it deploys the same technology as its successful cousin, Wikia is intended as a freewheeling forum for all kinds of topics—from *Star Wars* to pet diabetes—with argument and advocacy welcome. "Wikipedia is the encyclopedia," says Penchina. "Wikia is the rest of the library and the magazine rack."[24]

It is too early to measure the impact of Wikia, but its mere existence documents an awareness on the part of Wales and others that knowledge creation is inherently controversial. This latest project attempts to use a discourse of argumentation as an attraction point, much of which is now captured in Wikipedia in "talk" pages. Once a full version of Wikia is created, however, the divide between ratified knowledge and controversial statements might become more widely acknowledged.

So what should be the guideposts for living in a world with networked knowledge production? In the case of Wikipedia, it seems that even the founder of the site is advising us to exercise caution. By expressing surprise and disapproval at the fact that college students are citing the online encyclopedia in research papers, Wales would urge us to develop more awareness of how knowledge is produced and to make use of that awareness when interpreting and applying that knowledge. More bluntly stated, knowing where we get our knowledge is as important as the knowledge itself. The academy needs to react more quickly to the realities of knowledge production in a networked environment if it is to fulfill its role in creating and disseminating knowledge. But, as the Georgia chancellor and his academic audience's responses show, some three years after Wikipedia emerged in popular consciousness, there is more work to do in publicizing these new epistemological realities among college faculty and decision makers. In print culture, we have oftentimes erred by assigning too much credibility to the type of media rather than relying on the skills and reputation of a particular editor—we have found books more reliable than periodicals. Similarly, the challenge to applying knowledge from wikis to our existing knowledge production systems involves a willingness not to underestimate their capabilities. While no one wants to undergo an operation from a physician who has just referenced the procedure on Wikipedia, similarly we all want surgeons to share their knowledge from procedures among themselves. There are as many possibilities for knowledge creation on wikis as there are authors and audiences. The key lies in shared definitions of truth: it is very unlikely that a wiki created by disgruntled Wal-mart employees will produce the same types of knowledge claims as a wiki created for astronomers. But as long as there is an agreed-upon scope for any particular wiki, there is no reason not to apply this tool of networked consciousness to almost any endeavor.

NOTES

1. For more background information on the chancellor's remarks, see either the AAUP's newsletter, "Chancellor Davis Keynotes Fall Conference Meeting," *The Georgia Conference: AAUP Summary* 24, no. 2 (fall 2006): 1, http://www2.gsu.edu/%7Ehishdh/AAUP%20Fall%202006.pdf; or the summary of the chancellor's remarks at http://www2.gsu.edu/%7Ehishdh/Chancellor%20Davis%27%20Remarks.pdf (accessed December 15, 2006).

2. See Manuel Castells, *The Rise of the Network Society*, vol. 1 of *The Information Age: Economy, Society, and Culture* (Cambridge, MA: Blackwell, 1996), 171.

3. See chancellor's remarks, http://www2.gsu.edu/%7Ehishdh/Chancellor%20Davis%27%20Remarks.pdf (accessed December 15, 2006).

4. Like many public universities in the United States, the public universities in the state of Georgia are charged by the state with the missions of "teaching, research, and the extension of knowledge to the public. The personnel at its institutions recognize as two of their major objectives, the production of new knowledge and the dissemination of both old and new knowledge." *Board of Regents Policy Manual: The University System of Georgia*, http://www.usg.edu/regents/policymanual/policyman.pdf (accessed December 15, 2006).

5. There is more discussion of the *Nature* study later in this essay and in note 14, but the full citation is Jim Giles, "Special Report: Internet Encyclopedias Go Head to Head," *Nature*, March 28, 2006, http://www.nature.com/nature/journal/v438/n7070/full/438900a.html.

6. Most of the introductory articles were published in 2004, although the *Time* article came much later; Chris Taylor and Coco Masters, "It's a Wiki, Wiki World," *Time*, June 6, 2005, 40; Robert D. Hof, "Something Wiki This Way Comes," *Business Week*, June 7, 2004, 128; Brad Stone, "It's Like a Blog, But It's a Wiki," *Newsweek*, November 1, 2004, 34; Sebastian Rupley, "What's a Wiki? Even as Blogs—Web Logs Posted by Indi-

viduals—Proliferate, a Complementary Form of Online Collaborative Communication Is Taking Off: Wikis," *PC Magazine*, June 20, 2003, 23.

7. Hillside.net, "Hillside History," 2003, http://hillside.net/history.html (accessed October 24, 2004). See also "A History of Patterns," http://www.c2.com/cgi/wiki?HistoryOfPatterns (accessed December 15, 2006).

8. Ward Cunningham, "Wiki History," Cunningham & Cunningham, Inc., http://c2.com/cgi/wiki?InvitationToThePatternsList (accessed October 24, 2004). Another useful source on Cunningham's thoughts about the creation of the first wiki can be found at Bill Venners, "Exploring with Wiki: A Conversation with Ward Cunningham, Part I," Artima Developer, http://www.artima.com/intv/wiki.html (accessed December 15, 2006).

9. Wikipedia contributors, "Nupedia," http://en.wikipedia.org/wiki/Nupedia (accessed December 15, 2006).

10. Wikipedia contributors, "History of Wikipedia," http://en.wikipedia.org/wiki/History_of_Wikipedia (accessed December 15, 2006).

11. Ibid. This essay has been in process for some time; when I started writing it in 2004, Wikipedia had roughly three hundred thousand English articles. On November 24, 2006, it listed 1.5 million English language articles.

12. Robert McHenry, "The Faith-Based Encyclopedia," *Tech Central Station*, http://www.techcentralstation.com/111504A.html (accessed November 17, 2004).

13. Ibid.

14. Though *Nature* now has placed prohibitive charges on online access to portions of this study, there are five relevant components: the initial article; supplemental information by *Nature* published on December 22, 2005, about how the study was conducted; a rebuttal by *Encyclopedia Britannica*; *Nature*'s responses to the rebuttal, published on March 28, 2006; and a full list of the peer reviewed articles. Online access begins at http://www.nature.com/nature/journal/v438/n7070/full/438900a.html.

15. "Wikipedia Founder Discourages Academic Use of His Creation," *Chronicle of Higher Education*, June 12, 2006, http://chronicle.com/wiredcampus/article/1328/wikipedia-founder-discourages-academic-use-of-his-creation (accessed December 15, 2006).

16. John Seigenthaler, "A False Wikipedia 'Biography,'" *USA Today*, November 30, 2005, final edition.

17. Susan Page, "Author of False Wikipedia Biography Apologizes," *USA Today*, December 12, 2005, final edition.

18. Seigenthaler, "A False Wikipedia 'Biography.'"

19. Wikipedia contributors, "Wikipedia Signpost 2006–06–05 Oversight," http://en.wikipedia.org/wiki/Wikipedia:Wikipedia_Signpost/2006–06–05/Oversight (accessed December 15, 2006).

20. Seigenthaler, "A False Wikipedia 'Biography.'"

21. Ibid.

22. *The Colbert Report*, Comedy Central, production no. 101 (originally aired October 17, 2005).

23. *The Colbert Report*, Comedy Central, production no. 2096 (originally aired July 31, 2006).

24. Adam Lashinsky, "Cashing in on Wiki-ness," *Entrepreneurs* 154, no. 5 (September 4, 2006): 34.

Wikis and the Scholarship of
Teaching and Learning

Mark Phillipson

Wikis in the Classroom: A Taxonomy

What Kind of Wiki?

Wikis come burdened with a slightly ridiculous name and no end of claims about their transformative potential. Wikis drive collaboration, they promote community, they spur interactivity, they spawn archives: who wouldn't want one of these fantastic devices in the classroom? And yet, though many instructors have by now heard the term and its attendant claims, wikis can still induce bewilderment and even guilt among the uninitiated. Without codified examples of specific uses of wikis in classrooms, instructors are liable to deem this new platform as unmanageable or just too complicated for their purposes. By treating the wiki as an undifferentiated phenomenon rather than a variously applied tool, we risk alienating colleagues who might otherwise recognize its ability to facilitate long-standing and fundamental pedagogical goals.

After years of describing wikis to other educators, I've come to recognize stages of inquiry. When an open editing environment is described—and then qualified with reassurances that permissions, hierarchies, and rules may be nonetheless enforced—an intrigued instructor will naturally want to see a wiki in action. This is tricky: though the easiest response is to point to Wikipedia, its structure and aims are not readily correlated to many pertinent teaching and learning activities. Treating Wikipedia as the model wiki may in fact result in a distracting debate about the trustworthiness of this particular resource, students' reliance on it for research purposes, and the general importance of information literacy. If the conversation nevertheless progresses into ideas about a class actively building its own wiki, a teacher generally ends up asking for a readily appropriated model. Given that all kinds of wiki software is freely available, this kind of interlocutor will then often ask which one he or she should use. And from that question follows another: how do I use it?

Instructors rarely have time to wade through alternatives, test platforms, align pedagogical priorities with new technology—and, all too often, their educational technology support (if they're lucky enough to have such support) steers them to standardized course management software. Similarly, technologists do not always enjoy the luxury of collaboration with responsive and Web-proficient faculty. Still, the most productive answer to the "Which wiki should I use?" question is another question, however unsatisfying it may sound: "What do you want your students to do?" Wikis carry with them the DNA of the open source movement, for better and for worse: they are infinitely modifiable, adaptable for any number of locally conceptualized ends, and resistant to fixity. Such open-ended fluidity can only be tamed in the classroom by predefined purpose. In this context, wikis are best approached by thinking about how they can be used to effectively promote a specific outcome or end.

The goal of the broad classification I'm attempting here, then, is to highlight an array of wiki-enabled class activities by drawing on some early college-level projects that are (at the time of this writing) publicly accessible. But first, a few caveats. I am concentrating here on wikis specifically associated with courses (and therefore ignoring the burgeoning number of departmental or extracurricular wikis on campuses). The descriptions of class wikis that I offer often involve deduction and surmise; unfortunately it is not yet standard practice to provide background description to class wikis—and though instructors who have run classroom wikis are often glad to respond to inquiries, they rarely have the time to retrace initial expectations or measure them against actual outcomes. Indeed, first adopters of class wikis have had to approach this platform experimentally, discovering unanticipated benefits, purposes, and challenges; it is only now, with the benefit of (recent) hindsight and (scattered) evidence, that we are able to consider this tool as an enabler of specific educational activities. The characterizations of projects here will also be somewhat reductive since it is artificial to characterize wikis as facilitating just one activity or pedagogical goal; they often perform a gamut of functions (presentational, collaborative, archival) simultaneously.

Nevertheless, I hope that even a crude and reductive classification of classroom wikis may ease the trepidation that many instructors feel when confronted with infinitely malleable possibilities. If we can capitalize on the experience of early adopters to relate certain "types" of wikis to specific classroom assignments and dynamics, instructors may be able to approach this collaborative tool with a firmer sense of purpose. It is true that students often bring unexpected energy and ideas to a wiki project, but the real success of this venture in the classroom depends on initial vision from an instructor. You say you want a wiki? Very well then: what kind? In the rest of this essay, I'll run through five possible answers to that question: the resource wiki, the presentation wiki, the gateway wiki, the simulation wiki, and the illuminated wiki.

The Resource Wiki

Wikipedia's high profile makes it likely to dominate general discourse about wikis for some time to come. Instructors unexposed to other models may automatically associate their idea of a wiki project with Wikipedia and may even assume that the MediaWiki software developed for this venture is the natural form of a wiki. But it is worth stressing that MediaWiki was developed to support a specific purpose: Wikipedia is "first and foremost an effort to create and distribute a free encyclopedia of the highest possible quality."[1] If a class project is in line with Wikipedia's purpose—if students are to build an expanding reference resource—then MediaWiki software is a natural platform for this kind of project. It is not the only one, though, and it may prove unsuitable or overcomplicated in some circumstances.

A resource wiki is adaptable to a wide array of classes: its basic agenda, the assemblage of a collaborative knowledge base, may be applied to a great variety of subjects. Whatever the topic of a given course, such a wiki offers ready means for a "classroom [to] function as a knowledge-building community,"[2] inviting the rewards and perils of collective constructivism.[3] Thus we see students building wikis into encyclopedic resources that are specifically defined yet inexhaustible, such as the inventory of a natural environment in Skidmore College's NorthWoods wiki, the assemblage of a dictionary of population genetics at West Virginia University, or the self-styled "Micropedia" of educational games and simulations built some years back at San Diego State University.[4]

While acting as a register of class activity, a knowledge base (if properly archived and maintained) can extend beyond one class—and even one emphasis. In this way, a resource wiki can give students the sense of contributing to a large and unfolding project, joining preceding peers in a given course or department or topic of study; it can also allow instructors to continually drive study of fresh material. The Social Justice Movements wiki at Columbia University is a good example of this kind of expansion. Growing over the course of several semesters, it now contains the work of both undergraduate and graduate students studying at both Columbia University and Harvard University. The site represents itself as "a kind of portal into some of the key social justice movements in [New York City]"—a definition general enough that the wiki can grow in various directions, depending on the emphasis of a given course.[5] For example, a class in black movements built an index of social organizations on the wiki, while members of a later seminar in black intellectuals assembled information about individual social activists. (See the online version of this essay at www.digitalculture.org for additional figures.) (See figs. 2–3 in the essay "Wiki Justice, Social Ergonomics, and Ethical Collaborations" for other examples from the Social Justice Movements Web site.)

Representing a carefully assembled knowledge base, resource wikis are often turned outward to an audience beyond a classroom. Such wikis may announce themselves as under development, but a given entry will strive to be authoritative: commentary on finished pages tends to be hidden or deemphasized. Though students are often assigned the construction of individual entries, either alone or in tandem with peers, they may be expected to cultivate an impersonal voice. Evaluation of their activity will concentrate on effective ways of organizing gathered data, such as division into navigable content blocks, integration with images, regularized layout, and consistent attribution. Though entries are often linked to each other (ideally via category tagging), the majority of linkage on such wikis may be devoted to selective citation of outside sources, as the resource wiki claims for itself a place in the universe of reliable information.

The Presentation Wiki

In contrast to a resource wiki, which gathers student work for the theoretical use of later visitors to the site, a presentation wiki begins with more of an inward focus. Material in these wikis is generated primarily for the convenience of the class, for peer evaluation, and for providing practical experience in the effective use of a communication forum. A presentation wiki may aim, eventually, to represent the class to the outer world, and it may even hope to grow into a research resource in its field. Its primary aim, however, is to leverage wiki software in order to support a class in its efforts to access, organize, and manipulate information effectively. It is thus more self-conscious than a resource wiki and more likely to highlight the process of assembling the information it contains.

It hardly seems coincidental that many early presentation wikis emerged from composition and other writing classes—environments in which a wiki's support of brainstorming,[6] project collaboration, information literacy, and resource structuring resonates with perennial disciplinary concerns. The Digital Journalism In-Class Wiki Page at Stanford University brands itself as a "workspace"; it has students collaborating in teams, evaluating outside Web resources, and "organizing their findings on the wiki during class and presenting them."[7] Penn State's Epoche Wiki supports a rhetoric course whose "first axiom is: Think practically about what you are trying to do with words, images, sounds, smells, feelings, even chemicals. Composition is the practice of finding the right mixture for any given goal."[8] Student use of this wiki ranges from blogging to peer commenting to draft workshopping; the site's emphasis on practical assemblage has the effect of elevating mere journaling into peer-conscious and interactive presentation.

The self-conscious, performative display of presentation wikis makes them particularly suitable for education classes, in which future teachers practice curriculum organization and become conversant with strategies for communal presentation and review. At Penn State, a course that prepares graduate students to teach the aforementioned rhetoric class is itself structured around a wiki that supports "best practices clusters" and a practicum in "work[ing] together to develop sustainable teaching practices that can grow with us as researchers and teachers."[9] The Teaching English Language

Arts wiki at the University of British Columbia allows students to build work-shops, individually or in groups.[10] For these workshops, fledgling teachers assemble learning objectives, strategies, resources, and supporting media into lessons. They then present these lessons for evaluation (fig. 1). Work-shops are collected on the wiki over the course of several semesters, and, as a result of this archiving, a presentation wiki becomes an increasingly valu-able resource over time.

Presentation wikis are often more varied in style and tone than a more pol-ished resource wiki. They allow for the cultivation of individual voices and of-ten inculcate a dynamic of informal, spontaneous, inventive interaction. Stu-dents working in such an environment are likely to be evaluated on the unique engagement of their work and its communicative efficacy; standard-ization may be downplayed in order to highlight differing presentational de-cisions of small groups or individuals. While students building a resource wiki may think of themselves as banded together in a communal effort, stu-dents involved in a presentation wiki are more likely to regard themselves as unique contributors, open to individual assessment.

The more personal exposure of a presentation wiki requires forethought when access rules are set for the wiki. Brainstorming and other informal in-cubation of ideas may happen more freely in private or access-limited spaces,[11] with polished drafts or presentations pushed to more widely acces-sible areas of the wiki. Operating in a fluid, communal environment, a pre-sentation wiki must be especially cognizant of workflow: it is, after all, a means of generating content as well as displaying it. Defining a "finished" or "presentable" stage in this process is thus often a challenge for both stu-dents and instructors. It may mean, paradoxically enough, that at least part of a presentation wiki is best hidden from general view.

The Gateway Wiki

Resource wikis have been spurred by Wikipedia's well-publicized example; presentation wikis capture and facilitate a range of evaluative activities: their rise in pedagogical settings is thus not surprising, nor are examples of either hard to find. We pass into more speculative regions, however, with the gate-way wiki. This is an emerging model: no project that I'm aware of fully ex-

Back to UnitPlans
Back to MediaWorkshop

Media Literacy and Society
2005W

Unit Goal: To evaluate how the media can influence the perception of events.

Rationale: Students will examine the tools of the media by analyzing various genres and styles of "The News." Students will become critical viewers and readers of "The News."

I.R.P's
It is expected that students will:
- demonstrate a willingness to explore a variety of genres and media
- think critically about the messages surrounding them
- comprehend the role of mass media in society and their personal lives

SWBAT:
- identify how style and genre influences the way in which the news is perceived by the viewing public.
- interpret how reporters function in their roles as news broadcastors.
- analyze and interpret the "script" of a famous interview.
- compare, analyze and interpret how different types of newspaper styles influence their audience.
- interpret and analyze how images can portray powerful messages to their audience.
- analyze the language of the newspaper genre.
- create their own newpaper

Lesson #1 and Hook- Looking at Style In the Comedy/News Genre
Students will view a clip from the 'Daily Show' and brainstorm ideas about how they saw the news being presented to the audience ie. use of humour, persuasion
(The Daily Show Site∞ then click on "Spring Cloning")
http://www.cnnasiapacific.com/tc/file_manager/images/programs/the_daily_show.jpg∞
Source∞

Fig. 1. An education student assembles a lesson in media literacy (with a clip from *The Daily Show* acting as a "hook") and presents it for evaluation on the University of British Columbia Teaching English Language Arts wiki. Comments on this lesson's efficacy are on the same page.

emplifies it. Nevertheless, we can get a sense of the gateway wiki's particular potential from looking at a few pioneering social science and science classes.

While a resource wiki bolsters its authority through outside citation, it delivers itself to an end user as a self-contained project. Similarly, a presentation wiki strives to mix a range of student work into one communal environment—it is also, in this way, self-contained. A gateway wiki, in contrast, acts as a supplement, analysis, or elaboration of data that stands apart from a fluid, open-editing environment. Once documented, this data (which might consist of scientific measurements, statistics, calculations, survey results, metrics, and any number of other data sets) is fixed, though it may well be the subject of dynamic appraisal. A gateway wiki is thus marked by bifurcation; it stages the meeting of discovered data with evolving discussion and analysis.

Though it has yet to be fully developed by a class, the SaratogaCensus wiki recently set up at Skidmore College has laid the groundwork for a gateway wiki.[12] The agenda of SaratogaCensus is to explicate two data sets: U.S. census information for Saratoga Springs, New York, from 1850 and from 1860 (fig. 2). Though the wiki links to this data, the data is set apart from the wiki environment (figs. 3–4). "Information pages" in a familiar MediaWiki setting, all editable by registered students, provide a range of information that introduces, explains, illustrates, and supplements the census data. The wiki, then, offers a forum within which to collectively process raw data. Instructions on accessing and searching the census; illustrations, maps, and photographs; descriptions of buildings; biographical research; an invitation to community members outside the class to submit supplementary family information—all this comprises the ambitious (though as of this writing unmet) agenda of this gateway wiki.

We can see gateway tendencies in wikis set up to facilitate the study of science. In several cases, instructors have used a wiki environment as the place for students in a class to conduct interpretive or ethical analysis. This may in fact be meta-analysis, as students communally process literature about research. Though the scientific data being discussed may have receded beyond immediate linkage, it is still the organizing focus of discussion, and thus we can still consider such projects as gateways. Harvard University's Biotechnology: Academic, Government & Industry Interactions and Tensions wiki, for example, asks students to keep frequently updated journals, collaborate

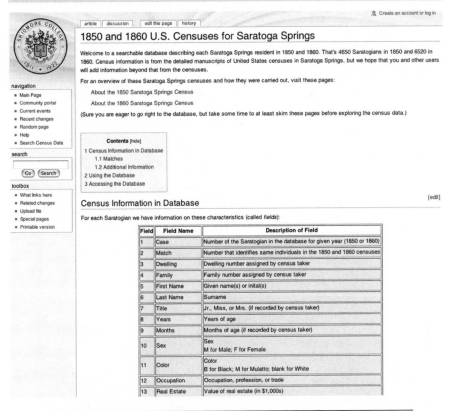

article | discussion | edit this page | history

1850 and 1860 U.S. Censuses for Saratoga Springs

Welcome to a searchable database describing each Saratoga Springs resident in 1850 and 1860. That's 4650 Saratogians in 1850 and 6520 in 1860. Census information is from the detailed manuscripts of United States censuses in Saratoga Springs, but we hope that you and other users will add information beyond that from the censuses.

For an overview of these Saratoga Springs censuses and how they were carried out, visit these pages:

   About the 1850 Saratoga Springs Census

   About the 1860 Saratoga Springs Census

(Sure you are eager to go right to the database, but take some time to at least skim these pages before exploring the census data.)

Contents [hide]
1 Census Information in Database
  1.1 Matches
  1.2 Additional Information
2 Using the Database
3 Accessing the Database

Census Information in Database

[edit]

For each Saratogian we have information on these characteristics (called *fields*):

Field	Field Name	Description of Field
1	Case	Number of the Saratogian in the database for given year (1850 or 1860)
2	Match	Number that identifies same individuals in the 1850 and 1860 censuses
3	Dwelling	Dwelling number assigned by census taker
4	Family	Family number assigned by census taker
5	First Name	Given name(s) or inital(s)
6	Last Name	Surname
7	Title	Jr., Miss, or Mrs. (if recorded by census taker)
8	Years	Years of age
9	Months	Months of age (if recorded by census taker)
10	Sex	Sex M for Male; F for Female
11	Color	Color B for Black; M for Mulatto; blank for White
12	Occupation	Occupation, profession, or trade
13	Real Estate	Value of real estate (in $1,000s)

navigation
- Main Page
- Community portal
- Current events
- Recent changes
- Random page
- Help
- Search Census Data

search

Go | Search

toolbox
- What links here
- Related changes
- Upload file
- Special pages
- Printable version

Fig. 2. The SaratogaCensus wiki provides an explanatory apparatus for a U.S. census database.

on class notes, supplement readings with links to current news, and draw each other into discussion.[13]

A University of Maryland class wiki entitled Eukaryotic Genetics and Molecular Biology is more focused on direct interpretation of scientific literature.[14] It asks each student to build a page that "will provide a critical discussion of the research of a researcher in translation or translational control."[15] Students working on this wiki kept research journals, annotated bibliographies, linked to a class glossary, and provided self-assessments of their use of the wiki environment (fig. 5). They also used the wiki to present research in teams. One student assessment of her experience with this wiki is typical: "I tried to pull in other sources for background information, as well as pic-

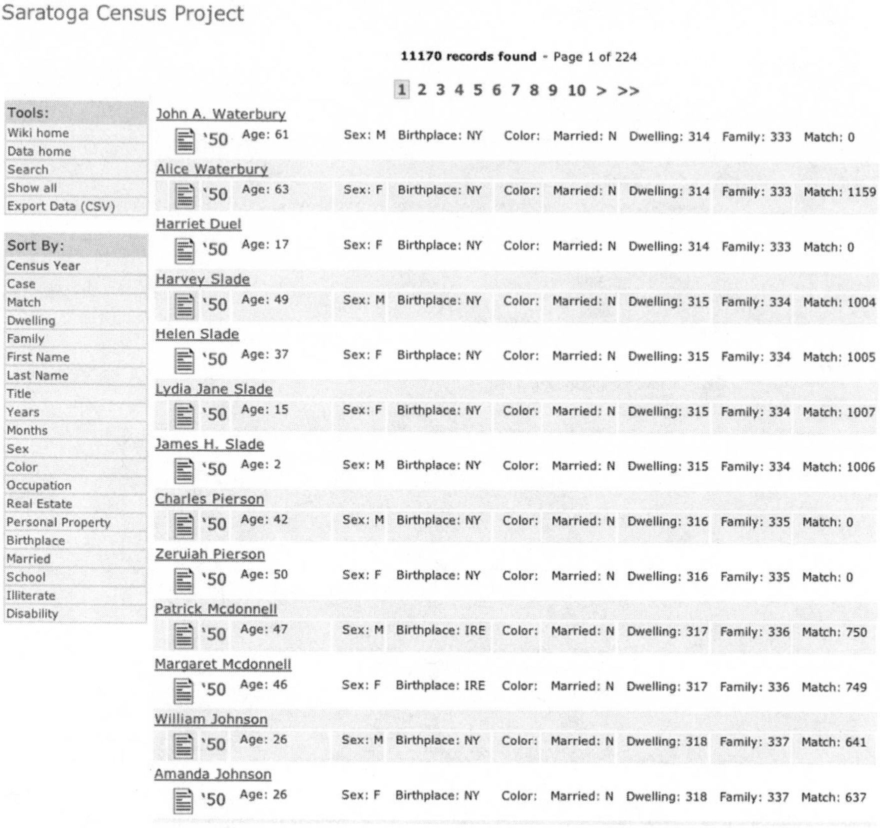

Saratoga Census Project

11170 records found - Page 1 of 224

1 2 3 4 5 6 7 8 9 10 > >>

Tools:
Wiki home
Data home
Search
Show all
Export Data (CSV)

Sort By:
Census Year
Case
Match
Dwelling
Family
First Name
Last Name
Title
Years
Months
Sex
Color
Occupation
Real Estate
Personal Property
Birthplace
Married
School
Illiterate
Disability

John A. Waterbury
'50 Age: 61 Sex: M Birthplace: NY Color: Married: N Dwelling: 314 Family: 333 Match: 0

Alice Waterbury
'50 Age: 63 Sex: F Birthplace: NY Color: Married: N Dwelling: 314 Family: 333 Match: 1159

Harriet Duel
'50 Age: 17 Sex: F Birthplace: NY Color: Married: N Dwelling: 314 Family: 333 Match: 0

Harvey Slade
'50 Age: 49 Sex: M Birthplace: NY Color: Married: N Dwelling: 315 Family: 334 Match: 1004

Helen Slade
'50 Age: 37 Sex: F Birthplace: NY Color: Married: N Dwelling: 315 Family: 334 Match: 1005

Lydia Jane Slade
'50 Age: 15 Sex: F Birthplace: NY Color: Married: N Dwelling: 315 Family: 334 Match: 1007

James H. Slade
'50 Age: 2 Sex: M Birthplace: NY Color: Married: N Dwelling: 315 Family: 334 Match: 1006

Charles Pierson
'50 Age: 42 Sex: M Birthplace: NY Color: Married: N Dwelling: 316 Family: 335 Match: 0

Zeruiah Pierson
'50 Age: 50 Sex: F Birthplace: NY Color: Married: N Dwelling: 316 Family: 335 Match: 0

Patrick Mcdonnell
'50 Age: 47 Sex: M Birthplace: IRE Color: Married: N Dwelling: 317 Family: 336 Match: 750

Margaret Mcdonnell
'50 Age: 46 Sex: F Birthplace: IRE Color: Married: N Dwelling: 317 Family: 336 Match: 749

William Johnson
'50 Age: 26 Sex: M Birthplace: NY Color: Married: N Dwelling: 318 Family: 337 Match: 641

Amanda Johnson
'50 Age: 26 Sex: F Birthplace: NY Color: Married: N Dwelling: 318 Family: 337 Match: 637

Fig. 3. The SaratogaCensus wiki links to the census database . . .

tures and diagrams, to help make the page more informative and understandable to those outside our field. I did enjoy using the Wiki for this type of project, and I think it provided a good way for all of the groups to share what they had researched."[16]

Finally, a gateway wiki can supplement student laboratory sections, providing a platform for students to log results, share experiences, air questions, and connect to theory. A wiki accompanying a physics lab at McGill University is taking steps toward such functionality.[17] Though the wiki is used primarily as a course management tool—instructors unidirectionally post schedules, instructions, and handouts on it—students are also asked to

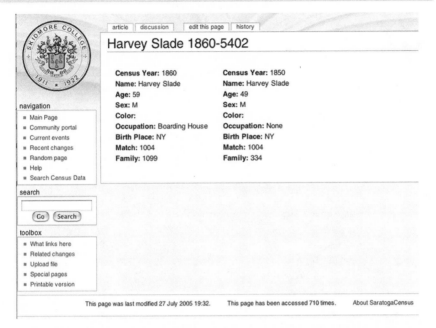

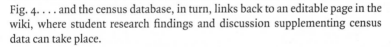

Fig. 4. . . . and the census database, in turn, links back to an editable page in the wiki, where student research findings and discussion supplementing census data can take place.

log descriptions of experiments and inventory equipment on the wiki. There is not much in the way of peer interaction on the site, at least at the time of this writing, but the logs do allow for reactive venting ("there is some terrible curse on the setup").[18]

The meagerness of student interaction in the McGill physics lab wiki may reflect a fast-paced, competitive learning environment. In an early consideration of disappointing use of proto-wiki software in engineering, mathematics, and computer science classrooms, researchers at Georgia Tech very sensibly concluded that use of a collaborative platform depends on context: "Content of courses and culture of a field can have a significant impact. If students do not expect to collaborate in a course, they probably won't."[19] Quantitative testing, single-answer assignments, and curve-based grading—elements common in science classes—may lead to a classroom culture resistant to open, communal interchange. If such is the case, gateway wikis, by drawing clear lines between objective data and analysis, offer a way for the article   discussion   edit   history

     Log in / create account

UMBC
AN HONORS
UNIVERSITY
IN MARYLAND

Zuberi

Group 3 Represent!!!

Annotated Bibliography Entries

biol414/biol414
- Home
- Syllabus
- Class schedule
- Readings
- Reviews
- Project
- Bibliographic database
- Old exams

students
- Class list
- Student groups
- Peer reviewing

help
- Online editing demo
- Editing help
- Editor Icons Help
- Wiki Etiquette
- Links

pages
- Recent changes
- List of all pages
- Try the sandbox...

search
[Go] [Search]

toolbox
- What links here
- Related changes
- Special pages
- Printable version
- Permanent link

(3/15) Ganesan S. et al. Engineering Cottonseed for use in human nutrition by tissue specific reduction of toxic gossypol. PNAS. 2006 vol 103 no 48 18054-18059

(3/26) Panstruga R. et al., 2003 Testing the Efficiency of dsRNAi constructs in vivo: A transient expression assay based on two flourescent proteins. Molecular Biology Reports. 2003 30:135-140.

(4/3) Gavilano L et al. 2006. "Genetic engineering of Nicotiana tabacum for reduced nomicotine content". J Agric Food Chem 54 (24): 9071–8.

(4/10) Tenllado F et al. 2004. "RNA interference as a new biotechnological tool for the control of virus diseases in plants". Virus Research 102 (2004) 85–96.

(4/17) Garcia S et al. 2006. " Viral suppressors of RNA interference impair RNA silencing induced by a Semliki Forest virus replicon in tick cells". JGen Virol 87 1985-1989.

(4/24) Stewart S et al 2003. " Lentivirus delivered stable gene silencing by RNAi in primary cells" RNA Society 9: 493-501.

Allen R et al 2004. "RNAi-mediated replacement of morphine with the nonnarcotic alkaloid reticuline in opium poppy" NBT 2004 vol 22 no 12 1559 - 1566

Self Assessment

RNAi applications in Biotechnology

Site Map
1) RNAi based Engineering of Plants
a) Making Inedible Plants Edible

     i) Southern Blot Analysis

b) Silencing Narcotics and Carcinogens

     i) Tobacco
     ii) Opium

c) Controlling Virus Infections in Plants
d) References

Rough Draft

This page was last modified 04:52, 23 May 2007.   This page has been accessed 605 times.   Privacy policy   About classes/biol414/spring2007   Disclaimers   Powered By MediaWiki

Fig. 5. A student presents a range of work on the UMBC Eukaryotic Genetics and Molecular Biology wiki, including assigned topic reports, bibliographic annotations, and a self-assessment.

innovative instructor to bring the interactivity of social software into environments that are not usually regarded as collaborative.

The Simulation Wiki

In contrast to the straightforward marshaling of information offered by a resource wiki, the simulation wiki presents an interactive experience: it is built as a world to explore. While a resource wiki will aim to expose the full range of its content through indexes, categorization, and other navigational facilitation, a simulation wiki is more unpredictable; its content might be browsed through negotiation of unique pathways, confrontation with decision points, exploration of one possibility over another, and comparison to real-life models. While its emphasis on the strategic assemblage of content may remind us of a presentation wiki, the simulation wiki is actually intended to mirror its subject: in other words, it doesn't describe X but rather mimics X. Such a project may be structured around the unfolding of a situation, which means that its authors conceptualize conditions and alternatives and work on building narrative paths. A simulation wiki is thus an intriguing choice for creative writing projects and also for the study of historical events.

The Holocaust Wiki Project, designed in an educational technology seminar at San Diego State University and run at West Hills High School in Santee, California, is a notably ambitious effort to engage students in the details of a historical event through role playing and wiki authoring.[20] Inspired by a static WebQuest learning module called Children of the Holocaust,[21] the Holocaust Wiki Project is modeled on the "ant farm" design pattern described in "Design Patterns for EduWikis—IncubatorWiki" in 2006: "A simulation of a selected time and place with multiple actors. . . . Participants carry a set of choices and consequences through for a single actor while coordinating with other participants working with other actors. Facilitator can require that paths cross to a particular degree."[22] Students working in small groups on the Holocaust Wiki Project first invented a family, based on background information. Then they imagined this family confronting a series of "decision points": moments of crisis involving two plausible choices (figs. 6–7). In essence, students (working in small groups) had to construct a branching structure, constantly plotting alternative outcomes. They also had to be aware of the movements of characters written by other groups: at some point during their narratives, they were required to intersect with another group's fictitious family at a geographic location.

If this sounds intricate, especially for high school students working on a two-week project, that's because it is: development of a simulation wiki like this requires charting, coordination within and between groups, attention to narrative flow, and plausible reflection of actual historical conditions and events. Evaluative guidance on the wiki detailed expectations for a successful simulation: protagonists with fully imagined personalities, detailed pros and cons worked out for each decision, plausible consequences, good pacing, skillful blending of fact and fiction, and a consistent narrative voice.[23]

article | discussion | edit | history

Log in / create account

navigation
- Main Page
- Community portal
- Current events
- Recent changes
- Random page
- Help
- Donations

search

[Go] [Search]

toolbox
- What links here
- Related changes
- Upload file
- Special pages
- Printable version
- Permanent link

MCDOWELL'S

Group4-18a

In the night Feuerstein wakes up to screams. He looks out the window to find Nazis smashing houses looking for Jews. Fabian wakes up and hears the chilling scream of a woman being shot. In the blink of an eye Feuerstein wakes the family up including Vogel and tells them the following. "Family and friends the time has come to transport the Jews out of Berlin. We have a desicion to make."

Runaway

Pros:

- Running away may provide you a chance to escape and be free from the clutches of the Nazis.
- Running away would get you out of Germany quicker than trying to escape from a labor or Death camp.

Cons:

- The consequences are greater if you run away and are caught by a Nazi.
- You and your family could possibly be killed if you are caught or sent to a Death camp for a painful death.

Go to a Ghetto

Pros:

- Going to a Ghetto will not get you killed right away and just maybe might give you a chance to escape for freedom.
- You may be able to go to a Labor Camp to work until the war is over.

Cons:

- Going with the Nazis to a Ghetto may eventually send you to a Death Camp.
- The Isidor's and Vogel may not all be together when they are transported to the camps, which may in turn lead to a few deaths.

This page was last modified 17:59, 6 June 2006.   This page has been accessed 263 times.   Privacy policy   About APWH Wiki   Disclaimers   Powered By MediaWiki

Fig. 6. A "decision point" on the Holocaust Wiki Project depicts choices for a Jewish family living in Berlin in 1941. Clicking on either choice leads the reader into more branching decision points.

Visitors to the site can now follow a family and choose between options, constructing a linear narrative for themselves; the authors of this project, however, had to imagine a complex environment of contingency and consequence.

Though it does not present users with branching alternatives, Skidmore College's SkidmoreGreekTragedy project is still an arena of invention and coordination that leverages a wiki for creative simulation.[24] In this project, groups of students (Alpha, Beta, Gamma, and Delta) collaborated to write their own Greek tragedies. They identified and described controlling myths, built outlines proving conformity to classic tragic structure, and submitted various process documents: progress reports, rough and polished drafts, and "final thoughts" on their productions (fig. 8). As becomes clear in those final thoughts, the demands that were placed on these groups as they apportioned, critiqued, adjusted, and knit together contributions—all the while

Progression of Events Chart

The Progression of Events Chart is the most important part of the project. It is here where you will do all of your planning. Before you can go on to developing the simulation on the Wiki, your instructor must approve your chart.

Directions

[edit]

- Using the format pictured below, begin planning out possible DecisionPoints for your family. During this part of the project, you are only looking for places where your family will have to make a choice between two options. Write a short summary of the decision point on your chart. *Remember you must have at least 12 major decision points.*
- Use the Country Links and Resource Links to ensure that the decision points are historically accurate and appropriate to your country.
- Use the provided maps of ghettos and camps to ensure that your geographic locations are accurate and appropriate. Plot your families location on the blank map.
- Do not worry about the details during this part of the project, focus on getting a general outline of the entire branching simulation. This plan may be altered during the development phase.
- Use the following format to label each decision point: group1-1A, group1-1b, group 1-1c, etc. This will be important when you start linking your decision points together.

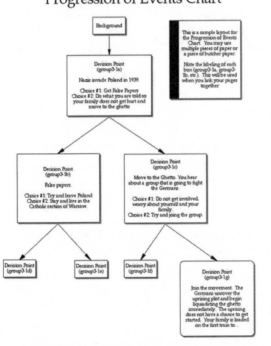

Fig. 7. A chart posted by the designer of the Holocaust Wiki Project helps students strategize decision points that they will narrate on the wiki.

Chorus

True love is perhaps the strongest bond between
mortals yet fragile enough to be broken by
a god in disguise. So quickly was the
love discovered between Hero and Leander,
yet faster was it destroyed. The love that
was found turned to misery and betrayal.
Hero's encounter with the unknown soldier
felt uneasy from the beginning.
Poor Leander, who swims against the raging
Hellespont, with a sad heart. Hero has
broken her vow with her true love, not the soldier.
Pandora

Fourth Episode   [edit]

> Still more logistics. The epiphany of Poseidon, coming as it does not quite at the end of your play, is an unusual
> move. As you know from Euripides, such appearances typically occur at the very beginning or near the very end
> (the *Heracles* is the exception that proves the rule). It is true that Athena appears toward the middle of the *Furies*,
> the last play in the *Oresteia* trilogy; but hers is not a one-off appearance like most others; she remains onstage
> until the end of the play, and for good reason. Poseidon's brief epiphany at this juncture would have struck an
> ancient audience as out of place. It seems to me you should swap the messenger speech of the epilogue with
> your deus-ex-machina in this episode.

(Enter Nurse)

Nurse
My lady I stood idle once before
As you let your innocence slip away.
Giving that which was pure and good to
Another, all for the sake of love proclaimed.
Donating that beautiful part of you
To he that stirred the fires of your heart.
Yes, I acted not against this because I felt
The intention to be taintless and
Unpolluted. But remain motionless

Fig. 8. A section from Beta group's rough draft of an original tragedy, posted on the SkidmoreGreekTragedy site. A comment from the instructor (in the box) criticizes an ill-timed epiphany.

constructing a coherent tragic drama—were considerable. Contributors to the project not only tried to adhere to the conventions of classical drama, but they also struggled to be faithful to the dramatic world they were creating: a coordination similar to the multifaceted imaginative demands of the Holocaust Wiki Project. As one student from the Delta group reported, "The whole time, I really got the sense that we were trying to write a play—our play. We wanted it to work for us as much as for anybody else."[25]

Though the Holocaust Wiki Project and the SkidmoreGreekTragedy project are quite different in emphasis and presentation, they both bring stu-

dents closer to specific objects of study through group-negotiated emula-
tion. In each case, coherence is predicated on sympathetic engagement with
fictional characters. Similar dynamics of patterning and interactivity can be
applied to purely imaginative projects. The success of such endeavors depends on rigorous attention to branching and coherence. A recent wiki usability study, analyzing a collaborative fiction project authored by French
children, identified several potential pitfalls:

> [S]ome subjects had trouble planning the topology of their story (8 out
> of 32). Others had difficulty with writing text so that it makes sense in a
> hypertext medium (14 out of 32). For example, they would write a page
> or chose its name in a way that made sense if the reader came to it from
> a particular page, but would not make sense if he came to it from an-
> other page (9 out of 32). Or they would not know what to write on a ter-
> minal page where the [character] wins or dies (7 out of 32). Or they
> would not know how to write a first page introduction for a story that is
> hypertext in nature (2 out of 32).[26]

Hypertext theory and hypertext fiction may strike us as rather creaky by now,
markers of the Web's infancy, but a simulation wiki in fact readily facilitates
authorship in the environment described by Ted Nelson: "nonsequential
writing—text that branches and allows choices to the reader, best read at an
interactive screen."[27] In 1992, Robert Coover lamented that hypertext fiction
was hampered by incompatible operating systems and transient applications, something that would have to change "if interaction is to be a hallmark
of the new technology."[28] Wikis authored by a class trained in elementary
coding techniques, built and distributed through platform-independent
browsers, can enable interaction long envisioned by hypertext enthusiasts.
Though I have been unable to find a college-level creative writing class using
a wiki to build interactive fictions, the examples of sites such as Wikipen[29]
and WriteHere[30] may inspire such ventures.

The Illuminated Wiki

Finally, we come to a type of wiki I have come to know quite well, though it is
as yet a rarity: the illuminated wiki. Unlike the encyclopedic resource wiki, an

illuminated wiki focuses on the act of explication; it is devoted to close reading and communal mapping. This focus on a particular object of analysis
may remind us of the gateway wiki. But the illuminated wiki is crucially different from its gateway cousin insofar as it incorporates the subject of study
into the wiki itself and, in so doing, alters or transforms the source material.
Students writing on an illuminated wiki mark up source text or images with
results of their work; they collectively imprint what they study. A developed
illuminated wiki will be therefore less a formal presentation than a record of
exegesis. Like a presentation wiki, it is a marker of work in progress and particularly useful as a spur to class discussion, but its most fundamental purpose is the communal markup of source documents.

The two Romantic Audience Project wikis developed by my students at
Bowdoin College, RAP 1 (2003) and RAP 2 (2005), are early models of textual
illumination on a wiki.[31] These projects focused on the explication of a de-
limited group of eighteenth- and nineteenth-century poems. Weekly assignments designated specific poems as the basis for required posting: students
chose a word or phrase from such texts and created links from this source
text to their analysis. As a result, poems were "lit up" by students, who were
individually staking ground in them, even as the class, collectively, was
defining broad patterns of engagement (fig. 9). Student work could thus be
assessed on an individual basis by the instructor, while the class could monitor its analytic proclivities as a whole.[32]

The topography of analysis rendered by an illumination wiki may be use-
fully compared across classes or, like a resource wiki, collected in a developing project over several semesters. For example, students marking up John
Clare's poem "I Am" in the 2003 Romantic Audience Project explicated different passages than those marking up the same poem in 2005 (fig. 10). An
illuminated wiki could become a repository of several classes' work over
time, as students picked through previously marked text and developed "still
open" ground. But the sense of gradual discovery fostered by an illuminated
wiki—the way it illustrates the progress of analysis as it unfolds—encourages a given group of students to isolate and consider their own interpretive
interventions as they proceed. A perhaps ideal solution for a multiclass illumination wiki would be a "layering" function, where the markups of specific
individual classes could be rendered visible or invisible, depending on an instructor's need.

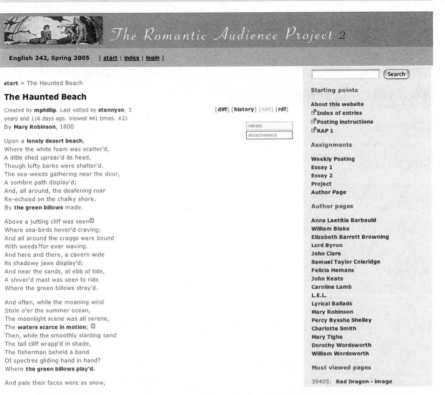

Fig. 9. Students illuminate passages of "The Haunted Beach" by Mary Robinson (1800) in the Romantic Audience Project 2. Two postings highlight passages involving "green billows."

As "mashups" of wikis and mapping software proliferate, we are likely to see class wikis directly illuminating topographical regions and other image mappings. Information maps set up in the wake of Hurricane Katrina in 2005, such as George Mason's Hurricane Digital Memory Bank, offer a simple model: contributors upload information and connect it to geographical location (fig. 11).[33] It is not hard to envision mappings undertaken by students studying specific works of art or manuscripts or sonic passages—any complicated surface that can be digitally rendered in the wiki and used as the basis of analysis.

Even though wikis naturally facilitate hypertext activity, as we've seen in simulation wikis, content on the majority of class wikis tends to be only

English 242, Spring 2005   [start | index |

Romantic Audience Project

I am

Created by **mphillip**. Last edited by **kmasters**
1917 days ago. Viewed 3781 times.
By **John Clare**, 1846

I am: yet **what I am none cares or knows**, ▣
My friends forsake me like a memory lost; ▣
I am the **self-consumer** of my woes,
They rise and vanish in oblivious host,
Like shades in love and death's oblivion lost;
And yet I am! and live with shadows tost ▣

Into the nothingness of scorn and noise,
Into the living sea of waking dreams,
Where there is neither sense of life nor joys,
But the vast shipwreck of my life's esteems;
And e'en the dearest - that I loved the best- ▣
Are strange - nay, rather stranger than the rest.

I long for scenes where man has never trod;
A place where woman never smil'd or wept;
There to abide with my creator, God,
And sleep as I in childhood sweetly slept:
Untroubling and untroubled where I lie;
The grass below - above the **vaulted sky**.

start > I Am

I Am

Created by **zmilner**. Last edited by **jbobsein**, 3
years and 95 days ago. Viewed 354 times. #8
By John Clare, 1846

I am: yet what I am none cares or knows,
My friends forsake me like a memory lost;
I am the self-consumer of my woes,
They rise and vanish in oblivious host,
Like shades in love and death's oblivion lost;
And yet I am! and live with shadows tost

Into the **nothingness of scorn and noise**,
Into the living sea of waking dreams,
Where there is neither sense of life nor joys,
But the vast shipwreck of my life's esteems;
And e'en the dearest - that I loved the best-
Are strange - nay, rather stranger than the rest.

I long for scenes where man has never trod;
A place where woman never smil'd or wept;
There to abide with my creator, **God**,
And sleep as I in childhood sweetly slept:
Untroubling and untroubled where I lie;
The grass below - above the vaulted sky.

Fig. 10. Two classes illuminate the same poem by John Clare, one in 2003 and one in 2005. Given the right archiving and programming, several classes could compare and contrast explications on a wiki project extending over several years.

modestly interlinked. This may be due to the current predominance of the resource wiki and the Wikipedia model; projects in this mode usually strive for the collective assemblage of "finished" entries. An illumination wiki, in contrast, is liable to be elaborately interlinked, as students weave together source text, analysis, and commentary. Such weaving seems intrinsic to the illuminated wiki's facilitation of what programmers have called a "documentation-enabled development environment."[34] In fact, constant interweaving of student work to source text may in fact help instructors control "the freewheeling, uncontrolled wiki environment," even as it vividly illustrates to

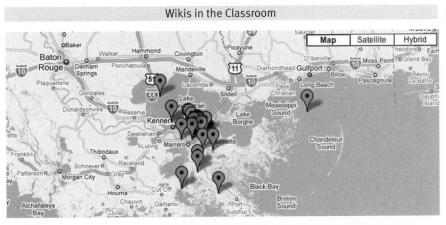

Fig. 11. A location-based wiki, set up by George Mason University's Center for History and New Media, uses a Google Maps API for the Hurricane Digital Memory Bank, at www.hurricanearchive.org. A similar environment could easily be used by a class illuminating a geographically defined field.

students that engagement with source material—their work as individuals and as a class—makes a difference.[35]

Wikis are proving natural components of Web application hybrids, or mashups—an increasingly prevalent and creative approach to building social software environments. Collaborative illuminations of maps, set within a wiki, can readily act as a rich yet easily navigated index to content, a way for students to discover geographically contiguous activity and ponder connections (Columbia University's developing religion studies project Sacred Gotham takes this approach).[36] It is becoming easy to imagine data visualization tools, desktop integration applications, audio-based forums, and any number of other applications being set within the parameters of a wiki. The malleability of this platform guarantees that any survey of its use will feel outpaced by innovation—especially a survey set within the slower and fixed parameters of print.

Application hybrids are liable to complicate conversations about what actually constitutes a wiki and may even present an unsettling prospect of unending development. A more productive conversation, for instructors, will start with defined pedagogical activities and work out to the collaborative environment that wikis foster. Resource building, presentation staging, data analysis, role playing, exegesis—such activities have been intrinsic to serious study for a long time and seem destined to persist long after the word *wiki* has dropped into disuse. In the meantime, attempting more extensive taxonomies of wikis as they continue to evolve in classroom contexts, we might remember a comment made by Ralph Waldo Emerson as he described the maturing spirit of a scholar: "what is classification but the perceiving that these objects are not chaotic, and are not foreign, but have a law which is also the law of the human mind?"[37]

NOTES

1. Jimmy Wales, "Letter from the Founder," Wikimedia Foundation, April 2005, http://wikimediafoundation.org/wiki/Founder_letter (accessed February 26, 2006).

2. Marelene Scardamali and Carl Bereiter, "Computer Support for Knowledge-Building Communities," *Journal of the Learning Sciences* 3, no. 3 (1994): 265–83, http://carbon.cudenver.edu/~bwilson/building.html.

3. Susan Loudermilk Garza and Tommy Hern, "Collaborative Writing Tools: Something Wiki This Way Comes—Or Not!" *Kairos* 10, no. 1 (2005), http://english.ttu.edu/kairos/10.1/binder2.html?http://falcon.tamucc.edu/wiki/WikiArticle/Home.

4. NorthWoods, Skidmore College, http://academics.skidmore.edu/wikis/North Woods/index.php/Main_Page (accessed April 18, 2006); EdGamesF03, San Diego State University, http://www.edwiki.org/edgames/pmwiki.php?n=EdGames.EdGamesF03 (accessed April 19, 2006).

5. "Social Justice Movements: About," Columbia University, 2006 (accessed April 19, 2006), http://socialjustice.ccnmtl.columbia.edu/index.php/.

6. Jonathan Davies, "Wiki Brainstorming and Problems with Wiki Based Collaboration," University of York, 2004, http://www-users.cs.york.ac.uk/~kimble/teaching/students/Jonathan_Davies/wiki_collaboration_and_brainst orming.pdf (accessed February 24, 2006).

7. Digital Journalism In-Class Wiki Page, Stanford University, http://traumw erk.stanford.edu:3455/Rheingold/117 (accessed April 19, 2006).

8. Epoche Wiki, Pennsylvania State University, http://epochewiki.pbwiki.com/ (accessed April 19, 2006).

9. Epoche Wiki:RhetoricAndComposition, Pennsylvania State University, 2006, http://wikipedagogy.schtuff.com/english_15_pedagogy_602_teachers_practicum.

10. Teaching English Language Arts, University of British Columbia, http://wiki .elearning.ubc.ca/tela/HomePage (accessed February 27, 2006).

11. Andrew Lincoln Burrow, "Negotiating Access within Wiki: A System to Construct and Maintain a Taxonomy of Access Rules," paper presented at ACM Conference on Hypertext and Hypermedia, Santa Cruz, CA, http://portal.acm.org/citation.cfm ?id=1012831.

12. SaratogaCensus, Skidmore College, http://academics.skidmore.edu/saratoga _census/wiki/index.php/Main_Page (accessed April 19, 2006).

13. Biotechnology: Academic, Government & Industry Interactions and Tensions 2006, Harvard University, http://web.archive.org/web/20070827140819/http://www.hcs.harvard.edu/~cyberlaw/wiki/index. php/Biotech (accessed February 28, 2006).

14. Eukaryotic Genetics And Molecular Biology, University of Maryland, Baltimore County, http://www.umbc.edu/bioclass/biol414/wiki/index.php?page=Home (accessed February 28, 2006).

15. BIOL414/614 at UMBC–Projects, University of Maryland, Baltimore County, 2005, http://www.umbc.edu/bioclass/biol414/wiki/index.php?page=Projects (accessed April 19, 2006).

16. BIOL414/614 at UMBC—Projects, University of Maryland, Baltimore County, 2005, http://www.umbc.edu/bioclass/biol414/wiki/index.php?page=Projects (accessed April 19, 2006).

17. PHYS-339 Measurements Lab—McGill University Physics Department Technical Services Wiki, McGill University, http://www.ugrad.physics.mcgill.ca/wiki/index.php/PHYS-339 (accessed February 28, 2006).

18. 339–2005 Speed of Soundsome—McGill University Physics Department Technical Services Wiki, McGill University, 2006, http://www.ugrad.physics.mcgill.ca/wiki/index.php/339-2005_Speed_of_Soundsome.

19. Mark Guzdial, Pete Ludovice, Matthew Realff, Tom Morley, and Karen Carroll, "When Collaboration Doesn't Work," Georgia Institute of Technology, 2002, http://coweb.cc.gatech.edu:8888/csl/uploads/24/CMCI-ICLS-final.pdf.

20. Holocaust Wiki Project, Dan McDowell, http://www.ahistoryteacher.com/holocaust/tiki-index.php (accessed March 2, 2006).

21. Dan McDowell, "Children of the Holocaust: A Webquest for 10th Grade World History and Humanities," http://www.guhsd.net/mcdowell/wq/children.

22. Design Patterns for EduWikis—IncubatorWiki, http://edwiki.org/mw/index.php/Design_Patterns_for_EduWikis.

23. Dan McDowell, "Holocaust Wiki Project Evaluation," http://www.ahistoryteacher.com/holocaustproject/holocaust-rubric.html.

24. SkidmoreGreekTragedy, Skidmore College, http://academics.skidmore.edu/wikis/Greek_Tragedy/index.php/Main_Page (accessed March 1, 2006).

25. "Delta: Final Thoughts—SkidmoreGreekTragedy," Skidmore College, http://academics.skidmore.edu/wikis/Greek_Tragedy/index.php/Delta:_Final_Thoughts.

26. Alain Désilets, Sébastien Paquet, and Norman G. Vinson, "Are Wikis Usable?" in Wikisym 2005: Proceedings of the 2005 International Symposium on Wikis (New York: Association for Computing Machinery, 2005), 9.

27. Theodor Nelson, Literary Machines: The Report on, and of, Project Xanadu Concerning Word Processing, Electronic Publishing, Hypertext, Thinkertoys, Tomorrow's Intellectual . . . Including Knowledge, Education and Freedom. Sausalito, CA: Mindful Press, 1981.

28. Robert Coover, "The End of Books," New York Times, June 21, 1992, 11, 23–25.

29. Jean-Christophe Chazalette, "Wikipen," http://en.wikipen.org/wiki/Main_Page (accessed April 19, 2006).

30. Matthew R. Bowen, "WriteHere.net," http://web.archive.org/web/20060310114550/http://www.writehere.net/moin.cgi/FrontPage.

31. Romantic Audience Project, Bowdoin College, http://ssad.bowdoin.edu:8668/space/snipsnap-index;jsessionid=16rfhc650fb6 (accessed April 19, 2006); Romantic

Audience Project 2, Bowdoin College, http://ssad.bowdoin.edu:9780/snipsnap/
eng242-s05/space/start (accessed April 19, 2006).

32. Mark Phillipson and David Hamilton, "The Romantic Audience Project: A Wiki
Experiment," Romantic Circles: Romantic Pedagogies Commons, http://www.rc.umd
.edu/pedagogies/commons/innovations/rap/index.htm.

33. Center for History and New Media, "Hurricane Digital Memory Bank," George
Mason University et al., http://www.hurricanearchive.org/ (accessed March 7, 2007).

34. Ademar Aguiar and Gabriel David, "WikiWiki Weaving Heterogeneous Software Artifacts," paper presented at 2005 International Symposium on Wikis,
http://www.wikisym.org/ws2005/proceedings/paper-07.pdf.

35. Jude Higdon, "Teaching, Learning, and Other Uses for Wikis in Academia,"
Campus Technology, http://campustechnology.com/articles/4062a (accessed November
16, 2005).

36. SacredGotham, Columbia University, http://sacredgotham.ccnmtl.columbia
.edu (accessed March 7, 2007).

37. The Collected Works of Ralph Waldo Emerson, ed. Alfred R. Ferguson (Cambridge,
MA: Harvard University Press, 1971), 1:54.

WIKIS CITED

Biotechnology: Academic, Government & Industry Interactions and Tensions 2006.
Harvard University (cited February 28, 2006). Available from http://web.archive
.org/web/20070827140819/http://www.hcs.harvard.edu/~cyberlaw/wiki/index.
php/Biotech.

Alain Désilets, Sébastien Paquet, and Norman G. Vinson. "Are Wikis Usable?" In Wikisym 2005: Proceedings of the 2005 International Symposium on Wikis, 3–15. New York:
Association for Computing Machinery, 2005.

Digital Journalism In-Class Wiki Page. (Metamedia software). Stanford University
(cited April 19, 2006). Available from http://traumwerk.stanford.edu:3455/Rhein
gold/117.

EdGamesF03 (PmWiki software). San Diego State University (cited April 19, 2006).
Available from http://www.edwiki.org/edgames/pmwiki.php?n=EdGames.Ed
GamesF03.

Epoche Wiki. (PBwiki software). Pennsylvania State University (cited April 19, 2006).
Available from http://epochewiki.pbwiki.com/.

Eukaryotic Genetics and Molecular Biology. (QwikiWiki software). University of Maryland, Baltimore County (cited February 28 2006). Available from http://www
.umbc.edu/bioclass/biol414/wiki/index.php?page=Home.

Holocaust Wiki Project. (TikiWiki software). Dan McDowell (cited March 2, 2006).
Available from http://www.ahistoryteacher.com/holocaust/tiki-index.php.

Hurricane Digital Memory Bank. George Mason University Center for History and New
Media (cited April 19, 2006). Available from http://www.hurricanearchive.org/map
_browse.php.

NorthWoods. (MediaWiki software). Skidmore College (cited April 18, 2006). Available
from http://academics.skidmore.edu/wikis/NorthWoods/index.php/Main_Page.

PHYS-339 Measurements Lab—McGill University Physics Department Technical Services Wiki. (MediaWiki software). McGill University (cited February 28, 2006). Available from http://www.ugrad.physics.mcgill.ca/wiki/index.php/PHYS-339.

Romantic Audience Project. (SnipSnap software). Bowdoin College (cited April 19, 2006). Available from http://ssad.bowdoin.edu:8668/space/snipsnap-index;jses sionid=16rfhc65ofb6.

Romantic Audience Project 2. (SnipSnap software). Bowdoin College (cited April 19, 2006). Available from http://ssad.bowdoin.edu:9780/snipsnap/eng242-s05/space/ start.

SacredGotham. (MediaWiki software). Columbia University (cited March 9, 2007). Available from http://sacredgotham.ccnmtl.columbia.edu.

SaratogaCensus. (MediaWiki software). Skidmore College (cited April 19, 2006). Available from http://academics.skidmore.edu/saratoga_census/wiki/index.php/Main _Page.

SkidmoreGreekTragedy. (MediaWiki software). Skidmore College (cited March 1, 2006). Available from http://academics.skidmore.edu/wikis/Greek_Tragedy/index .php/Main_Page.

Social Justice Movements. (MediaWiki software). Columbia University (cited April 19, 2006). Available from http://socialjustice.ccnmtl.columbia.edu/index.php/.

Teaching English Language Arts. (Wikka Wakka Wiki software). University of British Columbia (cited February 27, 2006). Available from http://wiki.elearning.ubc.ca/ tela/HomePage.

Wikipen. (MediaWiki software). Jean-Christophe Chazalette (cited April 19, 2006). Available from http://en.wikipen.org/wiki/Main_Page.

WriteHere.net (MoinMoin software). Matthew R. Bowen (cited April 19, 2006). Available from http://web.archive.org/web/20060310114550/http://www.writehere.net/ moin.cgi/FrontPage.

Jonah Bossewitch, John Frankfurt, and Alexander Sherman,
with Robin D. G. Kelley

Wiki Justice, Social Ergonomics,
and Ethical Collaborations

We don't stop with asking what a tool does. We ask about what
kind of people we become when we use it.
—HOWARD RHEINGOLD

The capacity for technology to promote certain modes of behavior has long been a topic of interest for social and cultural scholars.[1] Software in particular plays an obvious role in influencing creativity and production, as studies on topics ranging from word processing to PowerPoint have demonstrated.[2] Theorists claim that technology and the media it brokers are "transforming the way we know and think," impacting our cognitive styles much like language itself does.[3]

In the information age, more and more of our interpersonal communications are negotiated through the intermediaries of software. The structure and form of the interactions suggested by these environments are important in understanding their effect on society at large and especially within an educational setting. Many of the communication challenges that faculty and students encounter in the classroom resemble the communication challenges that are encountered within organizations, between organizations and their constituents, between companies and their customers, or between a government and its citizens.

In this essay we explore various theoretical, pedagogical, and historical aspects of wikis, focusing on three questions as points of departure: What is a wiki? How do you teach with a wiki? What is the point of a wiki?

Our essay begins by exploring the question, What is a wiki? Here, we propose a model that locates wikis within the university's pedagogy-technology context and describes their social and other impact. Our model postulates three layers: (1) the variety of pedagogical and technological environments a university chooses to support; (2) the sets of rules, policies, and content work flows that distinguish a social software (wikis versus blogs, forums, tagging, etc.); and (3) the social, cognitive, emotional, and personal impacts the engagement fosters. This model thus offers a powerful way to define and understand wikis.

Our second question—How do you teach with a wiki?—introduces a case study, a particular classroom implementation of a wiki, to illustrate the model. In spring 2005, the Columbia University Center for New Media Teaching and Learning (CCNMTL) collaborated with Professor Robin D. G. Kelley to launch a wiki in his undergraduate course Black Movements in the U.S. Throughout the semester, eighty students iteratively developed the content of a collaborative Web site about key social justice movements in the United States. Addressing the curricular challenges posed by using a wiki, we discuss why Kelley and CCNMTL selected the wiki platform, the advanced preparations that were necessary, and strategies for monitoring and evaluating the student work in the wiki.

With the model, the case study, and other examples of collaborative composition, we explore the historical context and significance of the wiki as a medium for writing in our third question, What is the point of a wiki? Specifically, how do the collaborative composition experiences of Kelley's students compare with notable collaborations from history? We explore the examples of Diderot's grand eighteenth-century communal effort, Encyclopédie, and Oxford's nineteenth-century thousand-contributor dictionary project. Has the wiki superseded these earlier techniques—can the process of constructing a social justice wiki really promote equality? Will the wiki earn an enduring place in the classroom, or will it go the way of blotting paper and fountain pens?

In an epilogue to this essay, Kelley reflects on the use of the wiki in his classroom. Additionally, he offers a personal word, comparing wikis to his expectations and prior collaborative curricular assignments and explaining how he plans to incorporate this type of technology into his future research and teaching.

The Model: What Is a Wiki?

Essence of Engagement

Our understanding of wikis can be enriched by looking at them in the various pedagogical and technological landscapes/contexts in which they operate. Generally speaking, new concepts are understood in relation to the network of concepts that surround them.[4] In keeping with this, any examination of technologies in an educational setting also needs to take into account the curricular goals and pedagogical strategies guiding the classroom experience. Wikis belong to a family of technologies informally labeled *social software*. Members of this family include familiar applications such as blogs, forums, and social tagging. A deeper understanding of wikis and their distinctive features emerges from studying their relationships to similar technologies.

For example, blog and wiki software can be used to support all sorts of activities that are not commonly associated with the activities of "blogging" or "wikiing." This includes activities like sharing syllabi, publishing announcements, and distributing files. These newer tools can also provide spaces for discussions, similar to "traditional" mailing lists and discussion boards. When maintained over time, these systems effectively describe a student portfolio system.[5] Some of the typical activities that these systems support range from the bureaucratic to discussion oriented, from collaboration to portfolios.[6]

The differences between these variations and approaches derive from the types of engagement they are trying to foster. Technology should be used to support existing educational objectives and can also serve to promote certain styles of behavior and engagement. Thus while many educational objectives and activities can be supported by a variety of technical devices, the selection of a particular configuration may provide structure and direction and encourage subtly different kinds of interaction. It is therefore useful to identify and describe environments that look superficially similar but are functionally different, as well as ones that look different but are functionally equivalent. By so doing, we will be better equipped to distinguish between raw software functionality and the varieties of engagements they support.

Culture of Use: Code = Law?

Social software environments encourage particular usages, but a complete understanding of the dynamics within these communities requires an examination of the written and unwritten policies that may be stipulated but are often not enforced by the system. Very rigid software systems constrain the degrees of freedom that users can exercise when communicating within these systems. For example, the software governing modern news publications strictly distinguishes between the roles of journalists, editors, and publishers by assigning particular capabilities to each. More flexible social software systems might combine user abilities, and the behaviors that take shape within these systems are best described as a social contract, ethical framework, or governance structure that delineates the interactions within the community.

Wikis are an especially poignant example of how policies affect usages, since their flexibility is both their greatest strength and weakness. Mark Phillipson, as explained in his preceding essay, "Wikis in the Classroom: A Taxonomy," has developed a taxonomy of wiki usages, all of which can be supported using most wiki software. The purpose that the software serves— the essence of the engagement—is determined by the way its participants agree to use it. Thus, in Phillipson's illuminated wiki, the wiki *software* does not prevent any user from altering the poem everyone is commenting on, but the wiki *community* using this tool prescribes leaving it intact, and their culture explains and enforces this. So, the software rules allow editing, but the social policies do not.

In most wiki environments, there are mechanisms that allow for policy to be corrected after the fact rather than prevented from occurring in the first place. In particular, the history and rollback feature, common in many wiki environments, changes the necessity for strictly enforced behavioral guidelines—in this respect, a degree of trust is extended to all wiki participants, although it is often tempered with the knowledge that all edits are preserved on the participant's permanent record. Only when we consider the rules embodied in the software, as well as how those rules are configured and combined with the software's culture of use, can we begin to appreciate the full dynamics of these tools.

Platonic Wikis

So far we have considered wikis as a part of the family of technologies informally labeled *social software*. From a technical vantage point, it is also useful to consider wikis in relation to their software predecessor, the content management system (CMS). A CMS is a set of processes and technologies designed to allow users with little technical knowledge the ability to organize, review, and publish digital content. In this respect, a wiki is also a kind of CMS where the rules are set so that anyone can edit it—anything you can see you can change.

All forms of social software can be described by the rules, policies, and work flows that are applied to their content. In this context we are using the term *content* in its most generic sense. From this perspective, articles, posts, comments, and replies are all just pieces of content. What differentiates these various types of content are the different rules and policies that are applied to them and the work flows they follow in their progression through the system. Discussion boards support the exchange of ideas between single authors and often do not permit the revision of a post. Wikis, on the other hand, support the exchange of ideas with multiple authors, potentially edited and revised over time. Rules such as these enforce who is allowed to perform operations such as creating, editing, and publishing.

Content management systems permit their users to control and refine the rules that the software enforces and are continually expanding the types of rules subject to adjustment. Such systems provide content administrators and developers the ability to create tools that enforce particular combinations of these rules according to the requirements of the situation. In a perfect CMS, which has yet to be implemented, the rules would be arbitrarily configurable, leading to the prospect of system designers who can focus their efforts on the deliberate arrangement and orchestration of the rules governing these environments.

To illustrate how imprecise the term *wiki* can be, consider "simple wikis"—those without categories or histories. Simple wikis don't group posts or ideas, and users cannot see what changes have been made or who has made them. Unlike the most common wikis today, it is hard to follow the thread of a discussion. Whatever is on the screen is the last word. Another illustration is the "despot wiki"—where the community is closed, you need to log in to participate, and then you can edit only your own section. These despot wikis foster controlling behavior by the editor—limiting users, limiting posts, and limiting change. Are all of these wikis?

We composed this essay in MediaWiki, the same environment used in Robin Kelley's course Black Movements in the U.S., our case-study class. One of the most commonly used wiki engines, MediaWiki powers Wikipedia. It can be configured to offer complete open access or require users to log in, with file upload enabled or not. It also includes a discussion space for each post and automatically creates a home page for every member. The malleability of wiki software makes it very hard to pinpoint and describe across installations. Simply referring to a software package's name is often not enough to specify exactly which software rules or social policies determined the online collaboration.

With this apparatus in mind, it is easier to understand and differentiate the proliferation of systems that have emerged around these themes. Thinking in terms of rules, policies, and work flows applied to content, it is possible to define the Platonic forms of social software: for example, a Platonic wiki can be defined as an environment where everyone can see anything that has been published, can edit anything they can see, and can easily create a new page. Similarly, a Platonic blog can be defined as an environment where the author can create a new post, anyone can comment on an existing post, and posts are displayed in reverse chronological order.

Currently, very few technologies aspire to implement the Platonic forms of any of these tools. In fact, it is the variations and riffs on these forms that are potentially the most interesting. It is pedantic to be so preoccupied with semantics that a particular piece of software can no longer be classified as a wiki if it supports fine-grained permissioning over different areas within the site. At the same time, identifying the ideal typical forms of these tools makes it possible to imagine the variations in rules that might inflect different behaviors among the participants. Figure 1 envisions the interplay between these distinct, yet related, social software systems.

The social software value-space postulates a continuum of values that software environments can directly affect by encouraging, facilitating, and catalyzing effects of specific types of engagements. The deliberate selection of specific policies to govern the environment will favor different types of interactions and experiences for the users within that environment. The axes of

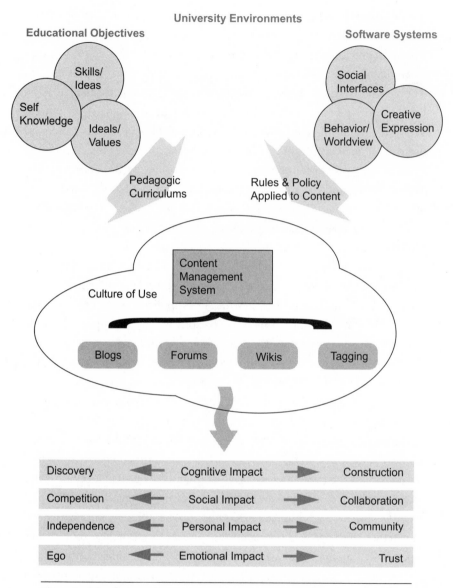

Fig. 1. Social software values

this value-space are meant to convey that these environments are capable of imparting more than subject matter. They have the potential to influence the values of the users in ways that ought to be considered by the designers of these environments.

These variations can even be seen across deployments of the very same piece of software and are even more pronounced as we begin to vary the design of the system. Consider the differences in dynamics between two classroom blogging situations: Contrast a situation where each individual student has his or her own blog versus an entire class that shares ownership and authorship of a common blog. Each of these deployments would likely be situated differently within the value-space defined previously. Should we expect different degrees of autonomy, trust, and competition across these different setups?

This is not to suggest a deterministic outcome based upon the selection of a particular technological configuration. Designers of these environments should be encouraged to deliberately consider the desired outcomes—that is, where are the participants ideally situated within this value-space?—and select the technology and its corresponding configuration accordingly. At best the environment will stack the odds in favor of certain kinds of interactions; it will not guarantee them. The obvious analogy here is to architects who design physical spaces with the aim of encouraging mingling or enabling mobility and flow. There is no guarantee that the final project will realize their intentions, but, in fact, they often do. In their essay "Disrupting Intellectual Property: Collaboration and Resistance in Wikis," Stephanie Vie and Jennifer deWinter explore variations on designing and using classroom wiki environments.

Social Interfaces: Software as Ideology

Software environments now influence psychology and culture in ways that have been historically attributed to architectural works. A contributing factor to the significance of architecture is the investment of large amounts of capital. The outcome of many building projects is determined before their design occurs—they will be built, one way or another. Similarly, the construction of software environments is often driven by requirements independent of the ethical design considerations examined in this essay. As we write this, the environments that mediate communications and learning are being constructed. These systems are now responsible for mediating the communication between individuals, organizations, and institutions. The rules of engagement are becoming set in stone or, more accurately, etched in silicon. We ought to be conscious and deliberate about their form.

The term *social interface* captures the idea that software environments create conditions for users that shape the nature of their interactions with each other.[7] Ergonomics is the study of designs intended to minimize the stress and discomfort of usage. Good hardware designs minimize physical stress, good user interfaces minimize cognitive stress, and good social interfaces minimize social stress. Examples of applications that present social interfaces include simple communications tools such as e-mail and news readers; social networking applications such as friendster, del.icio.us, and Flickr; and social software applications such as forums, blogs, and wikis.

Neither user interfaces nor social interfaces are specific to the digital age. Donald Norman describes the usability of door knobs and teapots in the language of user interfaces,[8] and theoretical architecture and anthropology have long described physical forms, spaces, and rituals in ways that could be described as social interfaces. The prevalence and malleability of software afford new media environments a degree of uniqueness, but this uniqueness is one of quality, not kind.[9]

As a corollary, since writing software is a form of creative expression it follows that the individual and community values invested in the creation of a system are almost inevitably embodied in the features that ultimately describe that system. A simple illustration of this idea is the default ability to assign a Creative Commons license using the GNU General Public License MediaWiki software, which would be a surprising default in an application produced in a proprietary setting, for example, an Adobe product. Software is now a cultural form, expressing an ideology (in this case, the importance of the freedom of knowledge) and capturing the logic of its birthplace.

It is not surprising that wikis gestated and were born within free and open source communities. The ecology describing a software environment's creation is an important inflection point when considering the values that environment might support. This does not mean that these systems will persuade their users to adopt these values, but, given our previous arguments, they may induce modes of behavior that will in turn lead to a heightened awareness and adjustment of perspective.

The case study we will now turn to is the story of the expansion and transformation of the participant's worldview. Technology was not the only influence on this educational journey, but it was the vehicle that helped them directly experience the living reality of the issues they were confronting.

The Case Study: How Do You Teach with a Wiki?

In spring 2005, CCNMTL launched a wiki in Professor Robin D. G. Kelley's undergraduate course Black Movements in the U.S. Kelley's class examines both historical and contemporary black activist movements for freedom, justice, equality, autonomy, and self-determination. The class explores, among other things, how movements were formed and sustained; the social and historical contexts for their emergence and demise; and the impact they might have had on power, on participants in the movement, on the community at large, and on a people's vision of a liberated future. Kelley wants his class to study activism not only as a written history but also as something that is relevant and alive today. It is out of this curricular goal—to teach activism as alive and meaningful today—that the need for a wiki for this class emerged.

Throughout the semester, Kelley required all eighty students in the course, divided into groups of three to four, to iteratively develop the content of a collaborative Web site about key social justice movements in New York City. In each case, students explored the broader political vision(s) of each of these movements (what they are trying to accomplish), the context for their emergence, their strategies and tactics, the impact they have had on the communities they serve as well as on struggles for social justice as a whole, and the kind of support they need to sustain the work they are doing. Students were required to interview organizers and conduct library research on the history and current activities of the organizations for which they were responsible. The idea to use a wiki was based on Kelley's need to have his students work collaboratively. Additionally, because this was effectively a semester-long project, Kelley needed to be able to check in and provide feedback to the students as they were working on their projects.

The Social Justice Movements wiki, created for this class project, was a collaborative work space for the student teams to develop their organization pages.[10] In order to develop and implement a wiki, Kelley approached CCN-MTL, a university resource for faculty interested in using technology in the classroom to advance specific curricular goals.[11] Working with Kelley, CCN-MTL initialized a wiki in development and production followed by a specific design skin for his class wiki. The next step was to add the initial content Kelley needed before introducing the wiki to the class, including, among other things, instructions for the class project and an alphabetical listing of the activist organizations to be assigned to the student groups.

Following the initial work conducted by Kelley and CCNMTL, an orientation of the Social Justice Movements wiki was given to the entire class, with the first assignment acting as a training session. Students were asked to visit a robust wiki such as Wikipedia and spend some time navigating the site. Following this, the students were asked to create their user page in the class wiki. The only requirements were that their user page take advantage of some of the basic wiki functionality: embedding an image, using various text fonts, and creating links to both external Web sites and new pages within the wiki. After the one week that was needed for orientation and the training assignment, the students began their work on their organization pages.

As a result of the painless technical demands to build a wiki page, the burden on the students for this project could be content driven. Student team members therefore had the opportunity to contribute directly and equally to their assigned organization pages. The Social Justice Movements wiki at this point was a password-protected site, available to the class only. The class-only status of the wiki was meaningful, as Kelley was able to encourage the class to use the wiki as a drafting space for their projects and not simply wait to publish their page at the very end of the semester. The process of researching and constructing the organization pages was useful to both the student groups to collaboratively work out the ideas, information, and aesthetic of their pages together and to Kelley to provide feedback. Similarly, with the history function in the wiki that allows a user to see what changes have been made to a page and by whom, Kelley was also able to make sure that the student groups were in fact working collaboratively. In summary, then, there were four elements of the wiki that were especially beneficial for Kelley's assignment:

1. The ability to introduce a new technology into the course with minimal technical training.
2. The ability for students to work collaboratively.
3. The ability for Kelley to provide feedback throughout the semester.
4. The ability for Kelley to monitor the student projects and ensure they were being constructed collaboratively.

Toward the end of the semester, the class met to present the latest versions of their assigned organization pages. Each organization page contained information related to mission, history, membership, and current activities, for instance, the page built for BlackOut Arts Collective, a grassroots coalition of artists and educators working to improve minority communities through the arts (see figs. 2–3).

In addition to researching the various organizations, Kelley required the students to propose what kind of activism the groups were primarily focused on—for instance, arts, economics, or sexual identity. Following this, the class as a whole had to propose these labels, associate them with each respective group, and then use them as metacategories to organize the assigned activist organizations. It is important to reiterate that, while Kelley selected the organizations at the start of the semester, he provided no labels. In fact, the only means by which he sorted the organizations was alphabetically, a generic taxonomy so that all assigned groups could be located by the students while not capturing any real sense of the specific activism conducted by each group. Indeed, the kind of activism these groups are conducting was part of the takeaway for the students. And because the categories had to apply not only to one group but to several, all eighty members of the class had to come to an agreement on how to classify the various organizations. The labeling of all the organizations into categories was a critical moment in the collective understanding of the class that each of their pages was part of one single site.

Generally speaking, wikis are well suited for collaborative projects where the intended outcome is a cohesive whole as opposed to a collection of independent or loosely related ideas. (See the online version of this essay at www.digitalculture.org for additional figures.) Wikis are also a good tool for iteratively developing ideas over time, allowing collaborators to revise and reorganize their contributions as themes emerge. Blogging software or a dis-

SOCIAL JUSTICE MOVEMENTS

SEARCH   Administrative Log in

Go Search

Navigation
Main Page
Organizations
Activist Intellectuals
Resources
Recent Changes
Credits
About
Help

NEW PAGE

Create New Page

TOOLBOX
What Links Here
Related Changes
Upload File
Special Pages

BAC: WHY?

+I+ **BAC: Who?** +I+ **BAC: What?** +I+ **BAC: Where?** +I+ **BAC: When?** +I+

Why is the BlackOut Arts Collective an effective social movement?

BAC artists performing

In this section we will discuss some general criteria for evaluating the effectiveness of a social justice movement based on class discussions and readings, and intermitently use those criteria to critically examine the BlackOut Arts Collective (those sections are in blue font)

Effectiveness of Social Justice Movements   [edit]

There are many elements that make a social justice movement effective. A movement can be assessed under three main lenses namely, *vision*, *leadership*, and **organization** (communication + mobilization).

The **vision** of an effective movement is one that organically cultivates compassion, inclusiveness, love, and freedom while the policy agenda is generated through collective and prolonged discussion and debate. In

---

Fig. 2. BlackOut Arts Collective

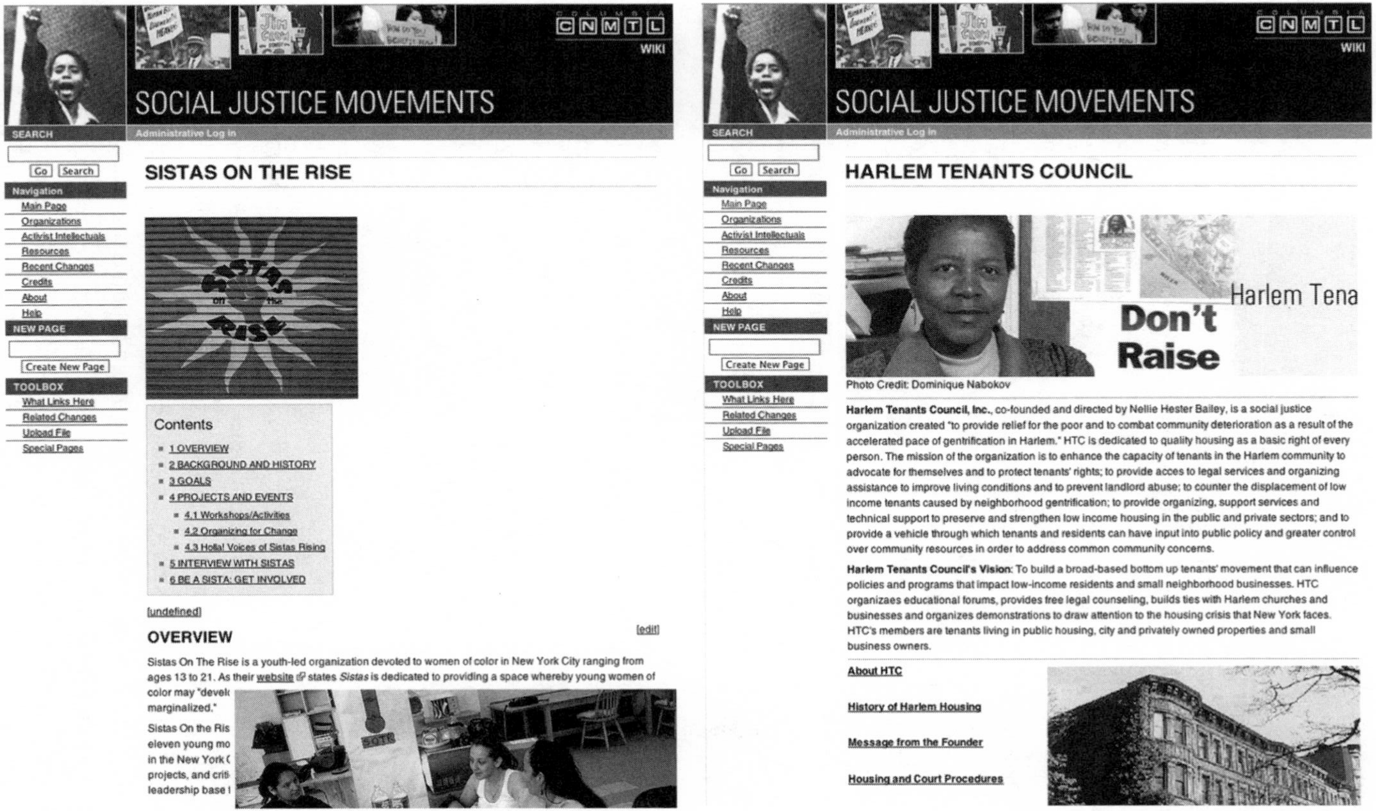

Fig. 3. Sistas on the Rise and Harlem Tenants Council

cussion board would not have allowed Kelley's class to perform these activities, which were essential to the project as a whole.

Along with the design, training, and implementation, Kelley and CCNMTL also developed methods to evaluate and eventually grade the wiki project. They developed four criteria for grading: the final product; response to feedback; collaboration; and, finally, the aesthetic of the page. The most important criteria for grading was the quality of the content; that is, Kelley evaluated each organization page like one does for the traditional print paper. Following the content, the next criteria for grading was the extent to which groups responded to Kelley's feedback during the work on the project. While Kelley did look at each organization page like a final paper, he took advantage of the "Discussion" field—sometimes known as "Talk"—in the wiki to provide students with feedback throughout the work on their project. Feedback on the organization pages ranged from the basic "no contact information" to the more complicated "need to better contextualize a mission statement." Kelley's perception of how much, or how little, students took advantage of his feedback was factored into the final grade.

Collaboration was the next quality factored in grading the wiki. Grading collaboration in the wiki in some ways presents the same problems as grading class participation—especially in a large class of eighty students like Black Movements in the U.S. Kelley and CCNMTL considered quantifying collaboration via the "History" section in the wiki, where every change is logged, or by introducing third-party visualization tools. Finally, however, it was decided to give a grade to the project as a whole as opposed to each individual student. At the same time, the in-class presentations—where every member of the student group presents his or her organization—gave a snapshot of the level of collaboration in the wiki.

The final quality Kelley considered when grading was the aesthetic of the site. Given that this was an online project, Kelley encouraged the students to take advantage of the powers of this environment when building their organization pages—for instance, posting pictures of organization members or events, adding maps to show where the organization is located, and providing links to external relevant Web sites. Similarly, the architecture of the site—where one clicks to find information—was also considered when grading. The students in Black Movements in the U.S. were not being trained to be Web masters, but Kelley wanted online pages that had a creative and informed navigation as opposed to simply being a long text document. In summary, Kelley evaluated and eventually graded the wiki project on the following criteria, in order of importance:

1. The content of each organization page.
2. The extent to which groups responded to his feedback during the work on the project.
3. The level of collaboration in each group.
4. The aesthetic of the site as it helps one to learn about each organization.

With the work completed on the organization pages and the categories agreed upon at the end of the spring 2005 semester, the Social Justice Movements wiki was released as a public site that anyone on the Web could view. With each organization page including a link to the respective organization's Web site, the Social Justice Movements wiki now serves as a portal into some of the key social justice movements in New York City. The organization pages in the Social Justice Movements wiki represent for some groups their first Web presence of any kind.

Following the public release of the Social Justice Movements wiki, Kelley has continued to introduce the wiki in other classes—including the two seminars on black intellectuals that he taught in fall 2005 at Columbia and Harvard. Instead of focusing on organizations, as was the case in the black movements class taught in spring 2005, the Columbia and Harvard seminars focused on individuals. Kelley required both seminars to work collaboratively in the Social Justice Movements wiki space: specifically, to build pages on activist individuals and connect them to the already created categories applied for the organization pages.

The collaborative work Kelley has his students conduct on either activist organizations or activist individuals supports one of the guiding aims of his courses, that is, to present activism not only as a series of past events but as living history. For the duration of a semester, Kelley asks his students to undertake research and also gain practical experience by engaging with the contemporary world of activism. With the Social Justice Movements wiki continuing to grow as a resource on activism, which offers potential strategies for social change, this particular wiki fosters an alternative online culture leaning toward the oppositional. The public sphere of this wiki, in this context, is defined by its distance from existing social and cultural norms that requires an active commitment and awareness of all its contributors, thereby resulting in the potential to learn new means to express critical public opinion. The Social Justice Movements wiki seeks to be a space that fosters a mode of self-creation through membership in a media-defined venue.

At the end of this essay, Kelley will discuss all the implementations as well as future plans for the Social Justice Movements wiki. As more implementations and uses of the Social Justice Movements wiki are planned, it becomes important to consider more not only the process entailed/generated/encouraged by the wiki but its products as well. What value, for instance, did the spring 2005 version of the Social Justice Movements wiki have for the fall 2005 seminars? Another issue with the fall 2005 implementation and its future uses concerned the role of the Social Justice Movements wiki as a public workspace: is it a public Web site where all site pages can be accessed by anyone online? And should all site elements be available at all times to all members of the class? Does the growing public visibility of the Social Justice Movements wiki—globally and in the classroom—change how students add to and modify the site? Do the students read more critically, contemplate more deeply, and respond and offer their own ideas more constructively? These issues and questions are ultimately at the heart of a much larger discussion about how transformative wikis and other genres of social software can be in both educational and popular/public contexts. Having offered a model of and discussion about a case study for using a wiki, the next section in this essay considers the wiki in the context of other collaborative enterprises such as encyclopedias and dictionaries in order to explore wikis as spaces of process and product.

The Context and Significance: What Is the Point of a Wiki?

Large-scale collaborations provide rich comparisons to wikis. Encyclopedias and dictionaries often require large-scale collaboration, and there are numerous historical examples of these, even from thousands of years ago. Two more recent efforts, *Encyclopédie* and the *Oxford English Dictionary* (OED) are both famous and well documented, and we will discuss both.

Each of these collaborative efforts reflects three key elements of Kelley's class's experience with wikis. First, an authority—teacher or editor—set the scope and wrote the rules and policies of contribution but did not set the categories for organizing the information. Second, these efforts live (at least partially) outside the ivory tower. Kelley asked his students to research, experience, and become part of the contemporary world of activism—a directive echoing these two earlier efforts. Third, since the readers and writers belong so closely to the same community, it is difficult to distinguish author from audience. Bear these three elements in mind as we consider the historical precedents of *Encyclopédie* and the *Oxford English Dictionary*.

In 1745, a Parisian publisher retained two foreigners to translate an English encyclopedia into French. When it came to preselling copies, though, it turned out they had not completed much work. The publisher tried a new translator but still had no success. In 1747, he engaged a French duo to work for about three years.[12] Denis Diderot and Jean d'Alembert, the two new editors, sat down to look over the work and planned a significant change, namely, the *Encyclopédie*. Rather than translating an English work, they planned to collect new information from throughout France.[13] Just as Kelley did setting out with Black Movements in the U.S., identifying the research topics, the editors sketched the entire content out thematically and then recruited writers to fill in the sections (for example, theology or arts and crafts) with alphabetical articles to be chosen by the contributor. In this way, the entire effort was centrally planned at the beginning. In fact, each article was distinguished as either "O" for contributor or "*" for editor—an early form of log-in.[14]

As with Kelley's class and most wikis, the readers and the writers of the *Encyclopédie* largely overlapped. In terms of raw numbers, when the first volumes came out in the early 1750s, the subscribers (a large number for the time) were hardly more numerous than the contributors and staff. In fact, it was so large a collaboration that roughly 1 percent of Paris was contributing to the project.[15] The authors and the audience (those who subscribed) both belonged to the literate and thinking folk of France, the salon set.[16] Even the censorious contributed—fifteen of the more than one hundred contributors also worked as government censors![17] In all, more than one hundred writers contributed 72,998 articles over twenty-six years to create the *Encyclopédie.*

The *Encyclopédie* set the tone for later collaborative works—fostering community as much as writing a document. In this case, the community was much more formal, perhaps because eighteenth-century French society itself was formal. After the volumes started coming out, the contributors met regularly—calling themselves Encyclopedists and meeting at Baron d'Holbach's every Thursday and Sunday. Similarly, but unusual for a wiki effort, Kelley's class also met regularly in person. (Writers about Wikipedia regularly comment on the vibrancy of the online community.) Strong social interaction supports social activism. In Kelley's class's case, activism included volunteering at social justice organizations. For the Encyclopedists, activism included atheism, erotica, and other activities deemed subversive by the French authorities of the day. In terms of activism, what better mark of service is there than serving jail time? The *Encyclopédie* nevertheless hit hard times when Diderot himself did "hard time" (albeit for the innocuous-sounding "Letter on the Blind").

The *Oxford English Dictionary* serves as another landmark in the history of collaborative writing projects. It took some seventy years to publish the whole first edition. The OED is the desert island book par excellence—or rather twelve desert island books, since it was published as twelve tomes totaling 15,499 pages. Most dictionaries include guides to definition and pronunciation. But, in addition, the OED offers 1,827,306 quotes to illustrate every meaning of 414,825 words. ("Salt," for example, covers fourteen columns over 6 pages—not counting "salt cote," "salt fat," or "salt like"— beginning with the pre–Norman the Conqueror "Wiþ blæce, wyl eolonan on buteran, meng wyþ sote, sealt, teoro.")[18]

When the Unregistered Words Committee of the London Philological Society launched an effort to write the OED in 1857, they had a rough idea that this would be big, so they adopted a new methodology that the Grimm brothers were using—recruiting volunteers to read and find different meanings.[19] In practice, the OED you read has been gathered from each of these volunteers—a system employing many authors, just like a wiki. Their complex interactions were governed by slowly evolving rules, just as wikis and other CMSs have specific rules. In the case of the OED, volunteers submitted their quotes of example usage of words, which were sorted by two people. (Originally, they thought that fifty-four five-inch pigeon holes would hold all the words in English—they were off by two orders of magnitude.) Then "re-subeditors" gathered these submissions by word and by part of speech. Then subeditors for "S" or "Q," say, gathered these chronologically and began distinguishing definitions. The editor at the top at last composed each definition and submitted it for publication.

Strict policies guided each collaborator's submissions, though the stringency of enforcement varied among editors. The first editor called these policies by their Latin name, *Canones Lexicographici*, setting out exactly how each volunteer should read, what centuries they should cover, even particular authors that were in short supply.[20] Like wiki policies, the rules guided how the information should be structured, and they even directed how the foolscap paper should be formatted!

By involving the eventual readers of the dictionary in its very writing, the Unregistered Words Committee intended a more collaborative undertaking.[21] Thus they launched an appeal to the entire English world to contribute. Two thousand appeals were distributed and reprinted in newspapers around the world, entitled "An Appeal to the English-Speaking and English-Reading Public to Read Books and Make Extracts."[22] In this sense, the authors and audience were one and the same.[23]

This broad approach was so successful that the project ballooned beyond all expectations. The contract signed with Oxford University Press in 1878 (twenty-one years into the project) stipulated ten more years of work. It took fifty-four more years. The contract stated seven thousand pages. The result was sixteen thousand. They expected it to cost nine thousand pounds. It cost three hundred thousand pounds.[24] The collaboration spawned its own sort of energy, making it difficult for anyone to get his or her arms around it at the beginning. As with many collaborations, the OED team faced the question, When is enough enough?

In order to highlight the benefits of wiki technology in general, it is probably useful to contrast the historical precedents we have described with a wiki larger than that created by Kelley's class. Therefore, let's consider the familiar case of Wikipedia.

The three collaborations resemble each other in size, namely, the number of collaborators and articles. These are each massive undertakings, engaging more people than the average person knows.[25] And the expanse covered in each case exceeds any one person's polymathy. The key point to understand is that the wiki-based effort is not larger than its predecessors just because it is a wiki. In fact, wikis have not yet engendered collaborative writing on a different scale than preceding technology. What they do is provide a new answer to an old problem, just as the ballpoint pen answered the ink-to-paper question differently than the fountain pen did. And even though ballpoints are a lot less effort, fountain fetishists persist with their Parkers and Penguins. Looking to the future, we expect new collaboration technologies to be even less effort than wikis, but a few pockets of people—for affectation or other reasons—will likely persist with wikis.

In general, it is difficult to deny that wikis are easier to use than earlier collaborative technologies: the wiki technology automates much of the effort that went in to the historical oeuvres. From editor to staff to the years of compilation, Wikipedia takes less effort. Most technologies today share this efficiency relative to their Enlightenment or industrial analogues. The ease of use and low price spread wikis quickly, but as the qualitative and quantitative comparisons to antecedents suggest, vis-à-vis collaborative tools, wikis are not doing anything radically new.

In other ways, wikis depart radically from previous efforts, in particular in the opportunity for ongoing revision. Consider the "Dewey Defeats Truman" blunder in 1948. Today, a mistaken report of election results could be corrected instantly. This speed not only helps accuracy but also encourages engagement. Unlike other collaborations, a wiki makes it possible to hit "save page" and see the effect of your effort right away. Speed encourages engagement—quality of process and sometimes quality of the product too. Wiki editors are instant stakeholders. You see your activism.

This historical perspective echoes our earlier theoretical perspective: that wikis are but a type of CMS—one specific family of rules and policies for organizing information. Neither theory nor history distinguishes wikis from other content systems or collaborative approaches. Our case study nevertheless bodes well for collaborative endeavors in general, however their content rules and policies are defined. The benefits of such endeavors are precisely those that became apparent in Kelley's class, namely, the role of originator, the real-world community, and the collapsing of author and audience. This last aspect of the wiki has two interesting facets.

The first facet is that of accuracy through exhaustion: these collaborative efforts are collaborative precisely because they require a massive amount of human effort. Their accuracy is judged by how exhaustively they cover the relevant bases. For example, the OED sought to plumb the depths of English, with the more citations per word the better.[26]

The second facet made plain by the collapse of author and audience is that of the general audience: perhaps wiki epistemology works best when the audience is general. For Diderot, his readers were his writers. The OED, believe it or not, was also intended for the general public, not the philological few. And Wikipedia is the first reference for generalists, not PhDs.

Viewed in historical context and in light of these notable similarities, wikis no longer appear to be an aberration in the history of composition. They are not revolutionary. The advantages of collaborative writing preceded wikis and will endure long after them as well. Wikis are a great technology, but they by no means offer a unique approach to composition. Consider for a minute the little magnetic words many people have on their refrigerators. They approximate a surrealist game from the 1920s—taking words out of context to find new meanings in them. The surrealists played games like exquisite corpse, where one person writes down a definite or indefinite article and an adjective, the next person a noun, the third person a verb, and so on, each without looking at what the previous person wrote. The final sentence often has unexpected meaning. "Surrealist texts obtained simultaneously by several people writing from such to such a time in the same room, collaborative efforts . . . brought out into the open a strange possibility of thought, which is that of its pooling."[27] The new collaborative meaning is precisely predicated on not reading what the others write before editing it. In this way, you discard your personal will and meaning and succumb to a group intention.[28]

This brings us back to the question, Can the process of constructing a social justice wiki really promote equality? As we saw, wikis, like other collaborative efforts, value the process as much as the product—the community engendered is a major benefit of writing in them. It is not the wiki technology per se that engenders equality but the collaborative effort on social justice (which raises the question, Would a wiki on social injustice promote inequity?). When we share an endeavor, perforce we share goals. Sharing goals and working together, we come to share values. The shared values and aspirations describe a world that we, as a group, believe to be better. Thus, wiki or no, together we make the world better.

What is a wiki? A content management system anyone can read or edit.

How do you teach a wiki? Set a topic and grade students on their ability to agree on meaningful categories.

What is the point of a wiki? Instant stakeholders and a collaboration where you see the impact of your effort.

Conclusion

The Internet, which most people are currently familiar with, is like an infinite glass wall. On one side of the wall are a small number of people with markers, writing on the glass for the rest of the world to read. Wikis fulfill one of the original intentions of the Web—bringing everyone to the same side of the glass and giving them all markers. The importance of providing individuals with this kind of autonomy and agency is exemplified in the historical discourse around the adventure playgrounds.[29]

In the detritus of World War II, the children of Europe played. Adapting the idea from the Danish junk playgrounds, the English let their kids loose on the sites destroyed by the Blitz.[30] The children played "with building materials, discarded objects and tools, and . . . buil[t] the playground according to their own ideas and for their own pleasure."[31] With few rules, they enjoyed building a fort one day and took just as much pleasure in destroying it the next. Proponents of this freeform play proposed that the war had alienated children by wresting away control of their lives and that this lack of control was causing juvenile delinquency. Adventure playgrounds offered freeform play, where the children were in charge. This exercise in control would engender broader civic participation and agency through their young lives.

If it is permissible to compare small things to large, similarly today the commercial wars have usurped control of the Internet. As browsers, we tread a battlefield of commercials. Flashing colors pop up willy-nilly on our screens. We are jerked from site to site. We don't even control our own names; anonymous corporations hoard our personal information. In the late 1990s and early 2000s, it seemed that any time you entered the Web you checked your personal control at the log-in. We were powerless, we were alienated, and we were delinquent. Is it any wonder the virus epidemic broke out so? Geeky delinquents asserted themselves, if at all, not as hollow beings but as lost, violent souls—wreaking damage on the rest of us.

Adventure playgrounds offered children the chance to reclaim the space around them. Wikis offer us the chance to reclaim the cyberspace around us. Once again, as silicon citizens, we determine what is written on our screens. Wikis offer the sense of control that the commercial wars blitzed. The best measure of the wiki will be not the number of articles posted, the number of edits made, or accuracy but rather civic and cyber engagement. Collaborative projects by their nature win over those who choose to engage. If wikis successfully engage people on civic issues like social justice, we may expect those folks at least to promote social justice (while still disagreeing about what it means). So the test of wikis will be, Are they easy enough to engage? Have we found the right way to work together to improve the world?

Epilogue
Robin D. G. Kelley

In past undergraduate courses, I always required students to collaborate on projects. Usually these collaborations took the form of classroom presentations of collective research or collections of primary documents relevant to the class that students organize, edit, and introduce in the form of a collaborative essay. But for Black Movements in the U.S., I decided to try something new: to turn what would have been classroom presentations into a permanent Web site focused on a movement for social justice. Initially, I envisioned these sites in HTML language and went to CCNMTL to show them how to build it. It was at that initial meeting with John Frankfurt and Jonah Bossewitch that I was introduced to the wiki.

Of the eighty-plus students in my course, very few were computer savvy. Indeed, many of the students considered themselves activists and were very hesitant when I announced that they would be building Web sites. Only three or four students in the entire class were familiar with HTML language and had had some experience creating Web sites, and fewer than ten had even heard of a wiki. Nevertheless, I learned some of the basics and introduced the basic syntax to the students. In addition, both John and Jonah visited the class and gave a brief but thorough presentation on the wiki. The students' first assignment was to create a personal page on the wiki site—a short autobiography along with photos and internal and/or external links that might be relevant. This assignment allowed students to become comfortable with the syntax, and very soon they were up to speed in terms of loading images and text and creating links to their own site or between sites under construction.

The wiki turned out to be the best teaching tool I've ever used. Not only did students conduct substantial library research, but the visual and audio requirements of the site compelled them to search for multimedia sources. They also had to write entries and essays about their subject matter for a public audience rather than for a professor or a teaching assistant. Thus they could not take anything for granted and had to create prose that filled in all the gaps in knowledge. More important, they had to create more internal and external links to names, concepts, and historical events with which few general readers would be familiar. Providing links to definitions, descriptions, and contextual information was much better than simply listing a source or a footnote.

Finally, the collaborative nature of the project compelled students to make links to other groups. For example, at least three groups were working on movements attempting to dismantle the prison system. It soon became clear that certain terms were used commonly by all organizations involved, most notably, *prison industrial complex* (PIC). Rather than create three different definitions of PIC, students from three different groups decided to write one definition to which all three groups might be linked.

I was especially pleased with the way in which these projects affected the activist community at large. In some cases, the organizations for which students created wiki pages had no Web sites. The wiki sites became their portal to the world. The members of these various social justice organizations became very interested in using the sites, and they, too, began to learn the wiki syntax. They wanted to use the wiki as an active site where they could add announcements for forthcoming events and possibly create space for discussion. Activists were especially drawn to the user-friendly nature of the wiki because they did not want to become dependent on a Web master or Web designer to create a site they could not change or alter on their own.

I am now teaching at the University of Southern California (USC), and my colleagues and some of the students I have met at USC are already talking about the Social Justice Movements wiki. I'm hoping to continue building the project, first by focusing on local Los Angeles activist organizations and taking advantage of students' knowledge of the city. I plan to have students add on to the existing site. One possible outcome is that USC students might be inspired to work with the Columbia and Harvard students who have already contributed to the site, not to mention the possibilities of collaboration across various social justice movements.

NOTES

The quotation at the beginning of the essay is from Howard Rheingold, "Rheingold's Rants," July 4, 1998, http://www.rheingold.com/rants/ (accessed June 13, 2005).

Editors' note: *Encyclopédie* represented the work of more than 1,000 contributors, to write 72,998 entries, with the effort of 21 editors, and took from 6 to 26 years to publish. The OED of 1878 represented the work of 1,000 contributors, to write 414,000 entries, under the supervision of approximately 1,000 editors, and took 71 years to publish. Wikipedia is an ongoing work of more than 15,000 contributors, to write more than 960,000 entries, under the supervision of about 502 editors, and is published continuously. This same information is presented as a table in the online version of this essay at http://www.digitalculture.org .

1. Marshall McLuhan, *Understanding Media: The Extension of Man* (New York: Signet Books, 1964).

2. Edward R. Tufte, *The Cognitive Style of Power Point: Pitching out Corrupts Within*. 2d ed. (Cheshire, CT: Graphics Press, 2006).

3. Michael H. Heim, "Heidegger and McLuhan and the Essence of Virtual Reality," in *Philosophy of Technology: The Technological Condition: An Anthology*, ed. Robert C. Scharff and Val Dusek (Malden, MA: Blackwell, 2003), 539–55.

4. "So in what direction will one discover the path that leads to the statesman? For we must discover it, and after having separated it from the rest we must impress one character on it; and having sampled a single different form on the other turnings we must make our mind think of all kinds of knowledge as being two forms." Plato, *Statesman*, ed. and trans. C. J. Rowe (Warminster, UK: Aris & Phillips, 1995), 258c.

5. A number of colleges are beginning to experiment with schoolwide student blogging solutions; a blog that students use for assignments for the duration of their college career effectively becomes a portfolio of their work.

6. From this perspective, course management systems are actually subsets of content management systems. Popular, general purpose, open source course/content systems include Plone, Drupal, Joomla, Sakai, Moodle, and others.

7. Joel Spolsky, "It's Not Just Usability," Joel on Software, September 6, 2004, http://www.joelonsoftware.com/articles/NotJustUsability.html (accessed June 13, 2005).

8. Donald Norman, *The Design of Everyday Things* (New York: Basic Books, 1988).

9. Lev Manovich, *The Language of New Media*. (Cambridge, MA: MIT Press, 2001).

10. The Social Justice Movements wiki can be found at http://socialjustice.ccn mtl.columbia.edu.

11. More information on CCNMTL can be found at http://ccnmtl.columbia.edu/.

12. Phillipp Blom, *Enlightening the World: Encyclopédie, the Book That Changed the Course of History* (New York: Palgrave Macmillan, 2005), 37–41.

13. Ibid., 48.

14. Ibid., 119.

15. Ibid., 58–79.

16. Ibid., 79.

17. Ibid., 111.

18. *Oxford English Dictionary*, 2d ed., s.v. "Salt."

19. Simon Winchester, *The Meaning of Everything: The Story of the Oxford English Dictionary* (New York: Oxford University Press, 2003), 43–44.

20. Ibid., 54.

21. Ibid., 44.

22. Ibid., 107.

23. Some think wikis distinguished for their anonymity—you don't need to be invited or qualified. Anyone can participate, unless the wiki is limited to members only. Actually, the OED was also open to anyone. As we now know, even certified lunatics were not barred.

24. Winchester, *The Meaning of Everything*, 88–94.

25. See Malcolm Gladwell, *The Tipping Point* (New York: Little, Brown, 2000), 176–81, referring to Robin Dunbar, "Neocortex Size as a Constraint on Group Size in Primates," *Journal of Human Evolution* 20 (1992): 462–93.

26. Winchester, *The Meaning of Everything*, 56.

27. Alastair Brotchie, compiler, *Surrealist Games* (London: Redstone Press, 1991), 141, citing André Breton, *Les Manifestoes du Surréalisme: Suivis de Prolégomènes à un Troisième Manifeste du Surréalisme ou Non* (Paris: Sagittaire, 1946).

28. Catherine Vasseur, L'Image sans mémoire. Les cahiers du Musée national d'art moderne, 1996, printemps. 71–91.

29. Christopher Alexander, *A Pattern Language: Towns, Buildings, Construction* (New York: Oxford University Press, 1977), 368–70.

30. Roy Kozlovsky, "The Junk Playground: Creative Destruction as Antidote to Delinquency," paper presented at the Threat and Youth Conference, Teachers College, Columbia University, April 1, 2006, http://threatnyouth.pbwiki.com/f/Junk%20Play grounds-Roy%20Kozlovsky.pdf.

31. Ibid., 1.

Dan Gilbert, Helen L. Chen, and Jeremy Sabol

Building Learning Communities with Wikis

As more and more students have access to technology and wireless networks, opportunities to collaborate, participate, and define how knowledge is organized are opening up at a dramatic pace. These opportunities make it possible for learning communities to engage more students, to operate in new ways, and to sustain collaboration over longer periods of time. To better comprehend these developments, this chapter introduces a framework for understanding how wikis can support the creation and maintenance of learning communities. This framework can be used by instructors to determine whether a wiki is right for their courses, as well as to troubleshoot and iterate new practices to gain more value from a wiki. Our framework has its basis in four case studies in which the authors analyzed the ways wikis were used in different classes at Stanford University—classes that included traditional undergraduate and graduate courses and also shorter workshops and special courses. Much of this information was first presented at the Educause Learning Initiative (ELI) conference in January 2006, and this chapter serves to expand upon and extend those initial findings.

Online experiences can supplement face-to-face encounters, and in many instances learning may extend well past traditional time frames such as the academic quarter or semester. In this new learning environment, wikis stand out as natural tools for facilitating and supporting the activities of a learning community, both during the official course period and afterward. The critical affordance of a wiki that fosters these activities is its versatility: the content, the navigation, and the interface of a wiki can be customized and updated to reflect the needs of a specific group of learners. Nevertheless, their chameleon-like features also pose a challenge: if wikis are able to be adapted to so many different tasks—tasks that other tools were designed to accomplish—how can we find out what wikis are *ideally* suited for? What are the chief virtues of wikis, and when are they most useful for achieving the goals of a particular learning community?

Background

Representing the perspectives of instructor, researcher, and academic technologist at the Stanford Center for Innovations in Learning (SCIL)[1] and the Center for Teaching and Learning (CTL),[2] the authors identified learning goals and pedagogical practices supported by wikis and designed a model for assessing how wikis can contribute to the development of a community of practice. Wenger describes a community of practice along three dimensions—what it is about, how it functions, and what capability it has produced.[3] Wikis are uniquely suited to address these dimensions because (1) they possess the flexibility to support the *joint enterprise* of the community as it evolves and changes (what it is about); (2) the wiki environment fosters the social aspect of engagement among the community's members (how it functions); and (3) wikis support the documentation of communal resources that represent the collective work and memory of the community over time (what capability it has produced).[4]

SCIL conducts scholarly research to advance the science, technology, and practice of learning and teaching. Through one of its programs, SCIL manages five experimental advanced resource classrooms at Wallenberg Hall,[5] where Stanford faculty and students work together to create innovative learning experiences for undergraduate and graduate courses from across the campus. An increase in the usage of wikis and other participatory technologies sparked the interest of SCIL staff and researchers in how these tools are being used to support learning communities inside and outside of the classroom. As a diverse collection of instructors and courses began to use these tools, patterns began to emerge that extended beyond any disciplinary boundaries.

At Stanford's CTL, wikis are introduced to faculty and instructors through faculty workshops on teaching and technology and through one-on-one consultations. CTL encourages faculty and instructors to use wikis in the classroom primarily as a means of supporting student learning in the context of a single course. Instructors use wikis as repositories of student-generated work or information; they also use them to foster more equitable communication among members of the course. This is especially the case in project-based courses or in courses that use student teams in some way. In addition to providing pedagogical support, CTL manages and maintains many wikis that are used in courses at Stanford.

Case Studies

Throughout this chapter we will refer to the cases outlined in table 1 to illustrate the different components of the framework. Observations, interviews, reflections on teaching, and analyses of the wikis themselves informed the development of the framework described in this chapter in each of these cases. It should be noted also that all of these classes took place at Stanford University and that the participants had access to laptop computers during most of the course meetings. In each case, there were fewer than thirty participants in the course.

Deciding which wiki technology to use for a particular learning community can be quite difficult. As of December 2006, Wikipedia identified at least sixty different kinds of wiki technologies.[6] In the cases that we studied for this chapter, four different wiki technologies were used: PmWiki, Swiki, TikiWiki, and ProjectForum wiki. Each had its own technical configurations regarding levels of participation and details of hosting. In all of these cases, the wikis were hosted locally on Stanford servers. Because the wikis were intended to benefit a specific community of learners who had come together for a course or institute, most of the wikis also used log-ins and passwords to manage the community. The only exception was the SCIL Summer Institute, which was open to anyone in the world. The rationale for having a completely open wiki in this particular instance was twofold. First, because exploring the technology was itself one of the pedagogical goals, the instructor felt that all parties should understand the risks and rewards of having an open community. Second, implementing a log-in/password system was simply too much work for a weeklong session that was not intended to create new proprietary content.

TABLE 1. Case Studies

Course and Wiki Tool	Description of Learning Community	Wiki Goals
SCIL Summer Institute: Designing Learning Spaces (Swiki)	A one-week intensive workshop for architects, academics, nonprofit staff, and graduate students to integrate learning theory into the design of physical spaces	Establish a Web presence for individual reflection and create a knowledge base for attendees to reference after course completion
Designing the Human Experience (TikiWiki, PmWiki)	A project-based introductory freshman seminar on design engineering experimenting with blogs and wiki environments	Facilitate student integration and synthesis of learning through increasing student awareness of learning and articulating connections between learning and the design process
Philosophical Stages Summer Program (ProjectForum wiki)	A three-week program for high school students that integrates ancient philosophy, drama, and interactive technologies	Create a forum for individual reflection and create a knowledge base for attendees to reference after course completion
Institute on Scholarship for Engineering Education (ISEE) Workshop (PmWiki)	A one-week workshop designed to build a community among twenty research fellows from five institutions, centering on doing scholarship with direct institutional impact	Give participants a place to document sources of learning, inspiration, and strategic planning during the institute, including links, documents, photos, insights, questions, and reflections

Cutting-Edge Technology Meets Preschool Board Game

The case study analyses revealed patterns that demonstrated how wikis could be employed to support emerging learning communities across disciplines, courses, contexts, and audiences. We have used these patterns to develop a framework for examining how wikis actually function in learning communities and determining whether a wiki is the right match for their courses. This framework will be useful in helping instructors decide whether a wiki is appropriate for the specific learning aims of their courses and in helping instructors make sense of how the wiki changes as their course progresses.

After identifying the elements of the wiki in relation to learning communities, we searched for a metaphor that would help explain how these different steps fit together. Initially, we explored ideas that related to the life cycle of a wiki and thought that the sequential stages in cell biology or water cycles might help explain how wikis develop, thrive, and die in academic settings. Retaining the idea of stages but noting that wikis often leap ahead or fall back into earlier phases, we eventually settled on the metaphor of a board game to illuminate the phases of designing, implementing, and sustaining a wiki. We used the classic Hasbro board game "Chutes and Ladders" as a metaphor for understanding the actions within a course that can accelerate the adoption of a wiki as a community of practice (ladders) or restrict or even set back the expansion of the community (chutes).

How the Framework Is Used

This framework can be used either by instructors who are considering a wiki for their courses or by larger communities of instructors, researchers, and pedagogy advisers who are examining the impact of wikis on learning. In each case, the participants imagine playing a game in which they advance by one square every time they answer one of the specific questions that is addressed to them. The first question, for example, asks them to determine what learning goals the wiki should support. After making these goals explicit, participants "move forward" to the next square, which involves developing a technology plan, and so on (fig. 1). When a faculty member is actively engaged with the wiki and makes it a central part of the practices of the course, this engagement acts as a ladder or a catalyst, which enables the learning community to become more robust in a shorter period of time. On the opposite end of the spectrum, if a faculty member tells students to "just put that on the wiki" but never responds or actively uses the wiki herself, then the community will fall into a chute and return to the beginning of the process. Both learners and instructor will thus be no closer than they were at the outset to achieving a full community of practice.

The key advantage of this particular game metaphor is that it enables instructors to understand quickly just how powerful their roles are in activating their learning communities. It acknowledges that, even though all partici-

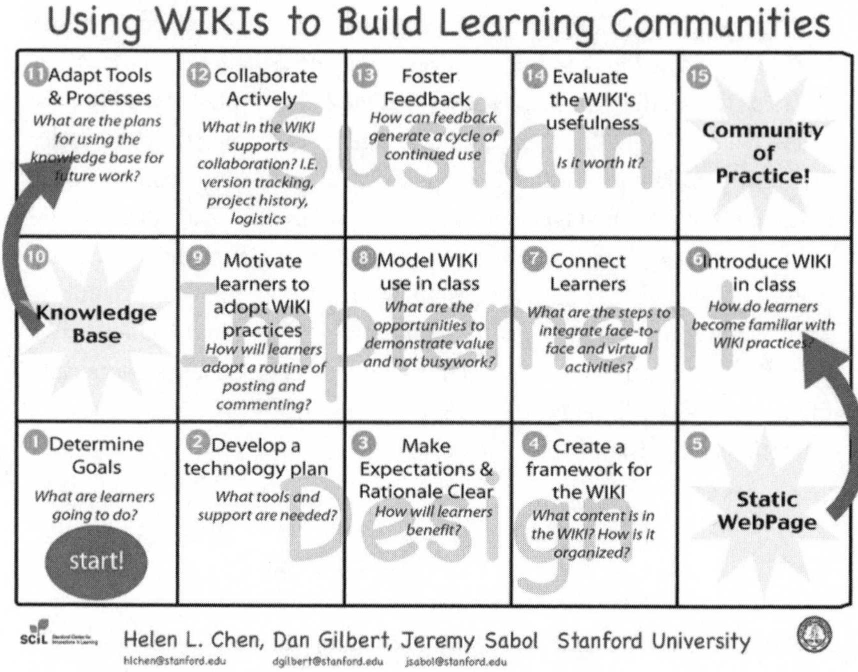

Fig. 1. Framework to analyze wikis in learning communities (from Helen L. Chen, Dan Gilbert, and Jeremy Sabol, "Using Wikis to Build Learning Communities: Successes, Failures, and Next Steps," poster presented at the annual meeting for the Educause Learning Initiative, San Diego, CA, January 29–31, 2006).

pants are peers from a technical perspective, the instructor retains a special status as someone who can create incentives for students to use the wiki. In the best cases, this special status can push the community forward when it might otherwise have stalled. One of the key disadvantages of the game metaphor, on the other hand, is that it implies the possibility of "losing"— that anything less than winning or reaching the end is not worthwhile. However, our experience suggests that this is rarely the case: communities of learners and instructors still gain value from wikis that help document a stage of their learning, even if that wiki is ultimately not active enough to sustain the community in the long term. For example, there is a value in having a static Web page emerge midway through a course; it is by no means a waste of effort or time. In our model, however, because "Static Web Page" is identified as only the fifth of fifteen distinct steps to building a community of practice, reaching that level might be considered a failure.

The game metaphor also reinforces the role of the instructor as the person who controls the action in the community. While the entire community of learners progresses through the various stages and is ultimately responsible for sustaining itself as a community, it is the instructor who leads the community and sets the tone for what the community values. The instructor is the "player," the person who made the initial decision to try the game in the first place and the one player who can choose to leave the game at any stage.

The following sections of this chapter narrate each step of the development of a wiki in more detail and offer concrete examples drawn from our case studies (fig. 2).

The power of collaborative technologies depends on their users' contributions. In the courses we observed, learners had a wide range of abilities and technical confidence. To get the most value out of their experience, all of the instructors first determined the learning goals for their course. How the course leader set the tone for the experience distinguished these cases from one another. As Elfving and Menchen-Trevino's case study amply demonstrates later in this volume, the structure of the learning community and the relative importance of the role of the wiki in that community are crucial for participation. The more the context of the learning community resembles a traditional class format, with lectures and individual assignments, the less the wiki can contribute to establishing and supporting community. However, that same case study points to the fact that the role of the wiki may be completely organic and cannot be decided upon in advance by a professor or other learning community leaders. Before deciding to use any kind of technology for learning, it is critical for the instructor to *determine learning goals* for their students. If those goals include collaboration, discovery, sharing,

❶ Determine Goals	❷ Develop a technology plan	❸ Make Expectations & Rationale Clear	❹ Create a framework for the WIKI	❺
What are learners going to do?	*What tools and support are needed?*	*How will learners benefit?*	*What content is in the WIKI? How is it organized?*	**Static WebPage**
start!				

Fig. 2. Squares 1–5: Designing the wiki experience in class

reflection, and a combination of face-to-face and virtual activities, then a wiki may be the right tool for accomplishing this kind of work. If the instructor's goals, however, focus more on individual research and writing, then a wiki may add no real value to the course. Lakeman stresses in his chapter, "Content and Commentary: Parallel Structures of Organization and Interaction on Wikis," that decisions about how to structure a wiki have both social and technical implications for the administration of the wiki and that these implications are interrelated. Users must actively shape the conventions that determine how they will participate and collaborate together.

A clear articulation of these goals should help decide the next step, which involves *developing a technology plan*. Building a technology plan requires answering several key questions:

- In what kinds of activities will students engage as a part of this course—collaborating, writing, researching, creating, and so forth?
- What technologies are available, supported, or supportable at my institution?
- How much training will learners need to use the wiki? While Net Generation learners are generally more familiar and comfortable with Web-based technologies, this does not imply that all students will master all technologies at the same speed.

After developing a technology plan, the instructors move from designing the activities that the wiki will support to designing the interactions themselves. To advance wiki usage and encourage class participation, the instructor needs to *make the expectations and rationale clear* to the learners. As with any activity, learners must see how they themselves will benefit from using the tool. In the cases that we examined, learners benefited from wikis by

- learning new processes and tools for collaboration;
- creating team archives and electronic portfolios to serve them in future courses; and
- developing a comprehensive view of their contributions to a project for evaluation during the current term.

In each of these cases, making the rationale explicit to learners proved invaluable to the basic use of the wiki itself. In the case of the SCIL Summer Institute, students were the most excited about using the wiki when it became clear to them that the resources and reflections that the entire community was assembling would be valuable throughout the remainder of the course. Their work on the wiki on days one and two would serve them on days four and five, so they had an incentive to participate in the wiki from the outset. One challenge, however, was that the perceived benefits seemed to disappear once the face-to-face community dispersed at the end of the course.

Before introducing the wiki itself, the instructor should design a basic structure for organizing its content, a structure that is typically seen by the learner as the front page. *Creating a framework* for the wiki not only seeds the community with some basic information and means for navigation but also helps set expectations concerning the kinds of tasks the wiki will support. In the SCIL Summer Institute, the framework simply consisted of the titles of the pages that were found in the wiki: course schedule, participant bios, useful links, images, and specific discussions. In contrast, in the Institute on Scholarship for Engineering Education (ISEE) Workshop, establishing the framework meant creating workspaces in the wiki for individual and small group work.

One of the more interesting things we found was that learners rarely changed the initial framework of the wiki. The wiki environment is unique in that any learner can change the navigation or reorganize the nature of the environment itself. This, however, rarely happened in the cases we studied (table 2). (See the online version of this chapter at www.digitalculture.org for additional figures.) In the ISEE Workshop wiki, while users were active in editing and creating pages, they were notably reluctant to edit the framework of the wiki shown in the right-hand column. We can speculate as to why this was the case. First, any tool that is introduced by an instructor is initially received as the property of the instructor and not necessarily a tool of the community. Because learners did not feel a sense of ownership over the wiki, they may have been reluctant to edit the pieces that they saw as fundamental to the environment itself. Second, users may have had a difficult time understanding that any changes made to the wiki could be easily reversed. Although this potential for "rollback" is central to the technology and philosophy of wikis as a tool, it is conceptually counterintuitive to the uninitiated. There may also have been some reluctance to change something that could affect every member of the community—in general, users were much more willing to add text rather than edit or delete existing text.

Even with an implemented framework, a clear rationale, and a technology plan in place with specified learning goals, the wiki may never solicit much collaboration among learners. In this case, the end result is a *static Web page* to show for the instructor's effort. In terms of efficiency, this result does not always benefit the students or the instructor. It is important to emphasize, though, that a static Web page in fact possesses several specific benefits. For one thing, it can still be valuable to students after the course is over, as a resource for future learning. Creating a static Web page can also be a community-building experience in which multiple people contribute to a process—building a class Web site—that has traditionally been the sole domain and responsibility of the teaching staff.

From the learners' perspective, the technological differences between a wiki and a static Web page are insignificant. Both are accessed through a Web browser from any computer in the world and therefore do not require any special installation or technical knowledge of computers. However, the two vary greatly in terms of the demands they make on learners as well as the potential range of practices they enable and encourage. In the case of a static Web page or traditional course Web site, learners are usually asked to simply read or otherwise passively participate in the Web site. In the case of a wiki,

TABLE 2.   Examples from Practice: Designing the Wiki Experience

Case	Goal	What Happened
Philosophical Stages	Empower high school students to see themselves as cocreators of learning experience	Used sleek, modern design to appeal to younger users Planned course in classroom equipped with laptops so that students and instructors could contribute simultaneously
Institute on Scholarship for Engineering Education (ISEE) Workshop	Encourage collaboration among small groups from each participating school Provide a continuous environment for brainstorming, project planning, project updates and reports, and document repository	Provided technical support by university staff Designated institute members to "seed" the wiki with content on a daily basis Sent daily reminders to post products of work sessions

learners are challenged to shape the content, the context, and the nature of the collaboration in the online setting.

A wiki offers much more functionality for supporting collaborations, such as creating documents with multiple authors or working on projects that require groups to coordinate and integrate their individual tasks. Yet, in order for these activities to get off the ground, instructors need to dedicate specific time to introducing the wiki in class (fig. 3). Devoting class time to this introduction sends a signal to the learners that participating in the wiki is a critical component of the course, and it offers instructors an opportunity to give students simple tasks that demonstrate the functionalities of the wiki. For example, in the SCIL Summer Institute the instructor asked students to find a useful site and post it to the wiki. During the first meeting, students searched, copied, and pasted URLs into the wiki in real time, clicked "save," and collectively created a single Web page with everyone's contributions.

These kinds of activities depend, of course, on having easy access to computers in the classroom. While it might not be necessary to have a one-to-one computer-to-person ratio, it is important that students have the experience of contributing to the wiki in the presence of others in the virtual community. In several cases, learners often made comments to each other, which reinforced the role of the wiki by instructing others in the class not to send content via e-mail but rather "to just post it in the wiki." These comments encouraged the learners to interact with the wiki on a regular basis and established it as the center of the community's interactions.

Having students make their first posts together in real time also provides them with a chance to connect with other learners in their community both physically and virtually. In the case of the Philosophical Stages course, the instructors invested a significant amount of energy in building connections among learners in person. Building on those face-to-face relationships, the

⑩ Knowledge Base	⑨ Motivate learners to adopt WIKI practices *How will learners adopt a routine of posting and commenting?*	⑧ Model WIKI use in class *What are the opportunities to demonstrate value and not busywork?*	⑦ Connect Learners *What are the steps to integrate face-to-face and virtual activities?*	⑥ Introduce WIKI in class *How do learners become familiar with WIKI practices?*

Fig. 3. Squares 6–10: Implementing wikis to build learning communities

instructors set the expectation that learners would participate in the wiki with the same commitment that they brought to their course meetings.

The implementation of any new practice in a classroom benefits greatly from the support and validation of the instructor. In the cases that we examined, the instructor *modeled wiki use in class* to demonstrate its value within the larger context of the course learning goals. In classrooms where the instructor's computer was projected onto a large screen, the instructor was able to make explicit to students the process and the rationale for using the wiki. In the case of the Designing the Human Experience course, the professor kept the wiki projected on one of the in-room computers so that it was a constant presence in the room. The constant presence of the wiki allowed the instructor to comment on specific wiki posts in a face-to-face setting. We suspect that the expectation that they would receive feedback from the instructor during class also motivated students to continue to post. Likewise, in the Philosophical Stages course the instructors often recognized and discussed student contributions during class time. In both of these courses, regardless of the activity, recognition from the instructor encouraged higher levels of participation in the wiki. The instructor's modeling of the tool set some baseline expectations for how students would use the wiki throughout the term.

Modeling the wiki use in class is critical to *motivating learners to adopt wiki practices* as a regular part of their study practices (table 3). Specifically, instructors need to encourage posting, editing, and commenting among their students. In each of the cases that we observed, instructors were able to motivate students in a face-to-face setting to post to the wiki. In Designing the Human Experience, three weekly assignments were created to encourage regular posting to the class wiki. With the "input capture" assignment, students were encouraged to post a relevant Web link, a sketch, or a photo of a project still in the design phase. The "immediate reflections" assignment asked students to share their thoughts on a class speaker, team meeting, or other activity by posting to the wiki in class or immediately following class. Finally, students were expected to distill materials from both their input captures and immediate reflections in the "epilogue" assignment, a well-founded reflection at the end of each design cycle that would highlight what they learned not only to themselves but also to their peers and to the teaching team.[7]

As the wiki fills up with posts, reflections, and edits, it becomes a knowl-

edge base for the course and for the discipline. As more learners post a diverse set of resources and reflections to the wiki, the online space is where learners go first when they have questions about the subject matter. During the SCIL Summer Institute the course wiki was the primary resource for information on designing learning spaces. As soon as the course ended, however, the wiki lost its importance in the community. Without the face-to-face community to keep the practices alive, this wiki slid backward from an active and growing knowledge base to a static Web resource that was only used occasionally by former students in the class. A follow-up e-mail from the instructor aimed at encouraging future posts generated only a few e-mail replies and no posts. In the instructor's opinion, generating content on the wiki would require bringing the learners back for a face-to-face meeting in order to create enough motivation to participate in a virtual community. In his chapter in this volume, Morgan describes a strategy of refactoring wiki pages for the purpose of synthesis and reorganization into a format that would be more suitable and accessible in a knowledge base.

In the best-case scenario, a wiki becomes part of a thriving and sustainable learning community. In such a community, learners must move from just adopting the practices to *adapting the tools* (fig. 4). In this stage, the com-

TABLE 3.   Examples from Practice: Implementing Wikis to Build
Learning Communities

Case	Goal	What Happened
SCIL Summer Institute	Strengthen relationships between learners	This wiki was a tool that learners used for the week they were in class; after class ended, so did their close connections with fellow learners.
Designing the Human Experience	Encourage students to develop habits of capture, documentation, and reflection about the design process and learning	Using templates and creating a structure for the wiki were extremely important in introducing the wiki to the students and getting them to use it. There was limited success with requiring weekly comments on other students' postings.

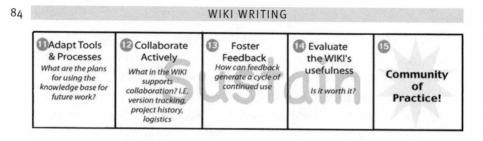

Fig. 4. Squares 11–15: Sustaining communities of practice

munity moves from a centralized top-down structure to an organic structure where all contributors feel ownership over the intellectual framework, the site navigation, and the wiki content. As a community, learners and the instructor collaboratively decide what information or media to include and how it should be organized. As the needs of the students evolve, they feel empowered to modify the tool to meet those needs. The community is also in a position to speculate what it might need for future work and can change the tools and work practices to support expected needs. In the case of the ISEE Workshop, two of four participant universities continued to actively use the wiki after the workshop was completed, and each of these universities evolved separate navigation and use practices, arising out of the specific needs of the groups at each of the universities. While one group continued to use the wiki as a project management tool, another used it more as an internal blog, sharing periodic updates both with group members and with other interested parties at the university. Significantly, the two groups with the most long-term wiki activity were also the most active wiki users during the workshop; these groups also had more structural support for sustained use, including designated roles for wiki use.

After developing a collective sense of ownership over the wiki, the tool is primed for learners, instructors, and even outsiders to *collaborate actively* on projects. To sustain the community, users revisit changes in versions of projects and comments and gain value from being able to compare processes as well as products. In this stage, complementary tools like electronic portfolios and blogs are valuable in helping learners reflect on their understanding of how the subject matter has evolved as well as to what degree the wiki has supported their learning. This active collaboration is not limited to specific projects that are a part of the course. Learners collaborate on a larger scale just by contributing to the development of the online community that the wiki represents. In the cases of the SCIL Summer Institute and the Philosophical Stages course, participants worked on projects as teams while also building the entire Web community that organized the experience of being in that class. In the SCIL Summer Institute this meant that all participants created a resource that was useful to the entire community, even if its organization was somewhat haphazard. Comments from both instructors and students demonstrated that the act of creating the wiki was in itself as important as any information that ultimately was available there.

In the best case, active collaboration on specific projects and across the site *fosters feedback* loops that keep the community engaged. Quality feedback from peers as well as instructors encourages greater use of the wiki and a higher level of acceptance and credibility. Participation in the online community becomes as valuable as participation in the face-to-face community in a course. The feedback must be provocative and engaging enough for community members to feel that their work is being read and taken seriously. For example, in Philosophical Stages the instructors posted their reactions to student posts on the Web and then analyzed their feedback with students during class. When students realized that their comments were being used as an assessment tool by the instructors as well as a means for structuring the nature of the class, they were extremely motivated to participate even further.

In the courses we observed, the final step to a community of practice was to *evaluate the wiki's usefulness* over the long term (table 4). Essentially, the learners and the instructor need to continually ask themselves, "Is using the wiki worth it?" The benefits have to be clear. In order for the community to be sustained, the benefits of efficiency, community building, and learning gains must outweigh the costs of time and energy expended into using a wiki. In most of our cases, the community could not consistently overcome this last hurdle, as users found that the wiki was much more useful in supporting existing practices by a community as opposed to building a new community of practice. In other words, learners had figured out how to utilize the wiki to support the activities already established by the community, but they never quite came to see the wiki as the core component of a community larger than themselves, a community that might produce new activities and practices. The wiki was a useful tool for collaborating, but learners did not recognize

TABLE 4. Examples from Practice: Sustaining a Community of Practice

Case	Goal	What Happened
Philosophical Stages	Keep high school students engaged with drama, classics, and each other beyond class	Most successful example of community enduring beyond limits of the course; students contributed to the wiki for months after course ended; students also contributed to the design of future courses
SCIL Summer Institute	Sustain community to generate enough interest in future workshops and build SCIL brand as center node of network interested in learning spaces	Strong feedback cycle existed through last day of class and even for several weeks beyond, but wiki was not a strong enough pull to keep community together after face-to-face community stopped meeting
Institute on Scholarship for Engineering Education (ISEE) Workshop	Sustain community in order to carry research project to conclusion and create impact at local university	Mixed results of community enduring beyond institute; some groups continued to use the wiki, while others stopped immediately when the workshop was complete; wiki activity not necessarily commensurate with completion of research project
Designing the Human Experience	Build a knowledge base of experiences for future students to reference and draw upon	Although previous years' wikis have been quite useful to the teaching team in improving upon curricula materials, the value to future students needs further exploration; issues of privacy, intellectual ownership, etc., need to be addressed.

the wiki as a cornerstone for establishing a new kind of learning community, nor did having the wiki available to them radically transform their thinking and their commitment to the learning community. Learners' commitments to the community and to the wiki were influenced most by the expectations set by the instructor.

Conclusion/Implications

The framework elaborated in this chapter can help instructors to better understand the practice of wikis in a variety of course environments. It offers strategies for determining whether a wiki is the right tool for meeting instructors' specific learning goals and for integrating the tool successfully in the life of the course. This framework may also help instructors to diagnose difficulties, stagnancies, or mismatches between course goals and participant activities. In his chapter in this volume, Phillipson proposes five models for wikis based on how they are used in learning communities. Our approach complements Phillipson's emphasis on the tools with reflective questions that push faculty to consider their pedagogical goals for the course. Used together, Phillipson's taxonomy and our framework could help faculty, students, and designers use a common language to describe their teaching and learning activities and make better decisions about learning activities and the role that wikis can play in accomplishing those goals.

Several additional insights about wikis and learning communities emerged from our research. First, wikis are by design participatory, collaborative, and engaging, and therefore they have great potential for community building. However, in practice, wiki activity must still be encouraged or driven by an instructor, a leader, or a group of advocates within a community. In the case of a class, that role is usually played by the instructor or teaching team, who can require wiki participation as part of the student grade. In learning communities that are not bound by a credit-bearing course framework, the leader or advocate role is all the more essential particularly for long-term sustainability. As with all Web 2.0 technologies, users need a reason to contribute and participate. In the cases examined in this chapter, where many of the participants were students, it was often explicit recognition—or fear of retribution—that encouraged community members to contribute during the course. In their chapter, Bossewitch, Frankfurt, and Sherman point to the importance of understanding the rules embedded within wiki software to understand the potential that this collaborative tool offers. The technical rules that govern the way wiki technologies operate are static for most users—we suspect that it is unlikely that students will make changes to the code of the tool itself in the context of a class. The social rules, however, are dynamic; they change as the term of the class goes on and groups form and instructors gain or lose interest in sustaining the wiki community. Sustaining the best social practices in creating communities (giving feedback, building on each other's ideas, encouraging reflection, etc.) is just as important, if not more so, as sustaining the work processes (posting regularly, linking to others' work, etc.) of using the wiki in a course. Our observations identify an opportunity to design creative and innovative approaches that demonstrate to participants the benefits of continued involvement after the completion of the formal course experience, both in terms of actual practices as well as new wiki features.

Second, in evaluating the value of wikis for educational environments, it is important not to overstate the leap in innovation they represent. Learning communities have thrived, formally and informally, long before wikis or virtual collaborative spaces existed. The cases studied here emphasize the importance of the face-to-face element of a community for the successful evolution of a wiki, particularly when the community extends beyond the time frame of the face-to-face experience. The virtual relationships that a wiki supports and represents are strongest when they are founded on social relationships that take root initially in a shared physical space. This is most important when considering the role of the instructor or advocate, who encourages others to use the wiki and models wiki practice in the early stages of the community's adoption of the wiki.

Finally, careful examination of how wikis and learning communities bolster or detract from the learning process will help elucidate what distinguishes wikis from other tools and practices, thus making their implementation more specific and focused. We believe this framework for analyzing wikis in learning communities is important in this regard, because it centers on the general activities of a successful learning community and situates the wiki as a tool to support that community. The wiki can maintain the life and activity of a learning community, but it can only do so if the wiki itself is sustained by the community.

NOTES

1. More information on the Stanford Center for Innovations in Learning can be found at http://scil.stanford.edu.

2. More information on the Center for Teaching and Learning can be found at http://ctl.stanford.edu.

3. Etienne Wenger, "Communities of Practice: Learning as a Social System," *Systems Thinker*, June 1998. http://www.co-i-l.com/coil/knowledge-garden/cop/lss.shtml (accessed March 6, 2007).

4. Etienne Wenger, *Communities of Practice: Learning, Meaning, and Identity* (Cambridge: Cambridge University Press, 1999).

5. More information on Wallenberg Hall can be found at http://wallenberg.stanford.edu.

6. Wikipedia, http://en.wikipedia.org/wiki/List_of_wiki_software (accessed December 7, 2006).

7. Helen L. Chen, David Cannon, Jonathan Gabrio, Larry Leifer, George Toye, and Tori Bailey, "Using Wikis and Weblogs to Support Reflective Learning in an Introductory Engineering Design Course," in *Human Behavior in Design '05*, ed. J. S. Gero and U. Lindemann (Sydney: University of Sydney, Key Centre of Design Computing and Cognition, 2005), 95–105.

Success through Simplicity: On Developmental Writing and Communities of Inquiry

Ward Cunningham called wikis an example of "the simplest thing that could possibly work."[1] Cunningham's Zen-like aesthetic was (and is) aimed at software developers, but educators should take notice as well. The virtue of absolute architectural simplicity pays off in the real-world dynamics of an emergent "community of inquiry." A wiki, stripped of features, bells, whistles, and other enticements, quickly becomes a working collaborative writing environment, knowledge base, discussion forum, media repository, and the evolving documentary record of a community of peers. Unlike a blog, a wiki focuses on the *group* instead of the individual, while the sheer simplicity of wiki editing keeps administrative tasks mostly on the pedagogical and textual level rather than the technical. Wiki is software that gets out of the way to allow more interesting dynamics to take center stage, and it is this shift that most interests us—as it does other educators.

Historically, the use of wikis in education is interestingly anticipated by a number of similarly motivated projects dating from the 1990s[2] and, it could be argued, by much thinking in the field of computer-supported collaborative learning.[3] What distinguishes wikis from these conceptual predecessors, however, is Ward Cunningham's gnomic statement of virtue: "the simplest thing that could possibly work." And, indeed, we are now seeing the simple wiki on terrain previously (and tentatively) occupied by content management systems (CMS), learning management systems, managed learning environments, and so on. In the late 1990s, Georgia Tech professor Mark Guzdial led an experiment to move his "anchored instruction" work into the simplest possible wiki environment, with the surprising result that instructors began to invent new applications on their own rather than struggling to adapt to the technology. But Guzdial's research is only a first step: beyond empowering instructors lies the much more interesting realm of empowering learners themselves. The wiki aesthetic of "radical trust" perhaps provides more generative possibility than a whole CMS full of features. As Brian Lamb reflects,

> To truly empower students within collaborative or co-constructed activities requires the teacher to relinquish some degree of control over those activities. The instructor's role shifts to that of establishing contexts or setting up problems to engage students. In a wiki, the instructor may set the stage or initiate interactions, but the medium works most effectively when students can assert meaningful autonomy over the process.[4]

Seemingly eschewing the need for software standards, learning object economies, and complex schemas, a wiki succeeds because it puts the emphasis simply on *writing* and—in Cunningham's terms—the emergent "system of names" that comes to embody a community's discourse and growing culture of learning. What could be more apt for an educational environment?

We have been experimenting with wikis in personal writing and classroom collaboration at the undergraduate and graduate levels for several years now. In 2005 we started a large-scale undergraduate peer review project in a wiki for an eighty-student Introduction to New Media course. This course featured the wiki as a core infrastructure component, encouraging student writing as a generative, developmental process. The results of this experiment in large-scale "radical trust" have been encouraging, to say the least. What follows is a discussion of these experiments and what we've learned through them. First, though, we will take a closer look at some theoretical touchstones that are useful in interpreting wikis in educational contexts.

Educational Wiki: Rediscovering Theory

According to Ward Cunningham,

> A wiki is a body of writing that a community is willing to know and maintain.[5]

The original WikiWikiWeb was not designed as educational technology. Ward Cunningham's foundational idea was simply to distribute the task of assembling the collection of software "patterns," a project Cunningham had hitherto housed in a simple Hypercard stack. As the collection grew, and more and more people were sending their contributions to Cunningham, he saw an opportunity in the (then new) Web to allow many contributors to add their own text to the database. Let people write their own cards, he thought, and he created a very basic Common Gateway Interface–based (CGI-based) system that would allow anyone to add and edit content. It was, as was the Hypercard stack that preceded it, the simplest thing that could possibly work.

It is not by accident, however, that such a system should become appreciated within educational technology circles. The use of wikis in education is intriguingly anticipated by a number of similar-in-spirit projects dating from the 1980s and 1990s in the field of computer-supported collaborative learning (CSCL). A little bit of historical hindsight allows us to use some of the high-water marks of early CSCL systems to better appreciate how wikis can work in educational settings (for more on wiki history, see Cummings's introductory essay to this volume).

Scaffolding Knowledge Building: CSILE

Computer-Supported Intentional Learning Environment (CSILE) was a pioneering "knowledge building" environment designed and developed in the 1980s and early 1990s by Marlene Scardamalia and Carl Bereiter at the Ontario Institute for Studies in Education and later commercialized under the name Knowledge Forum. Scardamalia and Bereiter describe CSILE as "a networked system that gives students simultaneous access to a database that is composed of text and graphical notes that the students produce themselves and a means of searching and commenting on one another's contributions."[6]

Drawing theoretically on Vygotsky's notion of the educationally generative "zone of proximal development," CSILE is *scaffolding* technology.[7] But as a group-oriented, collaborative tool, CSILE taps into the scaffolding normally provided by social settings through interaction with peers.

CSILE's emphasis on the *collective* fixes the unit of analysis in the group itself. Scardamalia and Bereiter write, "the community database serves as an objectification of a group's advancing knowledge," a move that almost subsumes individual voice—and individual learning—to the knowledge building that a group engages in.[8] This is certainly recognizable in wikis, as many have noted, from the community aesthetic of the original WikiWikiWeb[9] to Jesse Wilbur's fascinating comments in the "Value of Voice"—even the emergent voice that a project like Wikipedia seems to have developed.[10]

Scardamalia and Bereiter then ask the question, "Who is in charge of the zone of proximal development?" and suggest that we trust the learners themselves to "ask educationally productive questions" within a specially constructed environment. They write that "The community database of CSILE is created by students. Users produce public-access material, not simply material to be turned in for grading, and do so in a context that engages others on their behalf."[11]

Scardamalia and Bereiter are quick to point out the potential chaos lurking in strongly child-directed learning situations and indicate that the design of a structured environment is key to facilitating independent learning. CSILE is intended to provide such a support. The interesting question for wiki-based educators is just where the "design" issue is located. CSILE was far more structured than any wiki environment, which leads us to ask whether the important dynamic is indeed in the overt design of the environment or whether it is in the tenor of the interactions found there.

Perspectivity Technologies: Constellations

A different balancing of group and individual is found by the "perspectivity technology" approach of Ricki Goldman, whose Constellations system—a family of software developed over a decade at Massachusetts Institute of Technology, University of British Columbia, New Jersey Institute of Technology, and New York University—presents a decidedly different aesthetic and a different set of theoretical implications. Goldman's educational research is based in radically decentered video ethnography,[12] drawing notably on contemporary ethnographic theory from Stephen A. Tyler and others.[13] In a powerful response to Patti Lather's seminal article on research methodology, "Issues of Validity in Openly Ideological Research" (1991), Goldman developed the concept of "configurational validity," an idea with considerable currency for wikis in education. In her article of the same name, she writes:

> Research also gains strength by bringing together both the discordant and the harmonious. It gains strength by providing a forum for variance and diversity. In other words, *configurational validity* is attained through the construction of a "platform for multi-loguing."[14]

Constellations allows individual users access to "digitized video in chunks called 'stars' that could be assembled into larger groupings by different users/authors called 'constellations.'"[15] The metaphor is self-evident: a constellation is a configuration of objects that is apparent from a particular "point of view" or perspective. So, rather than a group's knowledge building activities, the constellations motif foregrounds the ongoing multiplicity of perspectives within a community of inquiry. Goldman's software serves as a platform for the construction of perspectives as well as their sharing and reinterpretation. "By linking the stars into constellations, users can interpret the data in diverse ways according to the themes they have assigned. In fact, the same data could be linked to a variety of constellations."[16]

Goldman's emphasis on perspectivity puts the emphasis on the *ongoing* interplay of personal and collective knowledge. Specifically, perspectivity reminds us that there is value not only in collective wisdom (often taken as the great virtue of sites like Wikipedia) but also in divergence and diversity of views. On the one hand, collaborative technology can be seen as "community memory" or the archive of group knowledge building; on the other, collaboration is seen as process, an ongoing dialectic between individuals and groups that is never complete, never finished. Successful wiki sites, like the WikiWikiWeb or Wikipedia, are fundamentally "ongoing" (a point that must be made clear to students who carelessly cite Wikipedia sources without considering this temporal aspect). Beyond the notion of a "knowledge base" or discursive trace, a wiki captures or presents the *evolving now* of a discourse community.

"Discovering" CSCL: Guzdial's CoWeb

In the 1990s at Georgia Tech, Mark Guzdial was engaged in building collaborative learning environments. The research surrounding Guzdial's

CaMILE project is recognizable in the mainstream of CSCL.[17] The key idea in the CaMILE project—a Web-based threaded discussion forum—was "anchored instruction," utilizing the World Wide Web's fundamental technology: the link. Guzdial's substantial research on collaborative discussion forums showed that these linkages were important to "create more sustained discussion than traditional classroom newsgroup discussions. But in our work, the anchors were always created by the teachers. Was it the anchor, or the fact that the teacher said to go there? Could students create anchors?"[18] Echoing Scardamalia and Bereiter, Guzdial asked who will be in charge of designing and developing educational applications. "Literature from the computer-supported collaborative learning conferences suggests it will be researchers and developers."[19] Forum software like CaMILE still required layers of instructional and/or administrative support, so that the actual deployment of CSCL systems was a major challenge, despite whatever cognitive or pedagogical wonders the software promised. Guzdial complained that it was all they could do to get faculty to "adopt" learning technologies, let alone direct them or exercise any creative agency.

The antidote, they found, was in Ward Cunningham's wiki concept, which Guzdial and his team implemented to create a new and simpler tool called CoWeb. By shifting to the simplicity of a wiki, Guzdial and his colleagues found they could devolve the organizational responsibilities to teachers or even students themselves. In their article "Beyond Adoption to Invention," Guzdial, Rick, and Kehoe report that teachers, rather than struggling to adopt a technology platform, were now *inventing* applications "that the developers have not considered."[20] Interestingly, CoWeb is not the result of extensive research into cognitive psychology, user interface design, or information architecture; rather, it is based on Cunningham's principle of the simplest thing that could possibly work:

> Though we have created over a dozen iterations on our version of Cunningham's tool in the last three years to make it work better for classroom applications, the core ideas and features that are making it so successful in encouraging teacher innovation are not ours. Rather, we are reporting on a *discovery*—that the CoWeb is an example of an application in which teachers actively invent their own uses.[21]

The radical simplicity of the wiki is undoubtedly what has led many educators to consider and implement it—and this is certainly true of ourselves. But this simplicity is clearly not its only virtue; a deeper examination of actual practice leads to an investigation of the cultural dynamics of communities of inquiry.

Using a Wiki in (Our) Classrooms

In our case, the initial appeal of using a wiki in the classroom derived from its simplicity. We are not newcomers to distributed learning, distance education, course management systems, learning objects, and so on. In many ways, our gradual adoption of the wiki has been a response to the unsustainable complexity and inflexibility of many existing tools and platforms. And, like Guzdial, we have been pleasantly surprised by what we've seen.

Our use of the wiki crept in gradually as an experiment in supporting group project work in a professional graduate program. Teams of six students would conduct research and development in a particular area over a six-week period, producing substantial documentation along the way. The work of writing, assembling, and refining this documentation was traditionally a significant task in itself. Documentation was traditionally written in various pieces in Microsoft Word and then later assembled for presentation in a layout program like QuarkXPress or InDesign. This composing sequence posed the all-too-common challenges of versioning (or keeping track of the different documents multiple writers will unintentionally create), collaboration, and the drudge work of formatting and (more critically) reformatting. The idea of using wikis was intended to minimize the hassles of the documentation. But almost immediately, the benefit of combining the processes of knowledge construction (organization and analysis of research findings, note taking, reflection, etc.), collaboration, and publication of results into one platform was apparent. The wiki spaces produced by the project groups grew quickly beyond the needs of producing documentation into complex information spaces tended by the students.

From this initial experiment came a simple research question: what if "everything" were to be hosted in the wiki?—that is, not just the students' project work but lecture notes and students' individual work as well: class papers, seminar notes, classroom discussions, and so on. This would allow open-ended commentary, peer review of student work, and an emergent— rather than preordained—information architecture. It looked easy enough to implement: what had previously been housed in discussion forums and courseware platforms could be dumped into the wiki. In fact, given the simple formatting conventions of wiki pages, this was almost a labor-saving device in itself: no more marked-up content. What had previously been a labor-intensive process of designing information spaces and navigation in a variety of tools gave way to the quick jotting down of WikiWords. Wiki Wiki indeed!

The real opportunity to test this idea came with the chance to teach a large (between eighty and one hundred students) lower-level undergraduate course on new media. Here, it seemed, was a case where we could try out these concepts on a fairly substantial scale and treat the process as part of the curriculum to boot (that is, if it fails you can still call it a teachable moment). The course in question had the additional characteristic of having been taught in recent years with a substantial student blogging component. One of the course assignments had required students to create a blog and maintain it throughout the semester by posting their thoughts and reflections on a course theme or topic that they personally found particularly interesting. Asking students to write in a wiki instead did not seem like too far of a stretch.

The bigger challenge was that of scaling up the notion of "radical trust"— an essential feature of wiki-enabled communities—to a class of eighty-plus undergraduates. Small groups of graduate students are fairly predictable in comparison, especially when everyone already knows everyone else. To unleash a class of nineteen-year-olds in a completely open collaborative environment requires a different level of "trust." The solution seemed to be in careful and thorough preparation, to guard against the chaos that typically ensues when people don't really know what will be required of them.

Possibly the key facet of this project emerged with the opportunity to teach the course under the guidelines of our university's "writing-intensive learning" program. The ideals and attendant requirements of making the course a "writing-intensive" course provided an additional—perhaps essential—level of scaffolding and structure.

Writing-Intensive Teaching and Learning

With the guidance of the Center for Writing-Intensive Learning (CWIL), faculty at Simon Fraser University (SFU) have begun to transform select courses to make writing more central to the curriculum. At SFU this means that *writing to learn* course material and *learning to write* in discipline-specific ways are explicitly tied to the requirements and activities of courses. In turn, and in an effort to ensure that graduating students acquire the writing and communication skills necessary for their discipline, some SFU programs now require that students complete a certain number of writing-intensive courses. The designation "writing-intensive" is something of a misnomer, since it foregrounds "intensity" and suggests that courses simply include a quantitative increase in course writing. Although this is certainly part of the requirement—at least 50 percent of the course grade in a writing-intensive course needs to be based on written work—the other significant aspect of writing-intensive courses is an understanding of writing as both an ongoing and generative process. However, this understanding is hidden from view by the naming convention "writing-intensive."

An SFU writing-intensive course further needs to explicitly incorporate revision into the process of formal writing. Here, formal writing includes written assignments and term papers and is distinguished from informal writing such as in-class or in-tutorial writing activities. Revision of formal writing may take one of two forms: a written assignment is divided into multiple stages (i.e., first draft, second draft, final copy) with students receiving feedback on their writing after each stage or, alternatively, multiple, similar assignments with students receiving feedback on each assignment that they can then use for future assignments. In both cases, writing is understood as an ongoing process, and students are given an opportunity to improve their writing throughout the duration of the course. The key requirement is to design assignments in such a way that the feedback generated as part of the revision process may be used to improve future writing and is not limited only to the specifics of the given assignment.

In addition, a writing-intensive course needs to enable students to use writing as a method of learning the course content. That is, in addition to writing that is demonstrative (i.e., students demonstrate that they have read and understand the course material) or used primarily as a method of recording (i.e., note taking in class or tutorial), writing to learn aims to provide students with opportunities to use writing in a generative way to explore and learn course content. In practice, this sort of writing often takes place in the classroom and/or tutorial and is worth few or no marks. For example, in a "quick write" students may be asked to write a few sentences or a paragraph to explain key concepts in their own words or to extend a key idea or theme. In both cases, students have an opportunity to write to learn and not just to record or recite course material.

For our course, which was a second-year communication class that serves as a historical introduction to information technology and new media, writing-intensive insights and approaches informed all aspects of the course. First, there were three short (three–four pages) essays. We asked students to select a course-relevant topic and explore it in depth by means of these essays. Students were to select a topic that remained the same across all three essays, but the evidence used to support each essay varied, so that students were able to gain experience with various evidential forms and styles of writing.

Second, we used various forms of informal writing to enable students to learn course material and to facilitate the revision process. In the case of learning the course material, both the instructor and the teaching assistants made use of "quick writes" to explore material presented both in class and through a tutorial. In terms of revision, students received feedback on their essays from the teaching assistant, who actually graded the essays, as well as from other students by way of peer reviews. That is, after the completion of each essay students were matched up in tutorial and asked to read each other's work using a structured peer review guide that directs reading and constructive feedback. The peer review guides were designed in such a way that students received feedback about their writing as well as the quality of their argument and their specific topic. In this way, we strove to ensure that the feedback for a given essay was relevant for the subsequent essay. Moreover, the third and final essay explicitly required that students integrate and synthesize arguments and insights from their first two essays.

Our adoption of wiki technology has been primarily motivated by a desire to extend and improve the key activities of writing-intensive teaching and learning. In particular, we have used the wiki as a platform that makes possible exploration of course content through writing and for expanding the writing revision process. In the first scenario, the wiki was used much like a discussion forum, with the instructor supplementing lectures with discussion questions via the wiki. Students were invited to respond to these discussions either by adding their own content to the page or by adding a wiki comment at the bottom of the page. In the second scenario, the peer review process was moved from the tutorial into the wiki. Each student was asked to create a page in the wiki and to publish each of the written assignments as they were completed. Upon completion of each essay, students were matched up in tutorial and asked to peer review each other's writing via the wiki.

Writing-Intensive Wiki

Based on this experience, we feel our experimentation with wikis in the classroom has been entirely positive and successful. In terms of exploration and learning of course content via writing outside of formal assignments, students have used the wiki both in the same ways as other technologies, such as discussion forums in particular, and in unanticipated and novel ways as well. In the case of the former, discussion questions, comments, and postings by the instructor have been followed up by students to a varying degree, from discussion starters that do not receive any feedback to others that receive much feedback and many comments from students.

With respect to conducting assignment peer reviews via the wiki in our undergraduate new media course, the potential benefits and advantages are clear. In addition to being able to conduct peer reviews, students have an opportunity to read the work of students other than their peer review partners, since all of the essays are published in the wiki. Thus, students are able to see the quality of writing of their fellow peers by reading other students' writing on a variety of issues and topics, some of which are different from and some of which are similar to their own. In the case of essays that address similar topics, this publication space not only may be a source of ideas, insights, and potential counterarguments but may also provide students with links to research sources and writing relevant to their topic. Although it is difficult to track the extent to which students read each other's work, some students submitted essays that directly referenced other students' work from the wiki.

Moreover, in the graduate seminar, students were entirely ready and willing to depart from one another's views in the wiki. In a spring 2006 seminar, the class of eighteen students were asked to write and "publish" three short papers to the wiki. By the third paper, cross-referencing of peers' work was common and ranged from background citation to direct responses to peers' work. The very idea of intra-cohort citation is rather novel but seems to us entirely appropriate, especially among "junior colleagues" in a seminar course. Indeed, this element deserves greater emphasis in the future.

Interestingly, even among the graduate students, direct editing of other students' contributions (as opposed to adding "comments") simply did not happen, except where pages were clearly understood to be group property. It would appear that the unwritten rules of academia (not to mention the sanctity of authorship) are so deeply ingrained as to exert a powerful influence on wiki use, despite the emerging ethic of sites like Wikipedia. In-page comments too tended to err on the side of courtesy and encouragement, despite the well-documented tendency of computer-mediated collaborative spaces to encourage outspoken exchanges.

As with other online technologies, some students proved more active online than others. This is not surprising given the diversity of interests, motivations, and time constraints underlying any class. From our standpoint, and keeping in mind that participation in wiki discussions outside of assignment publishing and peer reviews has been entirely optional and not graded, the fact that students do participate at all needs to be acknowledged as a positive response. It indicates both willingness to use the technology as well as desire to explore content beyond the strict requirements and graded components of the course.

Students have used the wiki to engage with course material in novel ways. Most notably, in the week prior to the midterm exam one student started a wiki page to collect notes on the course readings and lectures (titled "CLASS WIKI = GIANT STUDY GROUP"). The student advertised the new page via the class mailing list and invited other students to visit the page and to contribute their study notes and materials. The page introduction sets the tone, goals, and preferred forms of participation:

There are a whole bunch of us in this class so I suspect that we could come up with a pretty amazing collaborative study guide! My idea was to have a few different sections: People, Definitions, Chapters, Lectures. If *you want to contribute, edit the page, don't just comment.* However, comments are welcome too! We could use the comment section to discuss and/or debate more complex issues or ask questions of our peers.

The invitation was taken up by some of the other students in the class, and the page evolved to include content on key figures and important events in the history of media, definitions and elaborations of course concepts and issues, and concise summaries of course readings that highlighted key points and ideas. New pages were created and linked to the main page, and comments were used to ask questions and provide answers. The instructor participated in the discussion, answered certain questions, and clarified some of the responses from students.

The midterm exam was also a catalyst for the creation of a page by a student who invited other students to contribute questions and answers from tutorials that were held one week prior to the exam. In the tutorials, midterm questions and answers from the course readings were the primary focus, and students were informed that one question from each tutorial would be included on the midterm exam. As a result, most students took notes during the tutorials with the goal of improving their study efforts and chances on the exam. Although we had provided students with this opportunity to define a portion of the exam in the past, students had never used the available course online tools to collect all of the questions and answers from the various tutorials. For the first time, students from each tutorial posted their questions and answers to the wiki and provided each other with content that, given a total of eight tutorials, they would otherwise not have shared.

In both cases, the wiki was used to coauthor content and to engage with course material through writing. In our experience, the fact that other online tools such as course mailing lists and discussion forums have not been used by students in these sorts of ways in the past is perhaps an indication of two things. First, it may be the case that e-mail and discussion forums are not well suited to such activities. Although both technologies support online discussions, it is difficult to imagine how a class of one hundred students could collectively coauthor a study guide using either e-mail or a discussion forum. In the case of the latter, perhaps this could take the form of questions and answers and/or the use of threads to organize topics. Even though this is technically possible, the end result would still be awkward to navigate and read when compared to a wiki page, where all content is immediately visible either directly or via links to other pages. Moreover, the wiki enables students to organize (and reorganize) content in ways that would be difficult to emulate via threads or discussion topics. For example, the wiki midterm study guide included content that students had organized both by week as well as by readings and concepts.

Second, we believe that students' adoption and use indicate that they are comfortable using the technology and acknowledge at least some of its benefits. This is not to say that students are not comfortable with mailing lists and discussion forums but merely to suggest that our students' active and voluntary usage indicates that the technology has been accepted into their online tool and skill sets. Beyond course-related use, students have also used the wiki to complain about other courses offered within the department, to help each other with wireless connection problems on campus, to post and comment on each other's poetry, and to semi-anonymously announce their affections for other students in the class (titled "THE LOOOVE PAGE"). Although all of these uses are encouraging, only time and additional experience will help us discern novelty value from more enduring usage patterns.

Concluding Thoughts

Our emerging sense of wiki use in the classroom strongly resonates with the notion of learners as a "community of inquiry." To dig into the implications and connotations of calling a group of learners a "community" brings forward questions of culture and culture building. In our view, learning is a culture-building process. It is further a process marked by complex dynamics between individual and group development. In a very concrete sense, wikis provide an ongoing view of a culture as a *document*. Conversely, a wiki is the documentation of a culture, by its members, a kind of auto-ethnographic tool or environment (cf. Lakeman's essay in this volume). The educational implications of such dynamics are extensive, to say the least.

If we are to take the idea of constructivist or constructionist learning seriously, then the co-construction of meaning by a group is almost prototypically found in a community's self-documentation and collective self-repre-

sentation in a wiki space. The conceptual precursors invoked here—especially Scardamalia and Bereiter and Goldman—were prospecting for these
very dynamics, as well as the means of facilitating them. Guzdial's insight,
coming directly from the field of CSCL, was principally that the way forward
was to embrace simplicity.

Our experiences with wikis in our classrooms have been rich with examples of individual and group expression, both along the curricular lines we
have designed ourselves and—probably more important—according to the
emergent logic of the communities of learners themselves. The potential of
this particular approach to computer-mediated interaction has only begun to
be fully investigated. We will continue to experiment with the various facets
of wikis and eagerly watch the work of others in this regard.

NOTES

1. Ward Cunningham, "DoTheSimplestThingThatCouldPossiblyWork," Cunningham and Cunningham, Inc., http://c2.com/xp/DoTheSimplestThingThatCould
PossiblyWork.html.

2. See Ricki Goldman-Segall, "Learning Constellations: A Multimedia Ethnographic Research Environment Using Video Technology to Explore Children's Thinking" (PhD diss., MIT, 1990); Marlene Scardamalia and Carl Bereiter, "Higher Levels of
Agency for Children in Knowledge Building: A Challenge for the Design of New
Knowledge Media," *Journal of the Learning Sciences* 1, no. 1 (1991): 37–68.

3. Timothy D. Koschmann, *CSCL: Theory and Practice of an Emerging Paradigm (Computers, Cognition, and Work)* (Mahwah, NJ: Lawrence Erlbaum, 1996).

4. Brian Lamb, "Wide Open Spaces: Wikis, Ready or Not," *Educause Review* (September–October 2004): 37–48, http://connect.educause.edu/Library/EDUCAUSE+Re
view/WideOpenSpacesWikisReady0/40498.

5. Ward Cunningham, "WhyWikiWorks," Cunningham and Cunningham, Inc.
http://c2.com/cgi/wiki?WhyWikiWorks.

6. Scardamalia and Bereiter, "Higher Levels of Agency," 38.

7. Marlene Scardamalia, "CSILE/Knowledge Forum®," in *Education and Technology: An Encyclopedia* (Santa Barbara: ABC-CLIO, 2004), 183–92, http://ikit.org/full
text/CSILE_KF.pdf.

8. Marelene Scardamalia and Carl Bereiter, "Computer Support for Knowledge-
Building Communities," *Journal of the Learning Sciences* 3, no. 3 (1994): 265–83, 277,
http://carbon.cudenver.edu/~bwilson/building.html.

9. Cunningham, "WhyWikiWorks."

10. "if:book," Institute for the Future of the Book, http://www.futureofthebook
.org/blog/2006/02/the_value_of_voice.html.

11. Scardamalia and Bereiter, "Higher Levels of Agency," 51.

12. Ricki Goldman-Segall, "Configurational Validity: A Proposal for Analyzing

Multimedia Ethnographic Narratives," *Journal for Educational Multimedia and Hypermedia* 4, no. 2 (1995): 162–83.

13. Stephen A. Tyler, "Post-Modern Ethnography: From Document of the Occult to Occult Document," in *Writing Culture: The Poetics and Politics of Ethnography,* ed. James Clifford and George E. Marcus (Berkeley and Los Angeles: University of California Press, 1986), 122–40.

14. Ricki Goldman-Segall, "Gender and Digital Media in the Context of a Middle School Science Project," *Meridian, an Online Journal on Middle School Education* 1, no. 1 (1998), http://www.ncsu.edu/meridian.

15. Ibid., 175.

16. Ibid.

17. Mark Guzdial, "Information Ecology of Collaborations in Educational Settings: Influence of Tool," in "Proceedings of Computer-Supported Collaborative Learning 1997," Toronto, ON, 1997, http://www.oise.utoronto.ca.cscl/papers/guzdial.pdf.

18. Mark Guzdial, Jochen Rick, and Colleen Kehoe, "Beyond Adoption to Invention: Teacher-Created Collaborative Activities in Higher Education," *Journal of the Learning Sciences* 10, no. 3 (2002): 265–79.

19. Ibid.

20. Ibid.

21. Ibid., 6.

Wikis in Composition and
Communication Classrooms

Stephanie Vie and Jennifer deWinter

Disrupting Intellectual Property:
Collaboration and Resistance in Wikis

Mikhail Bakhtin and Michel Foucault have both explored the ways in which discursive practices are heteroglossic, simultaneously containing multiple voices and perspectives, and later work in rhetoric and composition has also continued to build on this notion of multivocality. For example, building on Foucault's "What Is an Author?" Kenneth Bruffee's landmark article "Collaborative Learning and the 'Conversation of Mankind'" calls into question the concept of individual textual authorship by establishing that the ability to write is learned only in a social context.[1] Kathryn T. Flannery draws on Bakhtin's theory of heteroglossia in her review "Composing and the Question of Agency," noting that "students are always caught 'intertextually'— they are never inventing a new language out of nothing, but patch together fragments of the multiple texts, the multiple voices . . . that are already available to them."[2] Finally, Rebecca Moore Howard argues that students often rely on "patchwriting," a practice that involves individuals' stringing together multiple authorial voices and sources and then adding their own voices to that conversation.[3] The scholarship of Bruffee, Flannery, and Howard all showcase our focus in rhetoric and composition on multivocal texts. Indeed, we advocate research and teaching practices that highlight multivocality such as citing sources, building upon prior knowledge in the field, and echoing the familiar terms of a discourse community.

But although the field of rhetoric and composition relies on these shared scholarly practices, true collaborative writing remains rare; our published scholarship commonly follows the model of the individually authored text. Recent work in computers and composition has nevertheless made a concerted effort to use computerized technologies to open up opportunities and possibilities for textual collaboration. For example, early work in computers and composition envisioned hypertext as a technology that might offer increased opportunities for collaborative writing. Since hypertexts are made up of many discrete subpages with multiple links among and between pages, their ability to enable multiple authorial voices to flourish seemed particularly promising. In theorizing his work with Storyspace, a hypertext writing environment designed to help writers map out large, complex projects, Johndan Johnson-Eilola notes that any social writing space must follow two main guidelines.

> First, it must allow writers and readers to work within the space of the texts (rather than downloading them, preserving the purity of the master text). Second, it must encourage more than one person to write within that space (in order to avoid pitting the weight of a published author against a single reader).[4]

In this way, hypertext environments can be seen to encourage, and possibly even demand, collaborative modes of authorship that challenge traditional notions of intellectual property in fundamental ways. Wikis build upon the earlier design of hypertext environments like Storyspace, but they attempt to address some of the obstacles to collaborative writing that have tended to limit the latter as well. Wikis, designed with multiple authors in mind, are generally stored on a server and can be accessed like any other online site.[5] In their most common configuration today, wikis are well suited to creating multivocal texts; the sheer simplicity of composing, editing, and publishing multiply-authored texts makes wikis appealing resources for fostering collaboration.

By challenging the authority of the single authorial voice, wikis also call into question traditional notions of intellectual property as a market commodity. These notions propagate the argument that ideas are a unique product of individual labor and can thus "belong" to a single person. It may be precisely because wikis challenge these established notions that some student users resist their use in the classroom. In keeping with this general theme, the questions that guide our research are as follows: What is the currency of intellectual property in the university setting? Do wikis, in fact, disrupt established, dominant notions of intellectual property? Can wikis be used as pedagogical tools that challenge capitalist power structures while still providing students the necessary skills to succeed in diverse writing environments?

In exploring these questions, we discuss the ways in which traditional authorship is upset by wikis. We situate wikis within the larger historical context of intellectual property. Having established a theoretical foundation, we then turn our attention to the practical application of wikis in the composition classroom. Our goal here is to explore how wikis can be used to foster and/or challenge collaboration. As well, we outline how wikis can be used in the classroom to promote critical discussions about authorship and intellectual property. Although we do not want to claim that wikis are an unproblematic means of fostering collaboration, we do explore the ways in which wikis can encourage students to move beyond traditional notions of ownership and academic writing and into more collaborative, public discursive practices.

Historicizing Intellectual Property

The foundation of intellectual property—the ability to create and own an idea—and even the very term *intellectual property* have been vigorously challenged in recent years. In particular, technology has made great strides in disrupting our traditional understanding of copyright law. For example, the ability of an individual to manipulate digital music files through ripping, copying, downloading, and remixing has set the stage for such highly publicized trials as *MGM v. Grokster* and *A & M Records, Inc. v. Napster, Inc.* Legal controversies like these continue to shape our collective views of how art and artists should be protected and how monetary gains should be assigned. These controversies are, as James P. Cadello asserts, driven by fear: Modern conceptions and practices of human freedom, self-possession and self-control, social organization, and moral assessment have enabled and influenced technological evolution in profound ways.[6] This fear partly explains resistance to new technologies. It also suggests that this resistance could produce further tensions in the future, if society becomes polarized between those who embrace the influence of computerized technologies and those who view these changes with anxiety and fear. However, the fearful attempts to sustain these modern conceptions are inherently conservative insofar as they seek to stifle the technological developments that spring from them.

Intellectual property has always been intimately connected with techno-logical developments that assist in producing and disseminating material goods. For instance, Gutenberg's moveable type printing press brought about changes in the way we consider the nature of writing as well as author-ship, laying the ground for many of our current beliefs about plagiarism and copyright. The printing press made the creation and dissemination of printed material simpler and more streamlined; ideas and therefore authors could be more easily commodified and marketed. Prior to the printing press, the idea of intellectual property was not as intimately tied to economic gain as it is today; the concept of mass production of texts on today's scale was impossible. Though texts were copied, this was a labor-intensive endeavor that required scribes to sit for hours and reproduce texts by hand. The many hours of skilled labor that went into the manual reproduction of books made them both rare and valuable; the printing press diminished the rarity of books, resulting in the loss of their economic value as art.

In *Standing in the Shadow of Giants: Plagiarists, Authors, Collaborators*, Rebecca Moore Howard notes five factors that worked in concert to support the emer-gence of the modern author: the printing press, the shift to viewing text as property that could be owned, the importance placed on the creativity and genius of the author, an expanded readership, and the ideology of individu-alism.[7] To this, we would add the emerging ideologies of capitalism, which focused on expansionism, knowledge as commodity, and consumption of books or ideas. The technological, economic, and ideological shifts afforded by the printing press resulted in an increased number of readers and a greater focus on the business of writing. These factors all helped modern copyright law take form.

Françoise Meltzer traces the emergence of the concept of individual own-ership of texts back to a single moment in European history: "John Locke's *Two Treatises on Government* (1690) are the paradigm of the European notion that an individual's work and the fruits of his labor are his own property."[8] An author could thus assert that he had spent time cultivating his work in the same way that one could own and cultivate land; indeed, the word *author* is derived from the Latin *augere*, a word tied closely to agricultural terms like *grow, increase,* and *augment.* The author has the first rights to the harvests born from his land.[9] But, historically, agrarian societies have shifted from the model of an individual or small group of individuals who toil together on their land for sustenance toward a commercialized, technologically driven business model. Today's crops have been planted, tended, harvested, and shipped thanks to the combined assistance of hundreds, even thousands, of workers. Similarly, today's texts are the collective efforts of many individuals working in concert. Though ownership rights of texts are afforded to the primary author, these rights often do not take into account the various individuals who assisted in the communal creation and dissemination of the text.

In many respects, we believe that wikis embody some of the best features of this new communal production model: they are community built, edited, and sustained. Wikis reflect both the values and the needs of specific communities or users. For example, most wikis have some form of code of conduct as well as rules and regulations that help shape the work contained within. Wikis are not, as commonly believed, uncontrolled and unfettered, with no sense of authorial or editorial control. On the contrary, most wikis have distinct hierarchies of users; each individual has a part to play. Though the memberships of these roles are not static, many of the positions themselves remain constant and often overlap: owner, editor, reviewer, proofreader, moderator, problem solver. Even defining and deciding what content stays and what goes is a communal decision, one that can be hotly debated. Like other collective systems, wikis depend on the shared responsibilities of the users who make up the community. Therefore, though different models exist for the creation and editing of wikis, they all rely in large part upon individuals working in harmony to create the best content they feel they can offer.

Wikis in the Classroom: Collaboration and the Creation of Knowledge

If wikis are so well suited to collaborative writing, it remains to be seen why more instructors aren't using them. If wikis are simple to set up and use, what holds people back? The perceived lack of control coupled with the potential for student disinterest and resistance are some reasons, we argue, that wikis are not commonly used in the writing classroom. Student authors must support and encourage trust in each other in order to offer constructive criticism and collaboration during the writing process. They must also accept that the wiki document or entry does not belong to them individually, which in many ways goes against how students are trained via tests, grades, and papers to view their work. Despite the fact that wikis do offer levels of control and despite the fact that classroom-based wikis would function under many of the same rules as traditional collaborative classroom writing, instructors often have a misguided sense, a fear, of the potential negative implications of wikis.

Instructors may fear that giving so much influence to the outside audience of the wiki may destabilize their classroom—that the traditional authority structure will be disrupted. But rather than feel stifled by the potential for such decentralization, we should instead embrace the possibilities that come with technological change. As Gail Hawisher and Cynthia Selfe aptly state:

> As teachers, we are authority figures. Our culture has imbued us with considerable power within the confines of the classroom: we are the architects of the spaces in which our students learn. Although the use of computer technology may give us greater freedom to construct more effective learning environments, it may also lead us unknowingly to assume positions of power that contradict our notions of good teaching.[10]

They remind us to resist falling into the conventional role of teacher-as-authority. And here is where wikis can step in: because wikis are built with notions of social constructivism in mind, they help us resist authoritarianism. They fight against "the banking concept of education" outlined by Paulo Freire. By resisting banking concepts of education, we can also resist systems of intellectual property that are both defined and controlled by the cultural elite and used to oppress.[11] But wikis are not a panacea. The challenge, of course, is how to critically employ wikis while consciously recognizing that they are not neutral tools. We examine two methods: using an in-class wiki created by the teacher for a specific classroom use and using a previously established wiki that enjoys popular use outside of the academy.

Method 1. Creating Classroom Wikis: Fostering
Collaborative Learning and Writing

When deciding which wiki to use in a class, a key concern of instructors is the ease of setting up and maintaining a particular wiki.[12] This question can only be answered effectively when it is considered in relation to the instructor's particular pedagogical goals. As Andrew Feenberg reminds us, computerized technologies are never neutral; technology is "not a destiny but a scene of struggle. It is a social battlefield, or perhaps a better metaphor would be a parliament of things on which civilizational alternatives are debated and decided."[13] Wikis too are far from neutral; they are a battlefield upon which concepts of intellectual property are challenged and sometimes attacked.

One of the best reasons to use a class-specific wiki is that instructors can adapt and create the wiki environment that best suits their pedagogical needs. Wikis can of course be used by solitary writers to compose individual works, but that is not the type of use we advocate. We see wikis as providing sites where communities of writers can collaboratively create a single written text. Instructors can work together with students in a wiki to create and revise syllabi, assignments, grading rubrics, or other negotiable classroom-related work that directly affects students. This approach helps decentralize power in the classroom; students have a greater voice in thinking through and defining a course's goals and objectives. Students can change, add, delete, and reject parts of (or entire) classroom documents. They are made responsible for accepting or revising those materials that directly affect their learning and their grade. While this concept is not new, wikis help enable the student-centered classroom by recording the messiness of negotiation within an electronic document that can be accessed in its newest form at all times.[14] The changes to the wiki are saved, and individuals' names are attributed to their changes, though the instructor or site manager has the final say. Here, it is important to remember Donald Murray's claim that "student-centered does not mean permissive. It does mean stripping away every impediment to learning, no matter how reassuring these impediments are to the teacher."[15] Wikis arguably help to strip away impediments to decentralized classrooms—the rigid, instructor-centric syllabi, rubrics, and other institutional documents. They assist in moving away from the banking model of authoritative power invested in the teacher and the institution, helping empower students in their own learning processes.

Not only can a classroom-based wiki challenge the idea of the classroom itself as an instructor's property by allowing students to easily negotiate classroom documents, but a wiki can also challenge students to work together in order to collaboratively write single documents for a group grade. Often, instructors ask students to work together in small groups on a single project, outlining methods to negotiate the shared responsibilities of a group or helping students to divvy up the work by assigning specific roles (such as researcher, writer, editor, and presenter). Wikis invite us to think of new ways to ask students to collaborate. With a wiki, groups of students have access to the most current draft of a project at any given time. They can easily revise, edit, and add to or delete sections of the wiki; they can revert to an earlier version if they choose. For those instructors who are concerned about the division of labor, wikis record their changes in an easily accessible history, which enables the instructor to see who is working on the project and what changes are being made by whom. Wikis, then, have embedded design features that allow instructors to manage project outcomes and record how individual students are performing relative to those outcomes. Further, wikis allow for the messiness of the drafting process as a recursive act instead of breaking the writing process into a series of discrete and disconnected units. Whereas in traditional collaborative writing, students often write separately and individually and then come together during class time to negotiate their work as a group, wikis encourage a more constant stream of writing, rewriting, and editing that does not rely on physical space or place for assistance. It is important to also note the ability of a wiki to extend the classroom beyond its physical space, allowing students to collaborate outside of their normal meeting times.

Though attempts have been made to use past computerized technologies (such as electronic mailing lists, threaded discussion boards, MOOs and MUDs, Microsoft Word reviewing features, etc.) to resist the limitations of the physical classroom, these software packages were not designed with collaborative, multivocal writing in mind. Therefore, the type of collaborative writing and revision that we see in wikis was not easily possible in prior incarnations. Furthermore, because wikis are often created with constructivist views of classroom practices in mind, they more easily lend themselves to the type of collaborative writing that allows us to upset traditional modes of intellectual property. Students are able to see how collaboration works to change and refine their ideas; at the same time, working together teaches them necessary negotiation skills. Finally, wikis bolster the view that no individual can "own" ideas—there is no solitary author. By adopting a collaborative pedagogy within wikis, we disrupt intellectual property.

Method 2. Using Established Wikis: Extended Audiences and Regulated Discourses

Whereas the previous section outlines some of the advantages of setting up an entirely new wiki for classroom use, this section describes some advantages of working within an already established public wiki such as Wikipedia. There has long been a disconnect between the goals of most writing courses—that is, to help students improve their writing by asking them to produce satisfactory work prepared for a particular, real audience and situation—and the actual setting or potential of the course as it is structured. That is, students are given assignments and readings chosen and developed by their instructor and are regularly asked to write in various genres in response to particular assignments; however, these students fail to find a particular, real audience and situation to write to aside from their instructor. Susan Miller describes this phenomenon in "The Student's Reader Is Always Fiction," in which she argues that students know that their ultimate audience is their instructor and that the instructor is always measuring students' writing next to a platonic ideal of text in order to mete out grades.[16] Consequently, composition students leave their course understanding many of the common formats and genres of writing, but they have often not yet learned how to write for an audience familiar with the particular requirements and needs of their discipline or discourse situation. They therefore lack an important component of rhetorical awareness. By working within an already established wiki, however, students will achieve a greater understanding of how to write for their discipline or chosen discourse community.

The benefits of having students write in an already established wiki, such as Wikipedia, Meta-Wiki, MeatballWiki, and so on, are threefold. First, presumably, there is already a healthy, thriving discourse community that guides and shapes the site. For example, as Robert E. Cummings notes in the introductory essay to this collection, Wikipedia is built upon a strong core of users who care about the project—enough that they put an immense amount of time and energy into maintaining the integrity and overall vision of the site. Thus, in a course that asked students to create or edit Wikipedia entries, students would be required to study previously posted entries to get a better sense of how the contributions operate: the language used, the background information assumed, and so on. Students would have to carefully analyze the writing within the wiki and ask such questions as "What are the criteria for a good wiki page in this community? and What criteria cause a page to be edited or deleted entirely?" Such a line of questioning allows for fruitful conversations about discourse, argument, and rhetorical awareness.

Most important, perhaps, is that students would be writing within an established community of authors and editors. Other community members will step in and comment on, edit, or change the students' work. Students receive feedback on their own writing without having to ask for it; as they analyze and respond to this feedback, they must negotiate their own sense of rhetorical awareness. In an active, already established wiki, it becomes clear to the students that they are writing for an audience beyond their classroom, peers, and instructor. Wikis assist in this goal naturally, whereas more conventional classroom settings often make it quite difficult for an instructor to reach an outside discourse community.[17]

The documents that our students create for us within the scope of our classrooms often have no real life of their own. As artificial documents created for an artificial situation, they live, breathe, and die within the scope of a semester. In contrast, documents created and housed online live on and are capable of reaching a far greater audience; entries in large, established wikis have the potential to continue to be read and edited long after the semester is over. Because students will likely be required to negotiate the process of meaning with an audience outside the classroom, they will more likely take it seriously; they will realize that their document, rather than living an artificial life within the classroom setting, is actually working to build an ongoing conversation regarding the topic they have chosen to write on. Within the classroom, students often resist peers' comments on their drafts or simply correct surface-level issues in their writing because they cannot conceive of any other way to edit their work. But in a wiki, students may find that their work is fundamentally changed and altered by other users and must then grapple with how to assess and respond to these changes. Wikis can therefore offer a much more powerful conceptualization of the ideal review process than our familiar pedagogies can provide.

Second, working within an already established wiki can relieve instructors of the sometimes daunting task of setting up their own wiki, which can take time, money, and effort and put a strain on instructors. Bob Whipple, in his contribution to this volume, "An (Old) First-Timer's Learning Curve: Curiosity, Trial, Resistance, and Accommodation," describes some of the difficulties that instructors who describe themselves as "wiki novices" may encounter when trying to bring wikis into their pedagogy. Also, some institutions have draconian rules and regulations regarding the establishment or modification of school-supported or -sanctioned Web sites; thus, the process of receiving permission to set up a wiki may be too daunting and deter instructors from taking advantage of the technology. Rather than searching for a hosting site, finding campus technical support in case things go wrong, and having to maintain the site themselves, instructors who use already established wikis can focus on what is more important: laying the pedagogical groundwork that will enable students to enter, understand, and navigate the discourse community the wiki supports.

Finally, working within an already established wiki can encourage students to work with concepts such as intellectual property and ownership from a critical perspective. To return to Rebecca Moore Howard's notion of patchwriting, wikis can help students play with sources, citations, and already written material in a relatively safe zone. Rather than asking students to become "instant experts" on a subject (an obviously impossible task), instructors ask students to practice patchwriting by adding their own voice to an ongoing conversation, thereby engaging with a variety of expert texts. This idea of contributing to an ongoing intellectual dialogue online echoes Kenneth Burke's metaphor of the "unending conversation."

Imagine that you enter a parlor. You come late. When you arrive, others have long preceded you, and they are engaged in a heated discussion, a discussion too heated for them to pause and tell you exactly what it is about. . . . You listen for a while, until you decide that you have caught the tenor of the argument; then you put in your oar. Someone answers;

you answer him; another comes to your defense; another aligns himself against you, to either the embarrassment or gratification of your opponent, depending upon the quality of your ally's assistance. . . . The hour grows late, you must depart. And you do depart, with the discussion still vigorously in progress.[18]

This metaphor almost perfectly mirrors many of the most heated debates in Wikipedia and similar large, community-based wikis. There is a commonly accepted language being used; there is often considerable negotiation about entries, ranging from small quibbles to major arguments in which an entry may be locked (preventing further editing) until the argument is settled; and, finally, the discussion often lingers after a particular individual departs.

As in the Burkean parlor, where many ongoing conversations seem to have no clear beginning, wiki conversations branch, connect, and cannot be traced back to a single root source or origin. They can therefore be thought of as rhizomatic. The metaphor of the rhizome has gained popularity to describe pages on the World Wide Web because of their lack of a central author or source and the dispersal of information via hyperlinks. Johndan Johnson-Eilola and Amy Kimme Hea, writing about hypertext, argue that rhizomes involve "a constant making and remaking" of knowledge, featuring "connections, heterogeneity, multiplicity, [and] asignifying rupture[s]."[19] The metaphor of the rhizome reminds us that, in wikis, control is dispersed, knowledge is constantly changing and being revised, and authorship is an issue in constant flux.

Conclusion: Engaging Generation M

As composition instructors, we have been searching for ways to engage the digital learners of *Generation M*, a term coined by the Kaiser Family Foundation in their 2004 study of the media consumption habits of these younger individuals.[20] "Generation M: Media in the Lives of 8–18 Year-Olds" describes an entire generation who has grown up immersed in media and technology, spending on average a quarter of every day interacting with new media; they have access to and are literate with computerized technologies. Their consumption of information is through smaller pieces and differently mediated forms; they rely more often on the Internet than the library for information gathering. This is the generation that we need to engage as educators, and, in order to do so, we must provide a rich learning experience that is grounded in critical and collaborative pedagogies.

Today's students are technologically literate, but only to a certain extent. Those students who are comfortable with computerized technologies often see them as a way to get things done, to find information rapidly and move on to tackle their next hurdle. Students are often proficient at searching the Web and using e-mail, but many have never been asked to find an article in an academic journal online, evaluate a Web site for bias, or look beyond common sites like Yahoo! or Google when searching for resources online. Just as we would not assume students know everything about writing upon entering our classrooms, we should not assume students know everything when it comes to using the Web critically as a resource.

Because wikis do force the issue of collaboration and confront stagnant and outdated notions of intellectual property, they are ideal for challenging instrumental views of technology. While wikis will not be able to topple a cultural history of intellectual capitalism, they can at least disrupt certain ideologies enough to make them visible and therefore discussable. And we must remember that certain disruptions are always messy—students and teachers simultaneously embrace and resist changes brought about by new technologies. These moments of "asignifying rupture" can provide rich moments for us to consider new ways of understanding the world and making meaning.[21] We find it important to always remember that technologies are ways of ordering the world and are not always compatible with culturally reified technologies. And this is "why wikis?" They ask us to rethink our relationships with collaboration, intellectual property, and the myth of the "author."

NOTES

1. Michel Foucault, "What Is an Author?" *Partisan Review* 42 (1975): 603–14; Kenneth A. Bruffee, "Collaborative Learning and the 'Conversation of Mankind,'" *College English* 46, no. 7 (November 1984): 635–52.

2. Kathryn T. Flannery, "Composing and the Question of Agency," review of *Writing as Social Action*, by Marilyn Cooper and Michael Holzman; *Reclaiming Pedagogy: The Rhetoric of the Classroom*, by Patricia Donahue and Ellen Quandahl, eds.; *Rescuing the Subject: A Critical Introduction to Rhetoric and the Writer*, by Susan Miller; *Expecting the Unexpected:*

Teaching Myself—and Others—to Read and Write, by Donald M. Murray; and *The Presence of Thought: Introspective Accounts of Reading and Writing*, by Marilyn S. Sternglass, *College English* 53, no. 6 (October 1991): 701–13.

3. Rebecca Moore Howard, *Standing in the Shadow of Giants: Plagiarists, Authors, Collaborators* (Stamford, CT: Ablex, 1999), 7.

4. Johndan Johnson-Eilola, *Nostalgic Angels: Rearticulating Hypertext Writing* (Norwood, NJ: Ablex, 1997), 213.

5. While most wikis are used collaboratively, some wikis are installed on solitary computers for individual use for activities like drafting, note taking, and so forth.

6. James P. Cadello, "Fears and Questions Concerning Technology," in *Technology, Morality, and Social Policy*, ed. Eager Hudson (Lewiston, NY: Edwin Mellen, 1997), 1–14.

7. Howard, *Standing in the Shadow of Giants*, 71.

8. Françoise Meltzer, *Hot Property: The Stakes and Claims of Literary Originality* (Chicago: University of Chicago Press, 1994), 54.

9. Ibid.

10. Gail Hawisher and Cynthia Selfe, "The Rhetoric of Technology and the Electronic Writing Class," *College Composition and Communication* 42 (1991): 55–65.

11. Paulo Freire, *Pedagogy of the Oppressed*, trans. Myra Bergman Ramos (New York: Continuum, 1993).

12. For a more detailed discussion of the types of wikis available, see Mark Phillipson's chapter in this volume, "Wikis in the Classroom: A Taxonomy."

13. Andrew Feenberg, *Critical Theory of Technology* (New York: Oxford University Press, 1991), 14.

14. See Peter Elbow, *Writing without Teachers* (New York: Oxford University Press, 1973); Donald M. Murray, *Learning by Teaching: Selected Articles on Writing and Teaching* (Portsmouth, NH: Heinemann/Boyton-Cook, 1982); David Nunan, *Collaborative Language Learning and Teaching* (New York: Cambridge University Press, 1992).

15. See Murray, *Learning by Teaching*, 133.

16. Susan Miller, "The Student's Reader Is Always Fiction," *Journal of Advanced Composition* 5 (1984): 15–29.

17. This audience connection is most commonly established through service-learning volunteer projects in the community, as advocated by Ellen Cushman, *The Struggle and the Tools: Oral and Literate Strategies in an Inner City Community* (Albany: State University of New York Press, 1998); and Bruce Horner and Min-Zhan Lu, *Representing the "Other": Basic Writers and the Teaching of Basic Writing* (Urbana, IL: NCTE, 1999).

18. Kenneth Burke, *The Philosophy of Literary Form: Studies in Symbolic Action*, 3d ed. (Berkeley: University of California Press, 1973), 110–11.

19. Johndan Johnson-Eilola and Amy Kimme Hea, "After Hypertext: Other Ideas," *Computers and Composition* 20 (2003): 425.

20. Kaiser Family Foundation, "Generation M: Media in the Lives of 8–18 Year-Olds," Kaiser Family Foundation, March 9, 2005, http://www.kff.org/entmedia/entmedia030905pkg.cfm (accessed May 2, 2006).

21. Johnson-Eilola and Kimme Hea, "After Hypertext: Other Ideas," 425.

D. A. Caeton

Agency and Accountability:
The Paradoxes of Wiki Discourse

In keeping with what is threatening to become a perennial trope in professional scholarship, this essay begins in earnest with the confession of a teaching crisis. Not long ago I experimented by including Wikipedia in my introductory composition course; the initial idea was to enhance the symmetry between my teaching and my research. Quite predictably (in hindsight), the impact of the experiment on my students was difficult to diagnose. Whereas a few of the students approached the wiki as nothing more than a curious novelty, an overwhelming number, and most notably a female student named Emina, found the software engaging—even though their engagement was often expressed as trenchant critique. The disturbance was so pronounced that Emina e-mailed me near the end of the semester to blame my class for making "things even harder to understand . . . because [she] had doubts on everything that [she] used to know."[1]

In dire need of reassurance and revitalization, I turned to a series of articles that I rely on to shake me from my idleness and prepare me for the challenges of a fresh semester. It was while rereading my heavily annotated and coffee-stained copy of Gail E. Hawisher and Cynthia L. Selfe's "The Rhetoric of Technology and the Electronic Writing Class" that I discovered what I needed. In the closing line of the piece, Hawisher and Selfe caution readers that "Unless we remain aware of our electronic writing classes as sites of paradox and promise, transformed by a new writing technology, and unless we plan carefully for intended outcomes, we may unwittingly use computers to maintain rigid authority structures that contribute neither to good teaching nor to good learning."[2] Because I had read it so many times before, the prescience of this statement struck me as a discomfiting—albeit fair—rebuke against the unintended outcomes of my first effort to incorporate a wiki into a university-level course.

Although wikis have been in use since Ward Cunningham first developed the WikiWikiWeb for the Portland Pattern Repository in 1995, they have only recently caught the attention of social scientists and humanities scholars.[3] To many readers the peculiar discursive modes of wikis manifest an open-ended realm of liberation that surpasses other technosocial arrangements. To be sure, wikis pose challenges to conventional academic structures and thus require fortitude and flexibility on the part of both students and instructors. Perhaps the most salient feature of wikis is that they orchestrate authorial effacement, which is to say that wiki discourse can confer authority on a singular position that has nonetheless been authored by multiple unseen contributors. As such, a wiki is a supple text written by people with unidentifiable identities. In light of this phenomenon, a perturbing question occurred to me throughout the previously mentioned semester: what are the social and pedagogical implications of a writing space where the benefit of open access is offset by an anonymity that ineluctably impedes authorial accountability?

At the heart of this question is a concern over power relations, a concern captured by Gunther Kress's observation that "when everyone can have the status of author, authority wanes or disappears."[4] And yet, wikis, unlike the more established forms of computer-mediated discourse that Kress considers, undermine the authority of authors while still maintaining the authority attributed to the seemingly solidified products of discourse. In other words, the dialogic and corporate mode of wiki discourse is translated into a monologic representation of knowledge. So, although wikis can be considered radically democratizing because they distribute the role of author, the same mechanism of authorial distribution makes it difficult to discern whose version of the truth is being represented. As such, the serious business of examining what James Berlin terms the "ideological predispositions" of composition as a signifying practice is potentially disrupted by wiki discourse.[5] For insofar as ideological analyses are often enough investigations of motives, the ability to assign and discern motivation becomes less tenable when authorial identity is concealed.

These considerations are significant enough that they cannot be suppressed by merely reiterating the benefits of wiki discourse. It would, however, be equally unreasonable to treat the challenges posed by wikis as irremediable failings. To be sure, wiki software is simple, but the discursive practices of wiki communities are highly complex, and they are doubly so when they intersect with the classroom. In an effort to help puzzle through these complexities, the remainder of this essay will focus on some of the more salient difficulties that Emina encountered while using Wikipedia.

"Crazy People" Invading the Cult of Facts

Since much of the ensuing argument deals with representations of knowledge and authorial identity, it is important to first have a sense of Emina's standpoint and her position in my course. Early on she displayed an extroverted confidence about her claim to an education as well as candor regarding her self-perceived limitations as a writer. In reply to a stasis question about students' expectations of the class that I posted to the course bulletin board, she wrote that "english was never [her] best subject, writing is hard; but it is necessary for the good jobs in America. . . . Everyone can dream big in America, but it takes education and writing good to get there." While this response seems typical of the initial attitudes freshmen have toward higher education—whereby a calculus of entitlement translates a college degree into a lucrative career, which then in turn translates into fulfilled happiness—Emina's further posts demonstrated progressively acute self-reflection. She offered an unsolicited explanation of her accent and her dress habits, which also provided readers with an understanding of her life both before and after America:

> So far I enjoy the university because people don't judge you as in high school. My family comes from Bosnia and when I first went to high school in America so many students would make fun of the way I talk or tease me for my head scarf. Nobody ever asked what was it like in Bosnia, or why we came to America. People would laugh at my head scarf and ask was I a nun? After I corrected them and told them that I was Muslim things were even worse for me. . . . Here in college people are serious about their studies and don't have the time to pick on people for being different from them. . . . I'm not a terrorist, I don't hate America and if anyone has any questions I would love to chat about things!

Clearly, Emina possessed a strong sense of who she was and a keen aware-ness of how her experiences added up to a coherent narrative that buttressed this sense of self. Far from adopting the role of an invisible victim, she was open about her life leading up to the fall of Titoist Yugoslavia. She candidly spoke to the class about growing up marginalized under a Communist regime, about how the carnage of war resulted in the death of uncles and brothers as well as the paralysis of her sister, and about her efforts to assim-ilate into a sometimes hostile American society.

This sketch of Emina provides a necessary foundation for the subsequent claims that I will make about the paradoxical growth that she experienced while using Wikipedia during the course. For example, despite her general intellectual curiosity and healthy distrust of unquestioned truth claims, she was incensed by the discursive maneuvering that she found on many of Wikipedia's discussion and article pages. The conversations that she read were difficult for her because they challenged the self-representation that she was committed to at the beginning of the course. The impetus for this hos-tility was an essay prompt that asked students to analyze the significance of keywords as they related to their sense of identity and to take into account the definition and usage of these terms by Wikipedia authors.

Rough and final drafts of the essays themselves were posted to the course Web site, where other students could respond. For one of her keywords Em-ina chose "Bosnian Muslim," which seemed to her at first to be an uncom-plicated epithet describing both her country of origin and her religious alle-giance. In her first rough draft she wrote that "it is not always so fashionable to call oneself Bosnian Muslim, but everybody knows what you mean whether you say Bosniak or Bosnian Muslim." The concluding sentence of her draft corroborated this simplistic pluralism: "It is up to the individual person's beliefs." This nonchalance, however, dissipated once Emina began studying the discussions that were catalogued on Wikipedia's entry for "Bosniak."

The first response that Emina posted to the course Web site after examin-ing the content of Wikipedia's information on Bosnia was unabashedly bel-licose. To be fair, her reaction, which I would characterize as bewildered dis-trust, was characteristic of many of her fellow students, although it differed in degree. She vehemently announced her frustration with "all of these opinions" that she saw expressed on Wikipedia. The information on Bosnia was anathema to her because she believed that "encyclopedias are supposed to be facts and this Wikipedia.com is not a fact! It's just made-up opinions by crazy people that I don't know!!" In an attempt to both mollify the class and seize what I took to be a teaching moment, I responded to her post by asking what exactly constituted a fact. A good deal of conversation was generated on this topic, but no student was able to offer a definitive answer that everyone was willing to endorse.

In the end, most of the students, Emina included, seemed desperate for a sign of authority that could end the controversy caused by Wikipedia's radical, anonymous discourse. In this way, they echoed Kress's articulation of the perceived differences between print and digital information systems: Where before the author was a publicly legitimated and endorsed figure, now there is no such gatekeeping. In *The Mode of Information*, Mark Poster, like Kress, demonstrates that the technologies of discourse are intricately related to questions of authority and fabrications of identity.[6]

But the problem that I saw occurring was not really a problem at all. Rather, Emina and her classmates were simply not familiar with actively producing knowledge and being counted on to referee truth claims for themselves. As the instructor, however, I was unprepared for this level of engagement and as a result failed to capitalize on the opportunity that their problems provided. Thus, though we were fluent in other computer-mediated modes of writing, our exposure to wiki discourse revealed that my students and I nonetheless viewed digital information technologies from a print-based schema. This print-based schema might be thought of in terms of Walter Ong's pipeline model of information transfer, which he faults because it "distorts the act of communication beyond recognition."[7]

Wikipedia and the Exposure of Discursive Spider Holes

Of course, these issues of textual authority and authorial legitimacy in Wikipedia are not only important to my students; they have also preoccupied a significant number of professional scholars. Both Besiki Stvilia et al. and

Andrew Lih have separately conducted recent studies of content production in Wikipedia and offered analyses of the relative quality of its articles. While Lih's piece, "Wikipedia as Participatory Journalism," pays particular attention to the ways in which Wikipedia was affected after specific articles had been cited in the mainstream press,[8] Stvilia et al. utilize methods consistent with library and information science. As such, Stvilia et al. include an impressive multidimensional framework with three distinct categories that are intended to gauge the merits of Wikipedia's Information Quality (IQ).[9] Methodological intricacies aside, Lih and Stvilia et al. focus on how Wikipedia articles compare with and conform to the standards of print conventions. Quality, of course, is a problematic term that connotes various things, depending upon usage and context; these studies seem to use it as a measure of legitimacy based upon reliability and fidelity to yet another problematic term: truth.

Thus the respective analyses of Wikipedia performed by Lih and Stvilia et al. are both limited by their inattention to the ways that wiki discourse disrupts standardized definitions of quality, truth, and knowledge. Rather than attempt to rehabilitate Wikipedia into the fold of received wisdom regulating textual legitimacy and the authenticity of truth claims, we should explicate the means by which Wikipedia problematizes the conventions of print culture. For example, as many of the other contributors to this collection address (cf. Barton, Lakeman, and Bossewitch et al.), the lack of traditional authority that distinguishes wiki authorship highlights the rhetorical aspects of discourse production by calling on both readers and writers to exercise responsibility for their acceptance of truth claims. While this rhetorical interplay is inherent in print, it is occluded by the artificial separation of textual production and consumption that occurs with print-based texts. In other words, print-based texts attain an illusory durability and authority because readers are unable to alter the text in any meaningful way, irrespective of how they rewrite the text through their own idiosyncratic interpretations.

George P. Landow's pioneering work on hypermedia's effects on composition in Hypertext 2.0 addresses this issue.[10] Landow maintains that collaborations between writers/readers and textual producers/textual consumers exist in the medium of print but that ever since Gutenberg the technology of the book "systematically has hindered full recognition of collaborative authorship."[11] In contrast, Wikipedia, and wikis in general, are vital because they reveal formerly hidden aspects of textual production, including the erroneous supposition that legitimate writing is produced in vacuums by solitary experts. What enables wiki software to expose the fallacies of print culture is that each writing product that they represent is highly textured. In the case of Wikipedia there is a clear distinction between the official discourse represented in an "article page" and the unstable discourse that appears in a "talk page" corresponding to articles. In effect, this means that all users are both readers and writers with access to the nebulous process that underwrites finished writing products, a process that is existent but indiscernible in the material production of print texts.

Despite Emina's exasperation with Wikipedia, and my inability to mediate these unforeseen problems, her aptitude for textual scrutiny developed in exciting ways. Over the course of the semester she gained the skills and the language to more thoughtfully analyze the writing of others as well as her own writing. Likewise, her general critical thinking skills heightened in the face of the problems posed by Wikipedia. For example, as Emina worked her way through the drafting process and paid closer attention to the ways that Wikipedians treated the term Bosnian Muslim, she became more invested in her writing.

During the archived discussion from December 2004, there was a lengthy exchange between a few Wikipedians who were debating the appropriate nomenclature for post-Dayton occupants of the former Yugoslavia.[12] Emina expressed annoyance over those who were arguing for the exclusive use of Bosniak because she felt that it was derogatory. Emina's entry indicates her view that this assessment had to do with her own experiences as a Muslim living in Bosnia and her fear that Bosniak, with its blank inclusivity, did not allow any room for recognition of the already oppressed Muslim population:

> Bosniak is fine if you don't care about religion or differences in Bosnian history. It is not that I don't want to be known as Bosniak because I think that Muslim's are better than the Orthodox or Roman Catholics. But, being Muslim is important to me. Some people think that it is nicer to say Bosniak like you wouldn't any more call African-Americans "Negroes", because nowadays times have changed. But, I don't want the world to pretend that our genocide never happened by calling everyone Bosniak.

This level of introspection and argumentation is markedly different from the laissez-faire attitude of Emina's first rough draft. After contending with the attempts of various unknown Wikipedians to define her ethnic and religious identity, she abandoned the anemic claim from her first rough draft that "everybody knows what you mean whether you say Bosniak or Bosnian Muslim." Ultimately, while her dealings with Wikipedia were uncomfortable, and although it was difficult for me to guide her through the process, Emina became more invested in the negotiation of knowledge by seeing the consequences of discourse.

Nearly an entire page of Emina's second rough draft was devoted to critiquing the claims put forward by the Wikipedian Vedran. During the aforementioned edit war of December 2004, Vedran emerged as the most outspoken advocate for the official change from *Bosnian Muslim* to *Bosniak*. It bothered Emina that she did not know who Vedran was or what motivated Vedran's strong argument for the substitution of *Bosniak* for *Bosnian Muslim*. Accordingly, she concluded in her paper:

> Why Vedran believes what she does about the name Bosniak is not clear. She gives list of reasons, but how do you know that she isn't supporter of Milosevic or if not, then at least anti-Muslim? She writes how Bosnian Muslims are "free to call themselves what they like. However, other people, such as me, who desire to be called Bosniaks—should be called Bosniaks." However, this is not clear because this Vedran might not be Bosnian, at all. Nobody even knows if she is real.[13]

This proved to be one of the most rhetorically potent sections of Emina's second draft. Not only does she argumentatively contest another writer's claims, but her refutation of Vedran's claim is highly significant because the claim paralleled one of Emina's own assertions from her first rough draft. Her growing dissatisfaction with the empty pluralism expressed in her previous assertion that "whether you say Bosniak or Bosnian Muslim . . . It is up to the individual person's beliefs" indicates her realization of the dire importance of epistemological turbulence. Vedran, Emina discovered, was basing a call for the universal usage of Bosniak by appealing to an uncritical personal belief, but the result of this personal belief was such that Emina would have her own conception of her identity infringed upon.

Perpetual Negotiation Machine

Emina's analysis was further complicated by one of Vedran's major justifications for initiating the change to *Bosniak*: namely, that "Wikipedia is about facts, it should aim to provide solid facts and not opinions. The Bosniak name is a fact today, accepted by everyone except a few persons."[14] Vedran's statement, coupled with Wikipedia's neutral point of view (NPOV) policy requiring contributors to post "fairly and without bias,"[15] served to erode Emina's credulous acceptance of truth. In effect, she had to submit to an intellectual struggle between her rejection of the Bosniak label and her commitment to preordained, objective facts. Ultimately, she found herself aligned with Nikola and Igor, two Wikipedians who rejected the *Bosniak* label and supported the reinstating of *Bosnian Muslim.*

Both Nikola and Igor shared Emina's opposition to Vedran's efforts to redefine Wikipedia's official representation of Muslims originating from the formerly united Yugoslavia. In response to Vedran's comment that the term *Bosnian Muslim* was separatist in nature and therefore problematic, Nikola, whose user profile revealed that he holds interests in "Serbia, Serbian culture and history,"[16] replied that "in this case Bosniak is ambigious, incorrect and derisive."[17] Igor, who like Nikola was listed in Wikipedia's directory of Serbian users, concurred that "the Bosniak name causes ambiguities and confusion."[18] But, while Emina appreciated Igor's and Nikola's positions on Bosnian Muslims, she was challenged by their understanding of discourse production and negotiations of knowledge.

Rather than resort to an uncontested, transcendent definition of factual truth, Igor and Nikola jointly proclaimed that "Wikipedia is about discussion and everything is open for debate."[19] Early on in the semester Emina had led her classmates in mutinous critiques of Wikipedia and what they perceived to be its faulty posturing as a source of knowledge. However, now that she was heavily invested in the discursive mode of Wikipedia, she began to experience slippage in her previous intellectual convictions. Determining whether Wikipedian authors held any legitimacy or whether their claims could be measured against a predetermined metric of authenticity had become difficult indeed.

Whereas Emina's initial dismissal of Wikipedia was based upon a relatively uncomplicated evaluation, her later analyses focused more on the interrelation of claims and the supple logic guiding collaborative writing. As such, her conceptions of truth became more sophisticated, and she began to regard knowledge as a composite of different claims and ideas. I interpreted this as evidence of her loss of faith in objective knowledge and textual permanence. While this was somewhat frustrating for her, it also galvanized her interest in constructing, acquiring, and negotiating knowledge. This shift away from a focus on discursive completeness and totality is reminiscent of Clifford Lynch's caution to avoid "checking the authenticity of an object as if it were a simple true-or-false test—a computation that produces a one or a zero" because it might be more "constructive to think about checking authenticity as a process of examining and assigning confidence to a collection of claims."[20] Lynch's conception of factual authenticity as an ongoing hermeneutic process is consistent with Emina's efforts to contend with the interrelated arguments that Vedran, Nikola, and Igor were making about definitions of truth and how it is represented. Thus, Emina was forced to confront both the ontological questions that she faced as a Bosnian Muslim as well as the epistemological considerations of how any of this knowledge was to be constructed and communicated.

In *What's the Matter with the Internet?*—a recent and important book dealing with the postmodern dimensions of cyberspace—Mark Poster devotes an entire chapter to what he terms *virtual ethnicity*. The problems that Poster describes in relation to virtual enactments of ethnicity closely correspond to Emina's experiences during the semester. According to Poster, "the fixity of ethnicity as an attribute of the self would appear to be the opposite of the identities constructed in . . . virtual spaces."[21] For Emina, the experience of not having any sort of physical referent, no matter how problematic physical referents may be, made it difficult for her to gauge the legitimacy of the claims made by Wikipedians about Bosnian Muslims. This significant obstacle, however, did not preclude her from evaluating the credibility or accountability of Wikipedia articles or contributors. Rather, she was forced to discover alternative means for discerning reliability, and, owing partly to her instructor's lack of experience in this novel writing environment, she had to design new strategies for grasping textual authority on her own.

Arguably the most important and certainly the most frustrating strategy that Emina developed was that of perpetual negotiation. Whereas she longed for a stable sense of identity predicated on apparently durable truths, the only way that she could understand Wikipedia was to stay open and mobile. In his study of what he describes as "cyber-Jews," Poster arrives at a similar conclusion: "the individual in a virtual object [is in] an unfinished, contingent state where identity is temporary . . . [and occupying a] subject position that is 'never before' rather than 'always already.'"[22] Because of this dynamic, Emina's essay assignment compelled her to probe her self-understanding more deeply than she had ever done before. I would hazard that this exhaustive analysis was somewhat disquieting for her, but it nonetheless produced startling results that neither she nor I had foreseen.

To be certain, some thoughtful readers might be tempted to dismiss the friction between Emina and Wikipedia as a case of semantics resembling a tempest in a teakettle, as did indeed a few of her classmates. However, I submit that Emina's analysis of wiki discourse in the context of her ethnic and religious identities helped to make her understand the material consequences of language use in a much deeper way. The project of naming—who is named, who gets to name, where the name comes from, what alternative names are elided—is central to understanding domination and possibilities for agency. This issue, of course, extends well beyond the case of Muslims in the former Socialist Federal Republic of Yugoslavia, as Emina herself pointed out when she alluded to the succession of labels that have been imposed on or created by black Americans. In post-Dayton Bosnia, where census statistics are being gathered to calculate the sickening impact of the genocidal ethnic cleansing that occurred during the 1990s, the effects of discourse and naming are very real. In response to a comment that her final draft received from a classmate about "taking Wikipedia and the essay assignment just a little too seriously," Emina reminded her classmates that the basis for much of the organized slaughter throughout the twentieth century began with sinister discursive regimes.

Artificial Denouement

Ultimately, then, what rescues Wikipedia from being a heavily flawed novelty is its capacity for infinite discussion. Students like Emina, who first found its lack of certainty and stability bewildering both with respect to authorship and credibility, eventually came to see it as a viable mode of discourse precisely because it was never complete. Such incompleteness put more at stake for the students, because the onus of accepting and creating knowledge rested on them; they could not simply defer to experts. Behind the relative stability of the articles themselves, which often enough were barely stable, lay the discussion pages where meaning was constantly in flux. Moreover, the lack of definition was counterintuitively the very mechanism that promoted most of my students from skepticism by allowing them to recognize integrity in the system. To put a finer point on things, collaboration, as it functions in Wikipedia, is liberating because it delays the suppression inherent in textual completion.

Unlike print texts, Wikipedia allows users to write back and to discern how the facts being represented have been negotiated by contributors. As a result, Emina and her classmates came to appreciate that wiki collaboration did not require complete agreement by all contributors. Rather, they understood that its collaborative efficacy results from distorted consensus, which I contend is consonant with John Trimbur's notion of "dissensus."[23] At the risk of being reductive, Trimbur's understanding of dissensus can be described as consensus that "depends paradoxically on its deferral, not its realization." Indeed, when he writes that he is "less interested in students achieving consensus . . . as in their using consensus as a critical instrument to open gaps in the conversation through which differences may emerge," he describes a tangled form of communication similar to that which occurs in wikis.[24]

Since so much of this piece is indebted to Emina's perseverance in the face of her instructor's incapacity to adequately prepare her for the challenges of Wiki discourse, it seems only fitting that she have the last words. At the beginning of the next semester Emina sent me an e-mail that clarified what she had gained from interacting with Wikipedia in my class:

> I still don't know about that Wikipedia.com. . . . But maybe that's good because it made me keep thinking about things that I had made up my mind about. I used to knew what being Bosnian Muslim meant and what war means, but really I think I stopped thinking about war and life and I just had answers that I told to people and myself. Probably I will never

know the truth about any of it. . . . But I want to keep discussing and "not get complacent" like you always warned us. Who knows, maybe I will get my friends together to tell that Vedran person what we know.

NOTES

1. As a gesture toward Emina's authorial integrity, I have reprinted her words exactly as she wrote them. Given the nature of the ensuing discussion I feel that it is important to protect the idiosyncracies of her spelling, syntax, and grammar.

2. Gail E. Hawisher and Cynthia L. Selfe, "The Rhetoric of Technology and the Electronic Writing Class," *College Composition and Communication* 42 (1991): 55–65. Reprinted in *The Writing Teacher's Sourcebook*, 4th ed., ed. Edward P. J. Corbett, Nancy Myers, and Gary Tate (New York: Oxford University Press, 2000), 138.

3. See Bo Leuf and Ward Cunningham's *Wiki Way* (http://www.wiki.org), a wiki that details the origins of Cunningham's original WikiWikiWeb.

4. Gunther Kress, *Literacy in the New Media Age* (London: Routledge, 2003), 172.

5. James Berlin, *Rhetorics, Poetics, and Cultures: Refiguring College English Studies* (West Lafayette: Parlor Press, 2003), 83.

6. Mark Poster, *The Mode of Information: Poststructuralism and Social Context* (Chicago: University of Chicago Press, 1990).

7. Walter Ong, *Orality and Literacy: The Technologizing of the Word* (London: Methuen, 1982), 176.

8. Andrew Lih, "Wikipedia as Participatory Journalism: Reliable Sources? Metrics for Evaluating Collaborative Media as a News Source," Proceedings of the Fifth International Symposium on Online Journalism, Austin, Texas, 2004.

9. Besiki Stvilia, Michael B. Twindale, Les Gasser, and Linda C. Smith, "Information Quality Discussions in Wikipedia," Technical Report, ISRN University of Illinois at Urbana-Champaign Information Sciences—2005/2+CSCW, 2005, http://mailer.fsu .edu/~bstvilia/papers/qualWiki.pdf.

10. George P. Landow, *Hypertext 2.0: The Convergence of Contemporary Critical Theory and Technology* (Baltimore: Johns Hopkins University Press, 1997).

11. Ibid., 106.

12. Wikipedia Contributors, "Talk:Bosniaks," Wikipedia, the Free Encyclopedia, http://en.wikipedia.org/wiki/Talk:Bosniaks.

13. Here Emina is quoting from Vedran's post on http://en.wikipedia.org/wiki/ Talk:Bosniaks.

14. Ibid.

15. Wikipedia Contributors, "Neutral Point of View," Wikipedia, the Free Encyclopedia, http://en.wikipedia.org/wiki/Wikipedia:Neutral_point_of_view.

16. Wikpedia Contributors, "User: Nikola Smolenski," Wikipedia, the Free Encyclopedia, http://en.wikipedia.org/wiki/User:Nikola_Smolenski.

17. See http://en.wikipedia.org/wiki/Talk:Bosniaks.

18. Ibid.

19. Ibid.

20. Clifford Lynch, "Authenticity and Integrity in the Digital Environment: An Ex-

ploratory Analysis of the Central Role of Trust," in *Authenticity in a Digital Environment* (Washington, DC: Council on Library and Information Resources, 2000), 40.

21. Mark Poster, *What's the Matter with the Internet?* (Minneapolis: University of Minnesota Press, 2001), 166.

22. Ibid., 169–70.

23. John Trimbur, "Consensus and Difference in Collaborative Learning," *College English* 51, no. 6 (1989).

24. Ibid., 614.

One Wiki, Two Classrooms

Faced with a daunting reading list and encouraged to work together, first-year graduate students at the University of Illinois at Chicago (UIC) Department of Communication created a wiki-based Web site in the fall of 2004. Since then, graduate students and faculty have employed it to varying degrees. Some have made extensive use of the technology, while others have used it peripherally, if at all. Two introductory courses provide an interesting glimpse into these variations.

Comm 500 and Comm 502 are graduate courses designed to introduce students to the field of communication and its key texts. Accomplishing this in a single semester requires significant reading and discussion. During the fall 2004 semester, both courses were attended by many of the same students. But while Comm 502 generated more than seven hundred individual edits and nearly one hundred pages of text, Comm 500 received far less attention over the same time period. The same students were using the wiki in one case but found it lacking in another.

Why did the same group of UIC students choose to use a wiki in one class only to disregard it in another? What factors contribute to the successful incorporation of a wiki into the graduate classroom? This essay explores these questions through a series of interviews with the students and instructors at UIC.

The Wiki

The initial courses taken by graduate students are designed to be overwhelming. This is to say that their intention, in part, is to steep new students in the basics of their chosen field and to establish a foundation of working knowledge. They also serve as a test of seriousness and rigor. If medical students are squeamish when it comes to dissecting a cadaver, they had best consider a change of career. If students of the social sciences blanch at a heavy reading load, they might wish to rethink their plan to pursue an advanced degree.

During the fall 2004 semester, in the Department of Communication at UIC, the test for incoming graduate students took the form of two classes, each consisting largely of the same group of students: Introduction to Communication Research (500) and Seminar in Media Studies (502). We knew we had a lot of work to do as we began our studies, but the true volume of our task became apparent when a second-year student shared a portion of the Comm 502 readings. With a smile, she handed over two phonebook-sized tomes, the sort of thing barbers might keep on hand to boost the seats of small children. Dozens of articles and chapters were spread across reams of paper, each page covered with tiny, photocopied text. Our professors, long used to seeing a mixture of panic and awe in the eyes of students, suggested we work together and help one another through the material.

After our first week of class, we met to discuss how to go about sharing the burden. It was suggested that each of us might focus more carefully on certain readings and then e-mail our notes to the group. This, however, seemed less than optimal. As our classmate Susan recalled:

> I knew that doing it through e-mail was not going to work. It'd mean that everybody would be sending documents that you'd have to download, and there's always a problem with the file. It wasn't what I think we wanted to do. Ultimately, it would be just every one of us looking at very specific texts, that's it.

We needed a way to work together, a way to write up notes and share comments collaboratively. None of the technologies familiar to us—discussion boards, e-mail, blogs—allowed for this.

At the time, only a few students (among them, us) had any notion of what a wiki was. Still, when the concept of collaborative authoring via wikis was brought up, it seemed like it might provide an ideal solution. After trying a free but extremely limited online service, we installed an open source wiki platform on a student-maintained server. There were some initial technical hurdles as newcomers to the technology wrestled with markup conventions and the unusual feeling that comes with editing and appending to the work of others, but it was nevertheless an almost immediate success. Students developed techniques for self-identification through color-coded comments and created a weekly schedule for publishing materials on the site.

The wiki worked. Not only did students use the wiki to share their thoughts and interpretations of the readings, but many relied on it to bolster their understanding. A mass of material that a single reader would have had great difficulty assimilating became clear when approached collaboratively. As the semester drew to a close and students began working on their first graduate-level papers, the wiki contained over one hundred pages of text that had been edited by students more than seven hundred times. We had, in effect, written our own textbook. Our Comm 502 professor, when looking over the material, was impressed. He remarked:

> There's a picture, it's an extension of the individualist picture of things, that each incoming class should suffer through the same exercises. As if they couldn't stand on the shoulders of students who went before them. And instead of that, what the wiki produces is a student written textbook. Textbooks aren't cheatsheets, they aren't answers to quizzes, they aren't papers to be turned in, they're a resource for you to go to. The students still have responsibilities to know and understand the material, but this way, they have a tool for learning it that is not a textbook that you just read, it's not an inert piece of paper, it's something that you go in and say "no that's not right" or "I don't believe that" or "Boy, I need to read more about this" so you're interacting with the text and with this resource that is much more valuable, and encourages more involvement, than any textbook.

But this use was lopsided. The vast majority of the content on the wiki focused on Comm 502. Comm 500 received far less attention over the same time period. The same group of students were using the wiki in one class and ignoring it in another. This disparity can be better apprehended by tracking the number of edits made to the wiki pages for each class over time. Figure 1 reveals that, throughout the semester, Comm 502 received significantly more attention than Comm 500. The peaks in the figure correspond with the

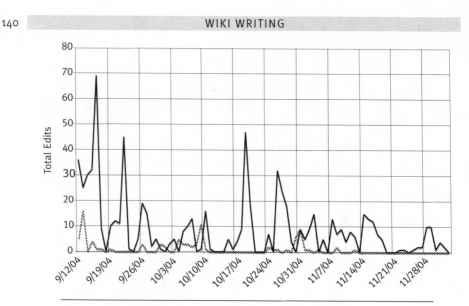

Fig. 1. Communication wiki edits, 500 versus 502

weekly schedule (initial notes were posted each Tuesday) developed by students.

Why did the same group of UIC students choose to use a wiki in one class only to disregard it in another? What factors contribute to the successful incorporation of a wiki in the graduate classroom? The answers lie not in the wiki itself but in the offline, social environments of each class.

The Classroom

Though the classes were attended by the same cohort of students, they were taught by very different professors and presented students with distinct challenges. While Comm 500 consisted of more traditional lectures and classroom activities, Comm 502 was designed to promote student collaboration. Its professor described it as follows:

> Basically, the course is about collaboration when dealing with the crush of literature—which is what all scholars must do. My approach forces collaboration, and students have always found ways to help each other out. In the past, they used photocopies and printouts. They would write

up summaries of readings, distribute them, and meet to discuss them. When universal access to reliable e-mail and the capacity to send attachments became available, students began using that medium instead. So what you have is an overload of work, and a clear indication that the students are in charge of how to deal with it.

It was clear to all that the Comm 502 workload was, in fact, too much for an individual student, while the Comm 500 course work proved more manageable. One student said, "I think it was the class structure itself. The fact that we were so overwhelmed with 12 or 13 articles every week and in Gary's class [Comm 500] it just didn't feel that way."

Being able to competently discuss those twelve or thirteen articles each week was of critical importance. In Comm 502, 35 percent of the final grade was determined by class participation and discussion. In Comm 500, the final grade hinged on a formal research paper and two exams—participation accounted for 10 percent of that grade. The varying importance of in-class discussion made for radically different classroom environments. Kristy, a student in both classes, compared the two as follows:

> Christopher [Comm 502] might guide the discussion, but we had to build it, we had to develop it. And we all knew that we were being graded on our participation, so we really had to read everything. . . . Gary [Comm 500] would talk a lot more. He would say, "this is what it's about" and maybe ask a few questions, but the discussion was not . . . we didn't guide it.

In essence, Comm 500 made plain what students were expected to learn from each of the assigned readings. In Comm 502, students had to determine the meaning and import of assignments on their own. Faced with an overwhelming task and explicit direction to collaborate, the Comm 502 class developed a certain cohesiveness not present in Comm 500. Susan felt that the wiki allowed for something beyond individual effort.

> We wanted to be a good class. I think we thought of it as a challenge, not just that we wanted to be good students, but also that we wanted to be a good class. I don't know if it was collective, but for me, the wiki was not just about me getting the article, but just getting ready to have a good discussion.

We weren't simply a class; we were a team that hoped to excel in the eyes of a demanding instructor. While the relationship wasn't adversarial, Kristy felt a sense of ongoing evaluation.

> I definitely always felt a little bit more nervous about Christopher's class [Comm 502] and I always felt like he wanted us to get to a certain place but he would never tell us how to get there. He'd make us go through this journey that was supposed to be wonderful, but it was just a lot of hard work.

The environment of Comm 502, then, was one in which the class felt it necessary to prove something to their professor, to figure out the meaning of articles and their place within the overall literature on their own. The environment in Comm 500 was markedly different.

Students described the atmosphere in Comm 500, with its more straightforward lecture style, as a more congenial one. The reading load was lighter, and the class discussion, rather than relying solely on the students, was directly led by the professor. Susan described it in the following manner:

> Gary [Comm 500] is less stressful. It's more pleasant. Christopher [Comm 502] is more stressful. It's high stress. You still have to do a good job for both of them, but it's the environment they create.

The fact that Comm 500 was experienced as more congenial did not mean that it was an easier class. The readings, though fewer in quantity, were nonetheless challenging. Also, the formal paper required of students made for a much more intense writing project than did the short exercises required of students in Comm 502. Where Comm 502 forced students to collaborate, Comm 500 encouraged students to research topics that were of interest to them as individual scholars. Where Comm 502 fostered teamwork, Comm 500 allowed for individual exploration.

Conclusions

The case of Comm 502 was a very special circumstance in which students with adequate knowledge about wiki technologies were faced with an appropriate task in a supportive social environment. A student-driven wiki project needs to have all of the right pieces in place—and this may only happen rarely. In contrasting the wiki participation of Comm 500 and Comm 502, it became clear that, although the wiki was not used actively in Comm 500, it was a mismatch of the technology and the circumstances rather than a failure of the technology or the people involved. It was the teaching styles of the professors and the nature of the assignments that shaped the wiki. While it is useful to talk about general circumstances where wikis can work or not, these cases are rich sites for exploration that moves beyond generality. Cases like Comm 502, which come about organically and are not directly incentivized by the instructor, have generated excitement about wiki technology. These situations are exceedingly difficult to replicate.

The bottom-up implementation of the wiki and its success in Comm 502 generated optimism about wikis and their role in the classroom. But the lack of participation by the same students using the same platform in Comm 500 is significant. We feel that it is important to recognize that minor differences in the nature of the classroom and the relationship between students may result in radically different usage.

The lack of wiki use for Comm 500 does not represent a failure of the technology, the students, or the instructor. The course simply didn't present a task requiring wiki collaboration. In this instance, a wiki was not a relevant tool.

We believe that attempts to replicate the Comm 502 environment would be challenging, if not fruitless. The success of the wiki in that situation was contingent on a number of intangible, social factors that cannot be readily duplicated. A better approach lies in simply making collaborative tools like the wiki available for student use. Vibrant collaboration via wiki can emerge, given the right circumstances, but this collaboration can't be forced. For all of the wiki-generated content produced, Comm 502 was not a more successful course than Comm 500. Both courses met their educational goals, but where Comm 502 was well suited for a wiki-based collaborative approach, Comm 500 was not.

Content and Commentary: Parallel Structures of Organization and Interaction on Wikis

It is my intention to suggest a number of ways in which the content and operation of wikis might constitute an unusually rich field of investigation for students of hypertext. Perhaps most significantly, I will suggest that particular qualities inherent to the operation of wikis often lead to the same questions that preoccupy the academic researcher being actively discussed by the writers of hypertext, the research subjects themselves. To simplify, we might say not only that many of the interests of academic researchers are understood and employed by wiki users but also that similar processes of critical inquiry constitute everyday experience on many levels of wiki writing. These user-led processes of discussion, comment, and ongoing critical evaluation are not only highly visible but also notable precisely because they employ the self-reflexive potential of hypertext authorship to ensure that the multitudinous networks of critical content generated by wiki writing are recorded as material in their own right.

It has been suggested by literary theorists and technologists alike[1] that one of the most significant aspects of hypertext as a form of communication lies in its potential to reconfigure the activities of its writers, substituting the isolated production of closed documents with dynamic webs of intertextuality that challenge the traditional relationship between readers and authors in fundamental and productive ways. This convergence is made possible by the capacity of hypertext systems to host a reading public that influences information networks as it traverses them, perhaps through forms of annotation and marginalia resembling the scholarship of the age of print[2] or, more radically, through a process of remediation that repositions texts, and the activities of reading and writing, within the fluctuating content of data networks that are both decentered and antihierarchical.

In light of this, it might be useful to analyze wikis in terms of their potential to host a diverse community of writers by functioning not only as a unique mode for the presentation and organization of material but also as devices for the practical organization of their individual contributors.

The Cumulative Processes of
Creating Communal Hypertexts

The terms of inquiry just suggested are of particular relevance to wikis, which can be analyzed as social formations organizing communities of writers and also according to a technological analysis that addresses them as specific implementations of hypertext theory, understood in this context as a model for the cooperative organization and transmission of information. These analyses converge through an exploration of the remarkable flexibility that enables wiki content to be shaped by the activities of its users, a noisy and sometimes anarchic process that nevertheless manages to sustain the production and organization of an enormous variety of written material.

I would like to argue that this flexibility is embodied in the specific ways in which the creators of wikis have chosen to implement hypertext authorship as a communal activity, utilizing techniques that render wikis relatively unique as a popular model of electronic writing, despite the fact that these same techniques are clearly inherited from the work of the earliest hypertext theorists. Most notably, wikis make good on the promises of hypertext evangelists such as Theodor Nelson and George Landow, who predicted that electronic texts would be fundamentally adaptive to the activities of their users and thus would encourage a participatory model of hypertext in which audiences can read, write, and manipulate any given item within a shifting network of interrelated pages. Wikis also situate these revisions of individual items within an organizational structure that is similarly distinguished by its plasticity and that allows material to be continuously edited, divided, and repositioned in ever-changing configurations. These perpetual revisions and shifting indices bypass traditional hierarchies of organization and are themselves documented as important webs of data, preserved through devices that chart the amorphous growth of content, comparing multiple versions of texts and recording each instance of editing and rearrangement.

The cumulative effect of countless, separate manipulations of text allows a loosely organized user base to maintain databases of remarkable complexity, and it is through participation in these collective efforts that the activity of authorship, insofar as the traditional implications of the term can be adequately transposed to wikis, fulfills its true potential. While newcomers to wikis are soon familiar with the way material advances through numerous revisions, a broader understanding of their operation hinges on the awareness that the historic development of a given text seldom occurs outside complex processes of rewriting and reorganization carried out by a community of wiki users. Once acquired, this perspective becomes an invaluable conceptual tool for understanding the functioning of wikis, not least to the degree that it reveals instructive parallels between the social composition of a wiki's user base and its organizational and technical peculiarities.

Critical analysts of hypertext participation such as Stuart Moulthrop have asserted that "the structure and specifications of the hypertext environment are themselves parts of the docuverse, arguably the most important parts,"[3] and I would suggest that the value of wikis as writing projects lies in the extent to which the user's awareness of these structures and specifications, a kind of "wiki literacy," is developed and indeed encouraged by the organizational idiosyncrasies of the wiki system. This can be best understood by observing the ways in which wiki users discuss these critical issues and the ways in which these discussions are then incorporated into wikis in the form of distinct levels of textual content. The recorded progression of a wiki page through multiple versions, paralleled by the visible interaction between multiple authors, produces a text that is richly annotated with the record of its own development, a body of supplementary material that provides social, historic, and even theoretical context for the growth of wikis, including the conditions for individual participation.

Interactive Commentaries and Visible Discussion

For many newcomers to the wiki system, the first wiki is Wikipedia. They become familiar with the significance of user interaction through the "discussion" pages that Wikipedia automatically attaches to each article, spaces in which the project's avowed implementation of encyclopedic "neutrality" is persistently renegotiated according to the exchanges between its individual contributors. These spaces, hosting preemptive dialogue for the development of both encyclopedic articles and the administrative aspects of the wiki itself, represent the public face of the process by which Wikipedia generates content, notable both for the frequency of bipartisan collaboration and for their periodic descent into a miasma of subjectivity, relativism, and factionalist rancor. Despite the precarious operation and occasional meltdown of this system, it is possible that the visibility of this quasi-democratic discussion process performs a crucial legitimizing function for Wikipedia's drive toward political neutrality. A counterbalance to the objective anonymity of Wikipedia articles might be perceived in the visibility of individuals in these marginal spaces, presenting their subjective viewpoints, and the terms under which they might collaborate, to produce a highly populated talking shop that complements the studied impartiality of the main encyclopedic text.

Conversely, many wikis strive to minimize the kind of conflicts that animate the discussion spaces of Wikipedia, not least by ensuring that dialogue takes place within the pages themselves, eschewing a segregated discussion space in favor of a process that continually refactors pages to ensure concision, while retaining a sense of plural, dialogic interaction within the text. Whatever the specific strategy adopted, wikis are notable for the degree to which users' understanding of a particular area of their content, including public administrative discussions among their organizers, may be enhanced by the study of an ongoing commentary threaded among multiple pages, previous revisions, and the activities of individual users. Any given interaction between users can be easily placed in context through a network of hyperlinks that signpost previous discussions on related subjects as well as a diverse network of information relating to writing precedent, arbitration, and dispute resolution. As a wiki writer, I often found that the tangential paths left by other users would place collaboration, and indeed disagreement, within a context that enabled me to refer to numerous similar situations and, as a researcher, to better understand the cumulative impact of countless loosely related interactions between a multitude of wiki writers.

The manifestations of this material might be as diverse as the content of the wikis themselves, indexical networks that connect a vast array of subjects, resembling argument, analysis, or simply conversation. Furthermore, as the locus of the interaction between their users, the talking spaces of wikis can be understood to host the virtual society of their writers, meaning that their content makes it possible to chart the ways in which the shifting conventions for the production and organization of material are influenced by social factors. The importance of this process for both wiki users and hypertext theorists alike proceeds from the way it presents the wiki as a truly open form of hypertext, which visibly expands the privileges of authorship to include the textual levels and locations that determine structural organization, social convention, and even technical administration. Understood as hypertext, a form that is inherently "antihierarchical and democratic,"[4] we might observe how wikis substitute the traditional roles of "reader" and "author" with the universal identity of "editor" or, in the terms set out by the introduction to Ward Cunningham's first wiki site, how they define themselves as "a moderated list where anyone can be moderator."[5]

According to Mark Poster, electronic writing under these conditions has the potential to undermine the formation of canons and authorities; it transforms texts into "hypertexts," which are reconstructed in the act of reading and which disrupt the status of experts or authorities by positioning the reader as author.[6] The reconstructive activities of wiki "editors" might coalesce into formal discourse, where projects such as Wikipedia incorporate sizeable resources detailing an enormous variety of administrative and organizational activities, or they might be manifested through the scattered conversational exchanges that can cause wiki pages to resemble the chaotic minutes of some arcane political society. At a local level, discussion drives a focused maintenance of specific pages in which users reconstruct texts by requesting more detail, collaborate to copyedit and peer-review material, and utilize a space that allows dissenting voices to articulate their concerns. In practice, this means that a text authored on a wiki is true hypertext, easily situated within a complex network of information sources, comprising references and influences[7] as well as arguments and challenges to its assertions.[8]

While particular software models, and indeed the reading habits of Internet users, might potentially marginalize these streams of commentary, the interactions that animate them must be understood as the catalyst for the constant evolution of wiki content. Almost any user is welcome to participate in these threads of dialogue, encouraged and even empowered by a visible process through which content is tangibly shaped by user input. The strategies with which wikis absorb the generative processes of this material, often influenced as much by traditional methods of knowledge transmission as by hypertext theory, should be understood as the basis of their potential to support innovative models of authorship and to widen participation. Their accessibility, visible as both discursive forum and reference tool, serves as both an introduction to wiki culture and a space within which wiki writers may continually renegotiate the terms under which they write.

Context and Annotation in Hypertext Theory

Hypertext theory can itself be defined by its attempt to reorganize the cultural processes that determine the creation, organization, and transmission of information. Accordingly, wikis might be situated within a historical lineage that sees Vannevar Bush's proposal to index encyclopedic materials according to a user-generated "mesh of associative trails" evolve into Theodor Nelson's vision of an online body of human thought, alive with the additions, revisions, and commentaries supplied by a global community of users.[9] In these terms, hypertext theory intersects with strains of postmodern literary studies at the point where writing, and indeed knowledge itself, is understood to function through an implicit network of links, references, and allusions embodied in the cultural cycles of the authorial process.[10]

Nelson's work in particular suggests that electronic writing must allow these connections to become more explicit, arguing that the dominance of paper-based sequences of argument, stored on separate physical documents, profoundly restricts the protean ingenuity of human thought.[11] For knowledge to evolve unfettered, Nelson proposes a shift from the fixed sequence of paper texts to the manifold associations made possible by computerized databases, which allow for the constant revision of materials and which situate these materials within a user-generated web of explanatory references and annotations. According to Nelson's proposals, every word within a nonsequential database of text could be accessed to branch into further documents or into definitions, lists of related concepts, or even literary allusions,[12] all facilitated by software that would automatically generate summaries and indices as the reader navigated through the information.[13]

Even a superficial investigation of wiki culture will reveal a variety of attempts to apply elements of these theories, most appropriately, to the ongoing discussion of the work of the hypertext pioneers themselves. The ability
to examine a separate discussion page, and the pattern of revision for both
that page and its host article, might hypothetically allow an interested reader
to discover that the Wikipedia article on Theodor Nelson had expanded to incorporate material situating hypertext theory within a wider history of public
knowledge, to link to a tangential discussion theorizing the hypertextual
character of the Jewish Talmud, or to parallel a detailed analysis of the differing taxonomies employed by the French *Encyclopédie* of Diderot and D'Alembert and the *Encyclopaedia Britannica*. The ability to edit these connections at
any stage encourages the reader "to treat the text as a field or network of
signs in which to create his or her own linkages," additions that "other readers may follow or change at their will."[14] The wiki user might provide new
context by inserting a reference to an academic study of wikis as hypertext or,
conversely, by requesting that the authors of these pages consider the benefit
of a beginner's guide to the more abstruse concepts of theoretical hypertext.
An article on the work of Theodor Nelson might branch outward from historical material to encompass administrative and even philosophical discussions concerning the operation of his own hypertext models, an appropriate
convergence in which a theoretical resource hosts the discussion forum for
its actual implementation.

This self-reflexive tendency, which may encompass an enormous variety
of philosophical and technical disciplines, becomes more apparent as the
user becomes more familiar with the parallel development of interrelated
discussions across many pages. In this sense, the networks of concepts and
allusions perceived by hypertext theorists achieve a new significance when
understood as evolving indices for the organization of content that replace
the inflexible hierarchical organization that characterizes paper texts. Even
within the field of hypertext, we might contrast this system with the organization of early models, particularly the expansions or conversions of paper-
based texts, which can be perceived as "axial" structures with a system of hypertext "branches" that spread out from a central, linear text.[15] In contrast,
true hypertexts are "network structured" and "borderless,"[16] possessing numerous pathways to wider webs of material and allowing production to oc-
cur simultaneously at multiple points.

The organization of wikis, in which every individual page is arranged side by side within a flat namespace, eschews linear or axial hierarchies in favor of the organic growth of linking structures, where the overall significance of an individual item proceeds not from its position in a preconceived index but from a shifting pattern of relevance determined by the accumulation of incoming links and the multiple associations inscribed by its users. The utility of a self-reflexive, "network structured" model for the transmission of knowledge proceeds from the potential advantages, both conceptual and social, that accrue from situating authorship within a malleable, nonhierarchical structure.

In abandoning a central index, wikis are free to adopt innumerable indices according to unlimited criteria, as idiosyncratic as the interests and abilities of their users. Unlike many other devices for the organization of knowledge, the flexibility of these nonlinear associations establishes the indexing and organizational systems of a wiki as an inseparable part of their content; where devices such as the content pages of a paper encyclopedia are transformed into active projects such as the "navigation links" area of Wikipedia, a catalog of catalogs devoted to a metadiscussion of the ever-evolving schema by which users organize its content.

Furthermore, these multiple indices, and their generation through user dialogue, are sufficiently diverse to invite and absorb the input of any interested user, at almost any level of expertise. The ability of wikis to host multiple, adaptable structures of organization can produce unusual and even abstract connections between different subjects, a tendency that reflects both Bush's and Nelson's insistence that human knowledge would thrive through new modes of association between creative individuals. The potential to discuss a subject at levels ranging from novice to expert, within a developing body of material providing context and explanation, allows textual material to remain responsive to the diverse concerns of a growing audience.

Wikis Communities and the Need for "Virtual Ethnographies"

Under these conditions, wikis might have the potential to radically influence communication, not least insofar as the global availability of open, public

hypertexts might diversify access to resources for the recording and transmission of human knowledge.[17] However, recognition of any democratizing
potential must avoid the precarious assumption that the expansion of the
material conditions that support hypertext readers, themselves made possible by a complex interaction of social and commercial factors, will automatically produce an active public of hypertext authors.[18] While there is no indication that the egalitarian potential of the wiki model of authorship will
automatically generate a varied community of participant writers, it is necessary to acknowledge that the complex networks of association and multiple
textual levels that comprise a wiki are themselves determined by, and are
equally dependent on, the relative diversity of their contributors.

Consequently, a critical analysis must incorporate numerous measures of
accessibility, addressing technical considerations alongside the social and
cultural factors that enable individual users to participate in wikis. The de-
mographic of their users could reasonably be expected, like that of Internet
users as a whole, to be heavily skewed toward the inhabitants of the affluent
West,[19] with the attendant risk that the same "democratic" qualities that allow highly populated networks of communal textual production to function
might obscure the voices of minorities, translating their inherent underrep-
resentation into invisibility. Although the organizational structures of wikis
are undeniably accommodating, their potential to expand their base of active
users depends on their ability to manage the contradictory interests of many
different individuals and to render this successful management visible in a
manner that encourages the participation of newcomers.

However, to assert that wikis are communally authored does not indicate
that their contributors are rendered invisible or marginalized, as some critics
of hypertext have feared. On the contrary, the intricate webs of user-generated material that constitute wiki writing reveal the presence of a multitude
of individual authors, working according to patterns of collaboration that
highlight the explicit parallels between the development of content and community. The talking spaces of wikis are often distinctly conversational, ani-
mated by personal, subjective dialogue that is archived to form rich bodies of
ethnographic data. The same networks of commentary that provide the context for ideas also describe their authors, recording their knowledge and interests and, crucially, allowing them to articulate their own concerns regarding bias, accessibility, and marginalization.

The ability of wikis to provide spaces in which these issues are explicitly discussed, and to incorporate them as one of the many contexts that describe the production of material, offers a potential solution to a problem commonly encountered in the ethnographic studies of what Howard Rheingold termed "virtual communities," namely, that discussions concerning identity, extended to include conditions of participation, are restricted by the impossibility of achieving holistic descriptions of any informant, location, or culture.[20]

A study of the social makeup of wikis might then be conducted according to Christine Hine's principles of "virtual ethnography," which embrace these restrictions to suggest that "ethnographers of the Internet can use their own data collection practices as data in their own right,"[21] a self-reflexive process in which conclusions are shaped by the researcher's own "intensive engagement with mediated interaction."[22] The advantage of employing a self-reflexive ethnographic technique lies in the degree to which the activities of the researcher must inevitably reflect the same process by which wiki users come to understand themselves as writers and to conceive of themselves as participants, readers, or even researchers within a community of individuals. Therefore, the process of research is conducted under the same conditions that inform the knowledge possessed by its subjects, producing data that is shaped by, even as it describes, the mediating effects of the wiki software. This process of mediation, which provides the structure for individual interactions and renders visible the user-created networks of content and commentary, represents both the context in which wiki writers become visible as individuals and the cumulative process by which they may come to conceive of themselves as writing communities.

While the data provided by these methods is necessarily partial, it offers the advantage of providing a picture of the community aspects of wikis in terms similar to those that are employed by their users. Although the activity of wiki writing might be interpreted as a "live" interaction among users, the ongoing processes of archiving and redaction are sufficiently visible that wiki communities can be said to develop self-knowledge by accumulating social interactions into the rich sedimentary layers that constitute bodies of content. Appropriately, many wikis allow their users to conduct ethnographies of their own, exploring the possibilities of community through a detailed reading of the accumulated products of specific conflicts and collaborations.

The ongoing commentary on a particular subject might direct the reader to a series of previous debates, thus allowing them to perceive the substantial influence of several competing groups of individual writers. Wiki writers might be grouped together through participation in loose networks of casual dialogue, in which users converse about their identities and interests and work under informal, ad hoc collaborations. Conversely, it might be possible for these users to organize into associations that are rooted in dedicated discussion spaces, where users congregate to develop writing strategies or form factions that are themselves determined by an enormous variety of political, linguistic, and philosophical affiliations.

These networks might be manifested in a great variety of forms. But their visibility achieves a singular importance when they are analyzed in terms of their ability to integrate patterns of social interaction with the broader tendencies that determine both the development of content and administrative activities. These administrative activities concern the organization and management of wikis on various levels, which ultimately determine systemwide policies. Most obviously, these levels might include the technical management of the wiki software and Web space, but large wikis such as Wikipedia also generate considerable bodies of content that determine language policy, uniform linking strategies, and the complex standards that govern acceptable user interaction. Assuming that these networks are sufficiently visible and intelligible, even novice users are thus equipped with the necessary tools to investigate the conventions by which particular wikis operate, the historical interactions between their established users, and the social histories of collaboration. This process of investigation might itself be applied to gauge the success of wikis in attracting and facilitating the participation of minority or marginalized groups, an activity of particular relevance if wikis are understood to thrive through the democratization of the processes of authorship and knowledge transmission.

I would like to suggest that the visibility of the diverse interactions between many kinds of wiki users is the single most important factor in determining which issues are discussed, described, and organized within wiki pages. The accessibility of these systems and the transparency of their operation determine the ease with which inexperienced users are able to understand the terms under which they might contribute as wiki writers. The importance of social interaction to this process means that the full privileges of wiki authorship, encompassing the organization and editing of material as well as the creation of new items, might be more readily extended to those users who quickly acquire a fluency in the conventions of social interaction.

This systemwide transparency could be seen as less important when the scope of the information discussed on wikis is restricted to a relatively narrow group of specialists, such as Ward Cunningham's original wiki focus on constructing an "Informal history of programming ideas," but becomes more relevant when considering Wikipedia's ambition to create "the largest encyclopedia in history, in both breadth and depth," written entirely by volunteers and distributed to "every single person on the planet in their own language."[23] The success of models of communal authorship, attracting a diversity of input and facilitating the participation of new users, attains a new importance when applied to projects that attempt to make recorded knowledge popularly accessible and at the same time extend the conditions under which knowledge is debated and reconstructed. Accordingly, the transparent processes of administration of a well-designed wiki make a case for the form as a unique development in a history of information technology, begun with writing that reveals "an increasing democratization or dissemination of power," accomplished through "exteriorizing memory [that] converts knowledge from the possession of one to the possession of more than one."[24] The terms *knowledge* and *memory*, in the sense in which they are best applied to wiki communities, come to include the types of social activities that have produced and organized content. This knowledge may, according to the interests of its users, be expressed in the language of ethnography and sociology; debates of authorship and authority; advanced and esoteric hypertext theory; or, ultimately, in the form of a metatext that integrates many competing methods of analyzing and organizing the same information.

It is this expansion of wikis as metatext, epistemological forums that discuss and record the development of both the user base and the content produced, that equips their users with the skills and knowledge necessary to participate in the perpetual growth and management of content. My own experience of editing Wikipedia quickly drew me toward an aphorism often cited by users drawn into unwanted debates about writing policy. This phrase simply states, "We're writing an encyclopedia, not talking about how to write an encyclopedia." However, I would suggest that the interplay between the branches of self-reflexive commentary and the ostensible purpose of the sites themselves in fact renders these activities inseparable, producing a distinct form of hypertext that embodies the conditions and conventions of its own growth.

Understood as both textual bodies and writing communities, the protean growth of wiki content might be seen to thrive through a profoundly nonlinear and interactive mode of textual production that allows the continual reconstruction of the text, "not as a fixed series of symbols, but as a variable-access database in which any discursive unit may possess multiple vectors of association."[25] The visible structure of these associations, which connect intricate patterns of social interaction, informational significance, and multiple authorial processes, is the context in which both wiki authorship and electronic literacy are made possible.

A wiki is therefore "both culture and cultural artifact,"[26] inscribed in which are networks of discourse that habitually resemble and even incorporate the concerns of academic research. The degree to which this tendency manifests itself on Wikipedia has prompted its description as a "self-documenting research population," one that hosts an active community of academic researchers at a meeting place called Project Wikidemia. Likewise, some of the most productive research for my own writing was carried out not at a physical library but in the archives of MeatballWiki, a network of wiki organizers and researchers that describes itself as "a community of active practitioners striving to teach each other how to organize people using online tools." The ease with which the researcher is able to delve into the histories of various wikis, following the rhizomatic connections between wiki discussions and the ongoing activities of their writers, leads me to believe that the accessibility of the discourse concerning the utility, communities, and evolution of wikis represents the most significant entry point into their culture and perhaps hypertext authorship itself.

Conclusion: Indices, Dialogue, and the Importance of Hypertext Literacy

Hypertext, in the sense in which it is embodied by wikis, is not just a new way of presenting material but a radical reconfiguration of the relationship between the recording and transmission of knowledge. The ability to freely annotate, link, and adjust texts, combined with the visibility and discussion of these processes, might hold the potential to popularize new methods of collaborative writing on a scale substantially different to anything that has preceded the personal computer, although it is equally true that it raises new questions about the physical and operational accessibility of technology. The significance of the visible commentaries that shape wiki content proceeds from the demands of transparency and accessibility, which mandate that an understanding of the individual items in a hypertext database is inseparable from the ability to comprehend the nature and operation of its overall structure. Stuart Moulthrop has articulated this concern in terms of a concept of literacy that can be easily applied to wikis and that extends beyond content in the traditional sense to include the reader's ability to perceive the operation of the associative structures and display strategies of texts. This literacy requires that its users "understand print not only as the medium of traditional literary discourse, but also as a meta-tool, the key to power at the level of the system itself."[27]

In order to express the cultural implications of electronic literacy, Moulthrop adapts Walter Ong and Marshall McLuhan's argument that the language use of television and radio produces a secondary orality to construct a concept of "secondary literacy," in which an approach to reading and writing includes "a self-consciousness about the technological mediation of those acts, a sensitivity to the way texts-below-the-text constitute another order behind the visible. This secondary literacy involves both rhetoric and technics: to read at the hypotextual level is to confront (paragnostically) the design of the system; to write at this level is to reprogram, revising the work of the first maker."[28]

I would like to suggest that the visible process of commentary that foregrounds the social, organizational, and technical aspects of wikis holds the potential for their users to develop a sophisticated electronic literacy of the kind imagined by many critical theorists of hypertext. In theory, the growth of this "electronic literacy" should help to democratize the processes that govern the social and technical operation of wikis, although it remains to be seen whether the growth of wikis will be paralleled by a similar expansion in the numbers of users interested in managing the complex processes so appealing to academic researchers. Nevertheless, the accessibility of this type of information, and the unique degree to which it forms new connections between more commonly accessed layers of information, raises the possibility of new interactions between the individuals involved in the authorship, organization, and research of hypertext systems.

NOTES

1. See George P. Landow, ed., *Hyper/Text/Theory* (Baltimore: Johns Hopkins University Press, 1994); George P. Landow, *Hypertext 2.0* (Baltimore: Johns Hopkins University Press, 1997); Theodor H. Nelson, *Literary Machines: The Report on, and of, Project Xanadu Concerning Word Processing, Electronic Publishing, Hypertext, Thinkertoys, Tomorrow's Intellectual Revolution, and Certain Other Topics Including Knowledge, Education, and Freedom* (Sausalito, CA: Mindful Press, 1990); Mark Poster, *The Mode of Information: Poststructuralisms and Contexts* (Chicago: Chicago University Press, 1995); Mark Poster, *The Second Media Age* (Cambridge: Polity, 1995); Mark Poster, "Cyberdemocracy: The Internet and the Public Sphere," in *Virtual Politics: Identity and Community in Cyberspace*, ed. David Holmes (Thousand Oaks, CA: Sage, 1997), 212–28.

2. See Landow, *Hyper/Text/Theory*, 90–91; Nelson, *Literary Machines*.

3. Stuart Moulthrop, "You Say You Want a Revolution? Hypertext and the Laws of Media," *Postmodern Culture* 1, no. 3 (1991), http://www.uv.es/~fores/programa/moulthrop_yousay.html.

4. Landow, *Hypertext 2.0*, 281.

5. Ward Cunningham, e-mail to the PatternsList, May 1, 1995, http://c2.com/cgi/wiki?InvitationToThePatternsList.

6. Poster, "Cyberdemocracy," 225.

7. Landow, *Hyper/Text/Theory*, 18–22.

8. See Charles Ess, ed., *Philosophical Perspectives on Computer-Mediated Communication* (Albany: State University of New York Press, 1996).

9. See Vannevar Bush, "As We May Think," *Atlantic Monthly*, July 1945, 101–8; Nelson, *Literary Machines*.

10. See Jean-François, Lyotard, *The Postmodern Condition: A Report on Knowledge* (Minneapolis: University of Minnesota Press, 2002); Moulthrop, "Revolution"; Poster, *Mode of Information*.

11. Nelson, *Literary Machines*, 2, 8–12.

12. Ibid., 47.

13. Ibid., 127–28.

14. Poster, *Mode of Information*, 70.

15. Landow, *Hyper/Text/Theory*, 90–94.

16. Landow, *Hypertext 2.0*, 79.

17. See Ess, *Philosophical Perspectives*; Poster, *Mode of Information*, 222.

18. See Ess, *Philosophical Perspectives*.

19. Manuel Castells, *The Rise of the Network Society*, Vol. 1 of *The Information Age: Economy, Society, and Culture* (Cambridge, MA: Blackwell, 1996), 375–77.

20. Christine Hine, *Virtual Ethnography* (London: Sage Publications, 2000), 65.

21. Ibid., 54.

22. Ibid., 65.

23. Ward Cunningham, "Informal History of Programming Ideas," Cunningham and Cunningham, Inc., http://c2.com/cgi/wiki?InformalHistoryofProgrammingIdeas.

24. Landow, *Hypertext 2.0*, 277.

25. Moulthrop, "Revolution," 5.

26. Hine, *Virtual Ethnography*, 64.

27. Moulthrop, "Revolution," 22–23.

28. Ibid., 24.

Above and Below the Double Line:
Refactoring and That Old-Time Revision

Here is a mantra for wiki authors:

> Writing on a wiki proceeds from ThreadMode to DocumentMode by way
> of Refactoring.

And here is how I explain it to students familiar with composing but new
to wikis:

> Writing on a wiki—because it's collaborative—changes not just what we
> write but how we write, and so we change the way we talk about the
> process. ThreadMode is a discussion. It's a little like prewriting to gen-
> erate topics and positions and arguments. DocumentMode is an exposi-
> tion, and it's a little like drafting an essay by drawing together the
> threads in ThreadMode. And Refactoring is something like revising, and
> something like reorganizing, and something like clearing away the tea
> table for another course. The word comes from computer program-
> ming.

When I introduce the process, with its odd terms, I feel like Humpty
Dumpty explaining Jabberwocky to Alice.

"But why do you smash some words together?" Alice asks.
　"Those are WikiWords. They are a little like portmanteau words. On
a wiki, WikiWords signal links to new topics that are open for elaboration. You follow the link."

Writing on a wiki means returning to a topic periodically to see what is developing. It means authors enter a page to work with the emerging text in a variety of ways. An author may refactor one section of a page and then go to another page and add to an emerging thread. She may add a WikiWord to still another page, point out a link from one topic to another, and then go have a cup of coffee to return to the wiki later to see what happened. A reader senses a difference, something left out, or an alternative way of thinking. She becomes an author and declares a new topic by creating a WikiWord on a page, going to the new page, and setting out some ideas, a summary, a direction for that page. The WikiWord is now a topic: a potential to be filled. She announces the existence of the topic. Or not. The topic appears in "Recent Changes" and "Index."

Others visit the topic, read, and leave. Or they begin to develop it in ThreadMode (signed) or DocumentMode (unsigned, above the Double-Lines). Others return frequently to see how things are going. More topics are generated for the developing topic as authors turn words into WikiWords to create new topics. Preexisting topics are linked into the developing topic as authors use WikiWords.

The parent of the page joins them. Or not.

The process continues as ThreadMode material bubbles up and is refactored into DocumentMode and as DocumentMode material spurs more ThreadMode exchange.[1]

That's the general idea, but, like all models, this one requires some backing up to cover details.

ThreadMode

ThreadMode is a dialogue, a discussion, a dialectic. It is open, collective, dynamic, and informal. It can develop as a page or develop on a page, but it develops organically, without predictive structure. Writing in thread mode is spontaneous, improvisational, but not sermonic, not preachy: those rhetorical postures close down rather than open up threads. Thread mode is public thinking: designed, considered, polite. Thread mode presents a position, a way of understanding, clearly and persuasively, but is not a soapbox so much as a sandbox.

This is to say that thread mode is tentative rather than absolute; opinionated but not seeking closure; exploratory and as such creating an understanding for readers rather than seeking to win ground from opponents. Thread mode writing is grounded in specifics to make sense of abstractions. Its end is to allow others to understand and create, not to win. It is an attitude.[2]

On one course wiki I manage, the BlogsAndWikis wiki, thread mode contributions are phrased in first person and are signed.[3] To this extent, authors initially see thread mode writing as similar to Web discussion board or e-mail exchanges. But threads are different than discussion board or e-mail exchanges. They are incorporated in the evolving shared document and eventually become the document; they cannot be separated from it.

Nor do threads necessarily follow a chronology of posting. Authors place their contributions near the materials they address rather than at the end of the exchange. Because they can be placed next to the passage they respond to, thread mode additions tend to be concise, pointed. Thread mode can start as a reply to a document mode beginning. After starting a page in document mode, others may choose to reply to the document rather than revise it or edit it. Those additions start threads of discussion that continue until someone is able or willing to refactor the page, deleting the original comments. Once the page is refactored into document mode, the process begins again.

DocumentMode

DocumentMode is expository, discursive, more monologic—but no less open—than thread mode. Document mode is written in third person, active voice, as a synthesis of the collective thinking on the wiki. Document mode pages and sections of pages become the collective understanding of the wiki. Generally, they are unsigned, but some authors add their names to the section as contributors. Others let the "Recent Changes" take care of crediting. While wiki pages are collective—or because they are collective—they are still active and continue to evolve. Authors return to revise, update, add to, or edit a document mode page.

In document mode, the ideas, not the authors, are the focus and the center. Document pages on wikis still have a point of view, a perspective, even a voice. But they don't call attention to themselves as pages, as writing. They are written in what Richard Lanham, in *Analyzing Prose*, would call a *transparent style*: a style that doesn't call attention to itself as writing.[4] Refactoring enters here: to guide authors in making compositional and rhetorical moves from thread to document.

By Way of Refactoring

In thread mode, wiki pages develop opportunistically as contributors return to them, read them, edit them, add to them, and reorganize them. Refactoring, however, is less opportunistic. It is a conscientious technique for developing a page, for moving it toward document mode.

Over time, as writers add comments to threads, a wiki page comes to look like a mess of posted bills and graffiti.[5] The initial point or purpose of the page can be lost in the shambles, the individual threads obscured in the tangle. The page becomes difficult to read, requiring mental energy to connect ideas scattered across screens. Authors don't read the entire page but skim and start adding comments willy-nilly, creating redundancies. Ideas that may help the page coalesce are lost in the tangle. Noise threatens signal. WardsWiki—at c2.com, also known as the Portland Pattern Repository— calls it Thread Mess: the page is developing by a drama of discussion rather than as exploration.[6]

Sooner or later, threads need to be synthesized into document mode, or refactored.

Refactoring is a kind of revision, but where composition and rhetoric types tend to see revision changing and developing meaning, refactoring attempts to preserve meaning. Refactoring is a matter of finding and making explicit an organizational pattern in the ideas of the ThreadMode exchange. It has the main purpose of making latent, implicit, possible meanings explicit and present enough to become a whole—a whole that can in turn be responded to, developed further, on another page, from another perspective. Refactoring is synthesis.

The term is borrowed from programming, where it refers to reworking program code for processing elegance, without changing the function of the code. An involved procedure might be refactored into one or two lines of code by using a less-known directive or procedure. Or variables might be given meaningful names.[7] We refactor in everyday life by devising mnemonics, by reorganizing a grocery list (on paper or in our heads) to map it onto the physical store.

Wikipedia notes that refactoring software systems serves further development and revision:

> Refactoring does not fix bugs or add new functionality. Rather it is designed to improve the understandability of the code or change its structure and design . . . to make it easier for human maintenance in the future. In particular, adding new behavior to a program might be difficult with the program's given structure, so a developer might refactor it first to make it easy, and then add the new behavior.[8]

Bo Leuf and Ward Cunningham seem to have been the first to apply the term to writing on a wiki. They mention refactoring in *The Wiki Way* (2001) as "an attempt to distill valuable information from earlier, less focused discussions."[9] They list four moves:

- add a comment
- edit older comments
- split conversations to new pages
- capture converging comments in a single paragraph.

On c2.com, refactoring is described this way:

> Replace a thread mode conversation with a monolog that says the same thing and preserving as much of the original text as possible. Change the 1st person singular to 1st or 3rd person plural. Remove the inline attributions and put them at the end under "Contributors." It is understood that individual authors may not have chosen the exact words used; that we have a consensus and hence probably compromises.[10]

Refactoring is an attempt to find or create a structure for the threads of discussion that allows them to be synthesized into a document. Of course, changing structure changes meaning, and "saying the same thing" is problematic. We know this, but in refactoring we bracket our concern. As a rhetorical act, refactoring is a declaration that the refactored document encompasses what the threads it replaces has argued. The refactored document makes explicit what was implicit in the thread, articulates what the threads dramatized. It might be considered an act of conversion or repurposing or of trying out alternatives. It might be considered something like reworking a drama into an exposition or an essay into a poem or remediating a print text into a hypertext.

But refactoring aims at stabilizing meaning—just for the moment—so writers can build on it further. Threads are refactored as summaries of positions and arguments. Writers create new WikiWords, invitations, and openings into other areas and alternatives to development. Entire threads are reorganized, questions and answers condensed into statements. In refactoring, discussion becomes collective knowledge, premises move toward locally accepted proofs.

The motives and purposes behind refactoring are local and rhetorical. A thread has gone on long enough; a page has become a tangle of threads. It is time to see what someone can make of the thread so all of us on the wiki can go further. Here's how we talk about the refactoring process in the StyleGuide on BlogsAndWikis:

> Re-working a passage to make it easier to understand (change the signal to noise, bring out structures in ideas, make it mean more than it meant before) means changing its meaning. We know that. And we know that refactoring favors some stylistic moves over others. We know that RefactoringIsProblematic. But we refactor anyway. Because we need to move on.[11]

Staying Close to the Ideas in Refactoring

In refactoring, authors are advised to not be cavalier but to keep close to the ideas in the thread as they synthesize the thread mode discussion into a document. Writers on c2.com comment on the difficulty, which is partly rhetorical and partly a matter of motivation. Refactoring threads seems like recovering old ground. The thread is there for everyone to work through; and in reorganizing and summarizing the arguments, we might lose a subtlety, might distort a point, so why bother? Refactoring is important to move the wiki along, but it is hard to do correctly. You need to synthesize the discussion in a way that is acceptable to most of the participants. Sometimes a discussion comes to an end, at which time it is easier to summarize it, but there is less motivation to do so. Discussions most need to be summarized when they get long, which usually means there are a lot of different opinions, making them hard to summarize.[12]

The concern is getting the synthesis wrong, especially thinking that you understand a point when you don't. However, the wiki is self-correcting: "Suppose I refactor a conversation and I (unknowingly, of course) get it wrong. The topic itself will show up in ChangeSummary and RecentChanges. There are good odds that one of the experts on the subject will read it and correct it."[13]

Techniques for Refactoring

Refactoring accurately is important. One slip and the wrong sense of things might be reified; and while the wiki will eventually self-correct, the shift in direction is frustrating. Refactoring is also difficult. Writers don't always read a page through before adding to the thread, so comments are scattered and often redundant. Refactoring can take time and repeated sessions, and writers might continue to add threads to the page even as others are refactoring.[14] The concern with staying close to ideas in refactoring is addressed by developing strategies and techniques for refactoring—strategies and techniques that the rest of this chapter will touch on. That is, to "be not cavalier" entails drawing on explicit, self-conscious, shared techniques for refactoring. So, to guide refactoring, rhetoric offers techniques. Here are two:

- use double lines
- use page patterns

DoubleLines

The DoubleLines are an ad hoc technique borrowed from c2.com and MeatballWiki for distinguishing document from thread. As c2.com offers, "Some pages use DoubleLines to separate a DocumentMode OpeningStatement, thesis, or pattern at the top of a page and (usually ThreadMode) discussion below. The top part is generally the page's payload—a short article on the page's title subject along with bibliographic information; while the bottom is meta-data about the page—discussion, suggested changes, categorization, stories, indirectly related links etc."[15] And here is how the double line appears in our StyleGuide on BlogsAndWikis:

> Pages on this wiki tend to have the DocumentMode section at the top of the page, followed by ThreadMode contributions. Use DoubleLines (two lines of four dashes) to separate DocumentMode from ThreadMode on the same page. This convention is not absolute, however, and we find that writers add comments and questions to DocumentMode sections. This is a Good Thing, and writers can refactor the page to address the embedded comment. But as a thread gets long, move it below the DoubleLines.[16]

Other wikis might place the threads on another pane or tabbed page (as on the MediaWiki engine). How the emerging document and the extending threads are distinguished may not seem important, but for the purposes I have in developing wikis, I would argue for the double lines. When the discussion is embedded in the evolving document, readers and authors have more context to draw on in developing meaning—and that context is significant for refactoring. There is a compositional and rhetorical virtue in keeping things together, in the same space.

Using double lines rather than separate pages is in keeping with Cunningham's original conception of wikis as quick and simple, as "the simplest online database that could possibly work."[17] Rather than creating yet another page or view, place the thread and the document in the same page, distinguished by the simplest of indicators: four dashes.

The double lines help coauthors and contributors determine the state of knowledge on the page—and so can be used as a powerful heuristic, similar to Ann Berthoff's technique of drawing a line down the middle of a sheet of paper to create a dialogic notebook.[18] The double lines can keep the state of knowledge on the wiki open and developing, keep the dialectic going, and remind authors that it is a dialectic.[19] I wouldn't suggest the split is simply one of "completed above/still at work below." The double lines can distinguish a range of functional and rhetorical oppositions that are useful to coauthors reading or refactoring: "payload" from "meta-data," or refactored material from content for further development and refactoring, or

- successfully refactored material/loose ends, discussion, suggested changes
- stable/volatile content
- opening statement/discussion
- generalization/specifics
- principle/examples
- thesis/support
- argument or structural pattern/discussion on pattern.

Authors can also use the double lines to suggest a rhetorical placement that invites and guides writers, suggesting where they might add to the text and what they might do next.

PagePatterns

In refactoring, pages born of discussion are given explicit structure. Like the use of double lines, the seed for using page patterns to refactor comes from practice on c2.com. The idea is that, as threads of discussion develop, the direction, the arguments, and the evidence suggest a possible pattern for organizing the page. The pattern, once made explicit, becomes a heuristic. C2.com lists a few (in keeping with c2.com's purpose as a pattern repository):

- ThereforeBut
- ThesisAntithesisSynthesis
- TentativeSummary.[20]

The logical terms are used as headings to indicate the structure of the page. In ThereforeBut, for instance, c2.com instructs users to "state the context and forces in a paragraph or several, then put a bold 'Therefore,' on a line by itself, and then state a tried and true solution in a paragraph or several."[21] Then (to continue where c2.com leaves off) use a bold "But" on a line by itself and state the qualifications. Material that doesn't yet fit the structure can be placed below the DoubleLines. Once the page is refactored, another author may see another pattern or an extension to the pattern that draws in the as-yet-unrefactored material.

In refactoring, the headings are not static but inviting, generative. The headings not only indicate the refactored structure of the page; they act as heuristics for further development. They signal where and what new material might be added. The headings are not typically WikiWords, of course. I write them as such to suggest that they carry the inventional potency of Wiki-Words. ThereforeBut—like a good WikiWord—invites StillOnTheOther-Hand; and StillOnTheOtherHand invites YesButIfYouConsider. . . . Potent page patterns guide structuring while also clearing space for more invention. For instance,

- ThereforeBut StillOnTheOtherHand
- ThereforeBut SeeAlso
- GivenThis . . . ThenThat . . . ButIfYouConsider . . .

Again I'll draw on Ann Berthoff, who anticipates refactoring in her dialectical model of composing that informs *Forming/Thinking/Writing*. She presents "workhorse" sentence patterns as "ways out of chaos": ways of moving from a collection of observations toward making statements, toward predicating. Here are two examples:

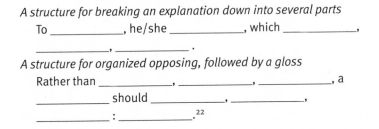

A structure for breaking an explanation down into several parts
To _____, he/she _____, which _____,
_____, _____ .
A structure for organized opposing, followed by a gloss
Rather than _____, _____, _____, a
_____ should _____, _____,
_____ : _____.[22]

Page patterns work in a similar fashion, guiding the refactoring of statements, arguments, and observations from the thread. Some prototypical page patterns might look like these:

A pattern for listing alternatives
- HowDoWeDoX
  - ByThisMeans
  - OrByThisMeans
  - OrByThisMeans
  - . . .

A pattern for stating and considering dependencies
- ItDependsOnThis
- AndOnThis
- AndOnThis
- WhichDependsOn . . .

A pattern for stating if-then, with an option
- IfThenOtherwise or IfThenElse

A pattern for breaking an explanation into several parts, with qualifications
- IfThisAndThisAndThis . . . ThenThis
- ButIfYouConsiderThis . . . ThenThis

A pattern for articulating parallel points or reasons in a series
- ThisAndThisAndThis . . . LeadToThis

A pattern for organized composing with a gloss
- OnOneHandThese . . . ButOnTheOtherHandThese . . . And-SoThis

Page patterns are rhetorically potent because the evolving thread drives the structural divisions. The weight for discovering the page pattern is on the authors who refactor, which comes of understanding the thread even as it develops.

And So

Since I began looking at refactoring as a technique for writing on wikis in winter 2002, many popular wikis have added notes and advice on refactoring, often in the style guide as on WikiFish[23] or as its own topic as on Wikipedia.[24] And as of spring 2006, the Wikipedia entry for refactoring now includes the use of the term *refactoring* for writing on wikis.[25] Refactoring is becoming mainstream, and we can expect to see the practice develop further and soon.

Refactoring, more than that old-time revision, is overtly social. And so customs of refactoring develop locally in the community of the particular wiki. For instance, on BlogsAndWikis, it has become the custom to list the contributors to the thread when a page is refactored.[26] BlogsAndWikis authors do not tend to use explicit page patterns, but they have developed a local way of thinking about writing on a wiki that incorporates refactoring. They see the wiki as a large, shared writing space that allows for different kinds of movement: Get in close to write, stand back to understand, scribble notes to start, and refactor to continue. Here is TheCollective's latest refactoring of their custom:

Online Chalkboard
When we write threads we scribble ideas as if we were writing with chalk.

- They need no order
- If the chalk keeps moving the brain keeps working
- Chalk comes in many colors
- You can make pictures with chalk
- A chalkboard can be taped over and posted to
- It's easier to read a chalkboard from a distance

Eventually, a chalkboard will be filled and it is at this point that we can look at what we wrote. TheEditor in us all can erase what isn't important, as well as summarize and refactor the information. With the extra space freed up we can then go back to scribbling notes.[27]

NOTES

1. For more on how wiki composition facilitates the processes of constructing knowledge, see John W. Maxwell and Michael Felczak, "Success through Simplicity," this volume.

2. ThreadMode is rhetorically governed by the social-epistemic rhetoric detailed by Thomas J. Nelson, "Writing in the Wikishop," this volume.

3. M. C. Morgan, "BlogsAndWikis: HomePage," Bemidji State University, http://ferret.bemidjistate.edu/~morgan/WeblogsAndWikis (accessed April 5, 2007).

4. Richard A. Lanham, *Analyzing Prose*, 2d ed. (New York: Continuum, 2003).

5. This is also noticed by Cathlena Martin and Lisa Dusenberry, "Wiki Lore and Politics in the Classroom," and Matt Barton, "Is There a Wiki in This Class?" this volume.

Bob Whipple discusses the generative value of thread mode messiness in "An (Old) First-Timer's Learning Curve," this volume.

6. c2.com, "ThreadMess," Cunningham and Cunningham, Inc., http://c2.com/cgi/wiki?ThreadMess (accessed March 31, 2006).

7. Wikipedia Contributors, "Refactoring," Wikipedia, the Free Encyclopedia, http://en.wikipedia.org/wiki/Refactoring (accessed May 31, 2006).

8. Ibid.

9. Bo Leuf and Ward Cunningham, The Wiki Way (Boston: Addison-Wesley, 2001), 333.

10. c2.com, "ConvertThreadModeToDocumentMode," Cunningham and Cunningham, Inc., http://c2.com/cgi/wiki?ConvertThreadModeToDocumentMode (accessed March 31, 2006). Another early contributor to the practice of refactoring on wikis is MeatballWiki, "a community of active practitioners striving to teach each other how to organize people using online tools," http://www.usemod.com/cgi-bin/mb.pl. I was aware of exchanges concerning refactoring in spring 2003, but much of the exchange of that time has moved on. The current discussion of refactoring is dispersed over 272 pages (as of May 2006), but refactoring on MeatballWiki tends to be seen as a means of building consensus. Refactoring is a way of inciting and reincing exchange.

11. M. C. Morgan and Blogs and Wikis Contributors, "BlogsAndWikis: Style-Guide," Bemidji State University, http://ferret.bemidjistate.edu/~morgan/Weblogs AndWikis/wikka.php?wakka=StyleGuide (accessed April 5, 2007).

12. c2.com, "ConvertThreadModeToDocumentMode," Cunningham and Cunningham, Inc., http://c2.com/cgi/wiki?ConvertThreadModeToDocumentMode (accessed March 31, 2006).

13. Ibid.

14. c2.com, "RefactorTowardsTheCenterOfThePage," Cunningham and Cunningham, Inc., http://c2.com/cgi/wiki?RefactorTowardsTheCenterOfThePage (accessed March 31, 2006).

15. c2.com, "DoubleLines," Cunningham and Cunningham, Inc., http://www.c2 .com/cgi/wiki?DoubleLines (accessed March 31, 2006).

16. Morgan and Blogs and Wikis Contributors, "BlogsAndWikis: StyleGuide."

17. Leuf and Cunningham, The Wiki Way, 15.

18. Ann E. Berthoff, "A Curious Triangle and the Double-Entry Notebook," in The Making of Meaning: Metaphors, Models, and Maxims for Writing Teachers (Montclair, NJ: Boynton Cook, 1981), 41–47.

19. Maxwell and Felczak also discuss the generative value of keeping the coauthoring visible in "Success through Simplicity," this volume.

20. c2.com, "Refactoring Wiki Pages," Cunningham and Cunningham, Inc., http://www.c2.com/cgi/wiki?RefactoringWikiPages (accessed March 31, 2006).

21. c2.com, "ThereforBut," Cunningham and Cunningham, Inc., http://www.c2 .com/cgi/wiki?ThereforeBut (accessed May 31, 2006).

22. Ann E. Berthoff, with James Stephens, Forming, Thinking, Writing, 2d ed. (Portsmouth, NH: Boynton Cook, 1988), 94–95. Originally published in 1978, twenty years before wikis were invented, Berthoff's dialogical text has a lot to tell us about writing on wikis and refactoring.

23. WikiFish Contributors, "Wiki Good Style," WikiFish, http://www.seedwiki .com/wiki/wikifish/wiki_good_style?wpid=77845 (accessed May 1, 2006).

24. Wikipedia Contributors, "Refactoring Talk Pages," Wikipedia, the Free Encyclopedia, http://en.wikipedia.org/wiki/Wikipedia:Refactoring_talk_pages (accessed May 1, 2006).

25. Wikipedia Contributors, "Refactoring."

26. Blogs and Wikis Contributors, "BlogsAndWikis: OffTheCuffBlogging," Bemidji State University, http://ferret.bemidjistate.edu/~morgan/WeblogsAndWikis/wikka.php?wakka=OffTheCuffBloggi ng (accessed April 5, 2007).

27. Blogs and Wikis Contributors, "BlogsAndWikis: TheCollectiveNotebook," Bemidji State University, http://ferret.bemidjistate.edu/~morgan/WeblogsAndWikis/wikka.php?wakka=TheCollectiveNote book (accessed April 5, 2007).

Wikis and the Higher Education Classroom

Is There a Wiki in This Class?
Wikibooks and the Future of Higher Education

> For teachers of writing, however, the most immediate need is for a
> pedagogy of collaboration, one that would view writing as always
> shared and social; writers as constantly building and negotiating
> meaning with and among others; and evaluation as based at least
> in part on a "range of selves" and on communal efforts.
> —ANDREA LUNSFORD AND LISA EDE

In one way, my intellectual life has become much easier. I can now tell my colleagues that "I study wikis" without sounding like I'm talking about a fuzzy creature from *Star Trek* or a Hawaiian mixed drink. As of 2006, the world knew about Wikipedia. After all, a Web site with 961,000 articles in English on every imaginable topic is as difficult to miss as the winter flu.

There is, however, also a downside to my colleagues' tacit knowledge about wikis: They tend to view them cynically, as though a Web site "that anyone could edit" is a Web site that only an idiot would trust. The very idea that a professor was referring students to Wikipedia or using it to teach her courses struck them as the height of absurdity. Wikis seem to represent an almost antiacademic perspective toward knowledge—the triumph of Vandals who have overrun the library. Some of us may agree with Wikipedia cofounder and expatriate Larry Sanger, who argues incessantly to anyone willing to listen that a little elitism is all Wikipedia really needs.[1] The academy understands the need for this elitism better than most. As Bruce Thyer points out in his book on scholarly publishing, "Generally speaking, the higher the rejection rate of a given journal, the more prestigious it is seen to be."[2] In the academy, an individual's prestige may partially be determined by how well he is able to suppress other voices.

How many of us have told our students, "Be careful citing Web sites—that professional-looking site about Jacques Derrida might have actually been written by a clever eight-year old!" or "Be on the lookout for telltale signs of authors lacking a PhD and a university affiliation!"? As for Wikipedia, it's suicide.

Meanwhile, adventurous "early adopters" and technophiles are discovering that adding wikis to their curriculum can be as painless as childbirth—and almost as life altering. Wikis are fundamentally different from more established technologies like blogs. True, blogs and wikis are both tools that make it easy (perhaps even *too* easy) to publish work online. However, the wiki and blog *genres* are as distinct from each other as a five-paragraph essay and a geometry proof. A "best practices" guide to wikis or blogs should begin with a thorough treatment of the myriad of social conventions that surround these technologies and lend form to their substance. An unfortunate but all too common tendency is to get so focused on the technical side of things that we miss the forest for the trees: Wikis are first and foremost communities of people, not databases of files.

Too many would-be innovators choose to ignore the conventions of the online writing communities they are introducing to their students—a mistake that no responsible teacher of writing can afford to make. Like proper blogging, good wiki etiquette means more than just knowing how to "put stuff" on a wiki. The "how" is the easy part—wikis are designed from the ground up to be simple to use. If you can surf the Net and use a word processor, you can wiki with the best of them. The bigger and far more baffling question for most of us is *when* to use them—for, despite what anyone else says, the Wikipedia does not suffer fools gladly. Knowing how to change a wiki page is one thing; knowing how to make an *appropriate* change that will be accepted by a wiki's community is another. Here is where the true challenge of integrating wikis into the classroom lies, and since it involves the verbal negotiation of authority within a given community, it is clear that this challenge is more rhetorical than technical.

My purpose here is twofold: First, I want to describe what kind of class assignments work well for wikis (and which ones don't), and, second, I want to discuss the value that good wiki assignments bring to the university and beyond. My main contention is that wikis have a strong civic or service-learning potential that tends to get overlooked (and compromised) by well-meaning instructors who do not integrate their wikis into their classroom properly. I will also unblushingly own up to having an agenda: I believe that it's important that we recognize the civic values and virtues of wikis and let those concerns trump our own initial misgivings about "security" and "ownership" when introducing wikis to students. Indeed, we should make this aspect of wikis our paramount reason for using them in our classrooms.

We can appreciate what is at stake here when we consider how the "citizens band" of the World Wide Web is rapidly eroding and being replaced by the same top-down corporate forces that bring us those self-proclaimed "fair and balanced" televised news programs. According to Ben H. Bagdikian, at the moment, only five megacorporations own most American newspapers, magazines, book publishers, movie studios, and radio and television broadcast companies.[3] The Internet, long seen as a haven from corporate-dominated media, is quickly losing its independence and autonomy from this corporate hegemony. Lawrence Lessig writes that "the architecture and law that surround the Internet's design will increasingly produce an environment where all use of content requires permission."[4] To my mind, no Web space stands so stalwartly against this commercializing, voice-squelching, "permission-based" trend as the wiki, the "Web site that anyone can edit."

A Tale of Two Wikis

I was first introduced to wikis three years ago in a graduate course called the Rhetoric of Technology. The goal of this course was to provide writing teachers with practical and critical experience with new writing technologies. The instructor, Joseph Moxley, used wikis primarily as an easy way for students to publish their scholarly works, textual commentaries, and biographies on the Web. Compared to the technical difficulties and fifty-step programs involved with publishing pages in HTML or XML and using FTP to upload them to a public directory, wikis are incredulously simple. A good example of this simplicity is the code required to link to another Web site:

- HTML: <a href="http://yahoo.com" target=_blank>Yahoo!</a>
- WIKI: [http://yahoo.com]

For Moxley (as well as many other wiki pioneers), the wiki's key selling point was the lightning-fast speed at which it could have neophyte computer users publishing material to the Web. Indeed, a few students were so impressed with Moxley's wikis that they continued to use them after the class was over, again primarily as an easier way to get material on the Web than conventional Web publishing. These wikis have nevertheless been long since abandoned, their authors having moved on to other projects. Bereft of contributors, the wikis are ghost towns on the wild frontier.

If Wikipedia boasts nearly one million articles and a bustling city of active participants, why do other wiki colonies end up as virtual Roanokes? One often-raised possibility concerns the security and integrity of wiki pages. After all, wouldn't it be just as easy for ne'er-do-wells to edit a wiki as it would be for the true owner of the page? To demonstrate (or perhaps exemplify) the problem, one rascal in Moxley's class took to making unexpected changes to everyone else's pages.[5] Suddenly, the rather serious and straightforward pages of my colleagues were rife with images of the *Beverly Hillbillies* and *Deliverance*. While these images invoked more laughter than anger, they posed a perplexing problem. How could anyone be serious about a Web space that was so vulnerable to sabotage?

The logical solution to this dilemma seemed to be a password scheme that would prevent other users from tampering with each other's wikis. Seemingly, the best wiki would offer a finely honed permissions system and a hard-coded hierarchy of control. Each page would have a single or small group of "owners," and casual visitors would have no more authority to make changes than they would at Foxnews.com. Only the best would be allowed to make changes; they would be like "real" publishers, who Paul Parsons describes as those who "help determine what is 'in' and what is 'out' in the marketplace of ideas."[6] All that was missing from this grotto of Web publishing paradise was an electrified cyclone fence and a squad of armed (or at least bespectacled) guardians.

While I certainly recognized the potential advantages of this approach, something about the whole affair buzzed and fluttered around my ear like a hungry Platonist. Were we, perhaps, somehow missing the point about wikis? Had we not yet grasped the *essence* of wiki? Perhaps a password "solution" would be one more instance of someone treating a symptom rather than a cause. Maybe the problem wasn't how to make wikis more secure but rather how to make them less needful of security. How could "vulnerability" be transformed/converted into an asset? I began to take a critical look at successful wikis like Wikipedia and Wikitravel, asking myself what it was about these wikis that allowed them to flourish despite, or perhaps even *because of*, their openness.

The more I thought about "best practices" for wikis, the further I had to retreat from the immediate issue of wiki vandalism in order to see the wider problem. What I noticed almost immediately was that the most successful wikis are encyclopedic in format. The pages tend to embrace a "neutral point of view" and conceal the traces of argumentation under a smooth veneer of "objective" prose. Furthermore, the individual identity of the users is elided along with the control or ownership of their contributions. Anyone attempting to edit a page of Wikipedia sees this warning at the bottom of the editing window: "If you don't want your writing to be edited mercilessly or redistributed by others, do not submit it." In other words, abandon all authority ye who edit here. Yet, even with this utter lack of concern for notoriety and authority, Wikipedia seems to have no shortage of volunteers. Why are so many smart people lining up to join this loser club?

I noted that the best wiki practices seemed to be those that resist traditional notions of authorship and textual ownership and take an impersonal and inclusive stance toward even the most controversial issues. Then it suddenly dawned on me why the world's most famous and successful wiki is an online encyclopedia: Reference works tend to be ideal for wikis because their content is not judged according to the same criteria as argumentative works. Obviously, we would not evaluate a book called *Foucault: An Introduction* with the same criteria we would bring to bear on Foucault's *Discipline and Punish*. We would reject the latter if we disagreed with Foucault's ideas, the former if we disagreed merely with the representation of those ideas.

This is not to naively suggest that a Berlin Wall stands between what we call "objective" and "subjective." What I am suggesting, rather, is that some knowledge workers attempt to synthesize ideas while others assert and defend them in a court of scholarship. To be positively ancient about it, the goal of one is to "inform," whereas the other is meant to "persuade." Of course, I don't expect, require, or even desire anyone to accept this easy distinction—the whole business is decadently drenched in rhetoric—but as long as we can agree that the stated (and suggested) intentions of the authors or contributors influence how they write and how they are read, then we can agree on two points: Wikis are a better fit for some types of projects than others, and the rhetoric *of* wiki is just as critical as the rhetoric *in* wikis. Effective wikis recognize and profit from the peculiar rhetorical implications of the genre, whereas less successful projects attempt to force fit or graft on conventions from other genres. Wikis turn out to be much better spaces for objective rather than subjective works. Wikis are better suited for composing *CliffsNotes* than literature. Like any good encyclopedia, wikis excel at making large quantities of expert information accessible to nonexperts; they democratize knowledge. Unlike traditional encyclopedias, though, readers are invited to directly participate in the process. Active contributors to wikis may not have PhDs, but they do share a sense of community and responsibility for the pages they work on. Indeed, a more "elitist" wiki that kept "common" readers at a distance would be very unlikely to succeed, especially if it expected contributors to work for free. It's precisely the openness and perceived vulnerability of Wikipedia that draws in so many helpful contributors, who feel they have a personal stake in the community and a privileged role denied them by traditional print media.

In short, Wikipedia flourishes not in spite of antielitism but because of it.

The Neutral Point of View

A wiki that sets out to inform the public is likely to gain more contributions from a wider variety of people than one that sets out to persuade or present a subjective view. Successful wikis like Wikipedia make neutrality and inclusiveness a matter of formal policy. The second "Pillar of Wikipedia" is worth quoting here:

> Wikipedia uses the "neutral point-of-view," which means we strive for articles that advocate no single point of view. Sometimes this requires representing multiple points of view; presenting each point of view accurately; providing context for any given point of view, so that readers understand whose view the point represents; and presenting no one point of view as "the truth" or "the best view." It means citing verifiable, authoritative sources whenever possible, especially on controversial topics.[7]

This policy reads, to me at least, like a recipe for delicious and enriching wiki projects. Note the similar policy at Wikitravel:

> Text should have a neutral point of view. We try to maintain a professional attitude towards all topics, and give an objective description of it. This doesn't mean watering down our guide—if some place is smelly, overpriced, ugly, loud, or just plain bad, we tell it like it is. But there are no whetstones here; people with axes to grind should set up their own personal Web sites.[8]

These policies are essential because of the nature of the wiki audience and its contributors; the "neutral point of view" policy embodies what I consider the *essence* of wiki: the tolerance, diversity, give-and-take, and collaborative nature of the wiki enterprise. To the extent that a wiki promotes and encourages these ideals, the better chance it has of becoming a truly useful online resource. A wiki that caters to "people with axes to grind" soon plummets into anarchy, as individuals gather into dreadful "wiki gangs" hell-bent on imposing their own myopic views even at the cost of destroying the wiki and its community. Such a wiki perfectly embodies the "tragedy of the commons," in which a public resource is razed by selfish, competing interests to the detriment of the whole.

In his book *Transforming Technology*, Andrew Feenberg reminds us that "technology is not a destiny but a scene of struggle. It is a social battlefield."[9] There are few technologies that illustrate the truth of this statement better than wikis. How does Wikipedia define Scientology? the Holocaust? Hillary Rodham Clinton? There is obvious power in being in control of these representations. Undoubtedly, an online dictionary owned and operated by Time Warner would impose a different understanding of the term *digital rights management* on the reader than another managed by the Electronic Freedom Foundation. The power of wikis is that no single person or entity has the authority necessary to impose a favored understanding on the public. Feenberg's opening commentary seems especially relevant here:

> What human beings are and will become is decided in the shape of our tools no less than in the action of statesmen and political movements. The design of technology is thus an ontological decision fraught with

political consequences. The exclusion of this vast majority from participation in this decision is profoundly undemocratic.[10]

Feenberg asks us to take a critical look at our technologies and the values that
shape their use. Will future generations find themselves delegated to the role
of mere "dead-end users," stripped of their ability to participate in online
discourse? Feenberg argues in his work that "instead of reducing individuals
to mere appendages of the machine, computerization can provide a role for
communicative skills and collective intelligence."[11] When I read this passage
of Feenberg's, I can't help but think *wiki*. Wikis are the type of computerization that will provide citizens with significant roles in the unfolding dialectic
of the information age.

Indeed, what is most exciting to me about wikis, and the reason why I
have dedicated so much of my scholarly energies toward understanding
them is this: They are not weapons of hegemonic domination but tools of
democratic liberation. Their power comes not from above but from below;
not from publishers but plebeians; not from a single proud tyrant but from a
thousand humble citizens. To use the language of Jean-François Lyotard,
wikis empower "groups discussing metaprescriptives by supplying them
with the information they usually lack for making knowledgeable decisions."[12] They give the public "free access to the memory and data banks."[13]
They command readers not to shut up but to speak up, not to "read silently"
but to "write loudly." The wiki way is to give our children a pen to write the
new age.

But let us return to the here and now and those everyday, run-of-the-mill
beliefs that make wikis better suited for well-fed idealists than hungry prag-
matists. At the end of the day, we do not wish to find our wiki work destroyed
or altered beyond recognition by some bucktoothed kid from Hackensack.
We're not going to cast our intellectual pearls before swine. Before we pledge
our time and expend our energies dredging up scholarship from the very
bowels of our being, we want some reassurance that Hannibal ain't at the
gate.

The question I always ask the skeptics is this: If wikis were as prone to
vandalism as so many of my colleagues suspect, then how can one possibly
explain the obvious success of Wikipedia? If there really were vast barbarian
armies out there whose sole motivation in life is to spray graffiti on bathroom

stalls and dump vulgarities and the prattling of mean-spirited idiots into wikis, then why isn't Wikitravel merely a poorly spelled guide to brothels? What protects these sites without fences, these authors without authority?

In their book *The Wiki Way*, Ward Cunningham and Bo Leuf assert that one reason wikis are spared by malicious users is that wrecking one just isn't a challenge: "It's so easy to wreck, there's no kudos in doing so."[14] It doesn't feed into one's ego; there are no bragging rights or kudos associated with peeing on the seat in a public restroom. While I agree that a wiki's lack of formidable technical resistance repels many a mustachioed malcontent, there are also far more compelling reasons why wikis flourish despite their openness. We should never downplay the significance of the role that the wiki community plays in its own maintenance and well-being. That is to say, we should not emphasize the *lack of pride* imputed to the would-be vandals over the *force of pride* felt by a wiki community fulfilled by its own achievements. As Cunningham and Leuf put it, "People are on the whole better behaved than one might imagine."[15] A flourishing wiki community is adequately protected by its own loyal citizen army rather than the hired, disinterested mercenaries of "trusted computing." As Machiavelli reminds us so well, no security mechanism in all of Redmond will long protect a prince hated by the people. Thus, from the outset, a wiki must be built with a community in mind, a community of contributors who will feel compelled not only to add to its store of knowledge but to protect that knowledge from ravage. This community must see its work as benefiting not only themselves but a great many others; they must dedicate their time and toil to no reward, save that of making the world a better place—or, at least, a place where they themselves would prefer to live.

The Celebrated Jumping Wiki of Calaveras County

So far, I have been mostly concerned with the underlying motives and the almost sacred duty that many effective wiki authors bring to their online communities. I have also alluded, by way of Lyotard and Feenberg, to the democratic function of wikis. Since I have already turgidly pursued this line of inquiry in depth elsewhere,[16] I will turn now to the specific kinds of value that good wiki assignments can add to the classroom.

The key pedagogical benefit wikis offer is epistemological. Wikis demonstrate, in a clear and obvious fashion, how knowledge is a function of communities engaged in ongoing discourse. Whereas conventional print scholarship tends to physically elide the evidence of its development, wikis highlight and preserve it in sedimentary or fossil layers. They also demonstrate and build upon the interconnectedness of knowledge and illustrate plainly that no discourse exists in isolation from other discourse. Finally, wikis make the fundamental importance of rhetoric clear to students. Successful wiki authors aren't just knowledgeable; they are persuasive. Indeed, I would argue that the "objective tone" is the "grand style" of our times. The "I think," "in my opinion," and "I believe" of so much student writing betrays a lack of confidence, a timidity that comes at a cost. The wiki author must speak with what is truly a public voice. After all—the most convincing opinions are objective facts.

The best wiki assignments are those that take fullest advantage of these traits and that work *with*, rather than *against*, the wiki way. My first example of such a wiki project is one I undertook last fall in an upper-level undergraduate course called Computers and English. The college catalogue describes this course in the broadest possible terms, allowing professors great leeway in customizing it to fit their own professional interests. I chose to emphasize new online writing spaces, offering students practical experience with wikis, blogs, and forums, as well as the theoretical background necessary to form critical metaperspectives toward these activities. Furthermore, I recognized that many students who would be taking the course were pursuing teaching careers, either at the primary, secondary, or postsecondary level of education. Though I had long been using blogs and forums in my other courses, I was unsure at first how to integrate wikis in a winning way.

As I was searching the Net and conversing with colleagues about good wiki assignments, I stumbled upon Wikibooks, a sister project of Wikipedia dedicated to producing and providing "open content" textbooks. These textbooks not only would be freely available in monetary terms but, more significantly, would be freely editable by anyone—even the students for whom the book was intended. After browsing and scanning through dozens of wikibooks on the site, I began to ponder what a composition textbook written by and for students would look like. I imagined it would be a very practical work that was more concerned with better grades than better writing. The advice it offered would probably focus on technique rather than theory, easily applicable *dos* and *don'ts* that harried students could seize upon to secure some slight advantage over their teacher's red marker and its terrible "*awk*-ing."

Above all else, I reckoned that it would be distinct from the textbooks offered to us by publishers. These textbooks, no matter what their publishers' marketing department claims, are written for the teachers who will select and require their students to purchase them, not the students whose top priority is just to survive college, teeth (and hopefully pocketbook) intact. At best, a good wikibook would be a work almost as useless and insipid as Aristotle's *Rhetoric* or the *Rhetorica ad Herennium*, both of which many scholars claim were written up by students from their lecture notes. Surely, if students of Aristotle and some chap whose name isn't even remembered could accomplish so much without so much as a good ballpoint pen, we could do all this and more with our powerhouse PCs. Puffed at every pore with overweening hubris, I went gung ho for wikibooks.

I knew, nevertheless, that I had a tall order in front of me. I would first have to "sell" the project to students who might already be skeptical of any kind of online writing, much less the "savage frontiers" of wiki writing, where anything they write might be deleted or modified beyond recognition by either their frantic classmates or a librarian from the Netherlands. I would also have to manage the project carefully, ensuring that everyone participated and that we would reach a satisfactory stage of development by the end of the semester. Finally, I would have to do something that most of us teachers find to be their most difficult challenge—namely, let these students find their own way. For I knew that the more I intervened and coerced changes that I thought were appropriate or important, the less the finished project would truly represent a textbook written by students for students. Honestly, I didn't know what I was getting myself or my class into. All I knew for sure was that we would undoubtedly find ourselves in places where no previous experience on my part would show us the way. Where would we find ourselves as my class sailed farther and farther past the edges of charted waters? The map simply said, "Here be dragons." It was time we introduced ourselves.

Looking back at those next few weeks, I still can't quell my pride. Of course, I'm proud that my hastily and recklessly concocted assignment turned out so well, but I'm far prouder of those students who soared. What professor worth his tweed wouldn't be proud of http://en.wikibooks.org/wiki/Rhetoric_and_Composition? In the course of one semester, some dozen students who had never used wikis before put together a usable (though, thankfully, imperfect) college textbook. Yes, this wikibook is a work in progress, just like all the commercial textbooks now entering their thirty-three and one-third editions. But what is so amazing to me is not the parts that are not complete or the parts that could be better but all the parts that turned out so well—so much better than I had dared to dream. I have no doubt that if more teachers could experience but a small part of the elation that comes from a successful class wiki project, we could put the fun back in poorly funded. These projects don't require elaborate hardware or labyrinthine programs. They only require an ounce of courage, two ounces of ambition, and sixteen tons of you-better-believe-it.

Getting It Right the First Time

I believe that I luckily stumbled upon a good recipe for wikis right away, without any of the "brilliant failures" I have seen described by my less fortunate colleagues.[17] Though I admit that my initial success might owe more to beginner's luck than pedagogical skill, my continued success suggests I'm on to something. There are only three keys to creating good wiki assignments: flexibility, camaraderie, and civility. For me, this last feature is the hardest—for, how can we convince our hardened students that the work they have so long labored to defend as "their own, original work" is no longer the goal and that their grade now hinges on some particularly vicious variant of the despised "groupthink"? These are students who have been told that forgetting to put their name on their paper may result in a zero. Now they are being asked to omit not only their names but also their very selves. All of this requires a heightened sense of their membership in a community and the well-developed skills of negotiation and abnegation necessary to speak not as private individuals but as a public. Interdependence, thy name is wiki.

What many people do not realize about wikis is how much rational-critical discourse goes on "behind the scenes." These conversations might take place in the rather clumsy fashion suggested by Leuf and Cunningham (the "thread mode") or more subtly by special software features. MediaWiki, the software responsible for Wikipedia and Wikitravel, has several built-in features to enable and organize this discourse on-site. One of the most common is "justification," which allows wiki editors to write a few words (generally no more than a sentence) explaining their rationale for instituting a change to the page. At times, this justification plays a critical role in determining whether the changes are kept or the page is "rolled back" to an earlier version. Thus, a wiki editor must be ready to defend her changes—a process obviously involving rhetoric.

Justification is not the only feature allowing such metadiscourse. Each page of these wikis has a sister page reserved for extended discussion. Here, a wiki's members can question or criticize the information on the page and even automatically sign and date their name on their comments. I used these discussion tabs extensively during our project, mostly to give tips and suggestions to the students. Sometimes outsiders would use these pages to offer their "thumbs up" to the project, but we also received our share of criticism. Sometimes this criticism came from folks who weren't interested in actually contributing to the project, but that wasn't always the case. A few bypassed the discussion page altogether and made changes directly, a few times very much to our chagrin.

For instance, early on someone decided that the graphic we were using as a "cover image" was unnecessary. I had stated in my project assignment that students could contribute in a variety of equally point-worthy ways, including designing graphics and images for the text. One of my students had leaped on this option and created a very nice image for the "cover" of our wikibooks. However, a well-meaning contributor took it upon himself to remove this graphic from our page. Incensed, we replaced the image and explained our rationale for keeping the graphic on the discussion page. Eventually, this contributor acquiesced, but only after shrinking and compressing the graphic so that it would load quickly in his browser.

Instead of seeing this little altercation as a problem, I seized it as a teaching moment. I had students who were used to handing in papers, having them graded, and getting them back (generally with no opportunity to revise them). They were seldom given the opportunity to explain to their professors why their papers were worth being graded in the first place. After all, professors are captive audiences for student discourse. It's our job to help students improve—to censure or coddle them, but not to oust them. We can show our contempt very liberally with our red pens, but few of us have the wherewithal to shrug off a stack of papers entirely.

"Some dog ate my homework!" Ah, yes, now that is an opportunity for some real writing instruction. These students now had to justify their work to an empowered audience who might very well chew up and spit out whole swaths of their "stuff." We often tell students to "consider their audience" but not how to duck when the audience launches fruit. A wiki audience is not some august body of passive-aggressives with colorful markers. I, for one, can think of few things more conducive to a good college education than being asked not just to acquire knowledge but to convince others that you possess it. Those of us who teach are all too aware of the difference, but we should not take this for granted in our students. Feeling like a tongue-tied, conceited ignoramus without anything worthwhile to say is a useful first step toward wisdom. It is the meek who shall inherit the wiki.

Still, when students do feel the sting of wiki rejection, it's nice for them to know that their classmates are also their comrades. During the whole cover image fiasco, the other students provided outstanding moral support to the artist. When we discussed the issue in class, several students who had expressed distaste toward the very idea of collaborative work were suddenly eloquently and spiritedly speaking of "our" project and insisting that these "outsiders" had no right to change it. Indeed, in many ways this challenge served as a serious "kick in the pants" for my students; motivation and enthusiasm for the project increased considerably. The students felt an invigorated sense of comradeship; they were united against the intercessions of "others." My task was to convince them that these outsiders were also comrades, even if they did live in other countries and had different ideas about where our project should go. We could not assume ownership of this project; we had to work instead toward making such a fine product that no one would feel *compelled* to alter it. Such a high level of polish and professionalism would only be possible if we all worked together.

I realized from the outset that we would all be bringing different skills, experience, and knowledge to the project, so I wanted to make the assignment as flexible as possible. To that end, I only required that students spend a certain amount of time on the wiki each week. They chose their own way to contribute. Several announced that they would specialize in producing text. To help them out, I let them borrow some of my composition textbook desk copies, none of which, I'm thankful to say, turned out to be very helpful. Other students took on the rather significant task of editing and revising content, ensuring that the style and tone of the wikibook remained consistent across sections. The rest of the class divided among themselves the responsibility for layout and design.

Though each student's enthusiasm for the project waxed and waned over the semester, by the final weeks the project was coming together nicely. I announced our achievements on several blogs and electronic mailing lists dedicated to computers and writing but, despite my several entreaties, was never able to secure the assistance of any of my colleagues. This reluctance of so many of my fellow teachers to join our efforts was disappointing. The dream of students and teachers working together fell flat. The few colleagues I talked to about it claimed that they were hesitant to get involved until after the semester was over; they did not want to intervene or possibly challenge my authority with the students. Clearly, if there is one aspect of this project that I would like to improve, it's securing the involvement of other teachers and scholars of writing. Perhaps Lisa Ede and Andrea Lunsford have it right—we're "more comfortable theorizing about subjectivity, agency, and authorship than we are attempting to enact alternatives to conventional assumptions and practices."[18] Book 'em, Dano.

I plan to revisit this project again next fall, when I will have a fresh batch of Computers and English students to work with. My goal is to patch in the holes left by the last class and generally to strive to improve the wikibooks as much as possible. I am curious to see how the existence of so much prior content will affect their attitude and performance toward the project. Eventually, I hope to use this wikibook to teach my first-year composition courses.

Training Wiki Jedis

If there is one question about wikis that still keeps me awake at night, it's how they can be used to change the nature of scholarship and our understanding of knowledge. I know very few serious wiki enthusiasts who do not also constantly ask themselves this question. Where, if anywhere, will this collaborative approach to knowledge get us? Stanley Chodorow predicts that the scholarship of the future will be "one in which the information used by the teams of scholars will be in liquid form."[19] Chodorow's vision of future scholarship sounds surprisingly like the wiki way, where "constant change—addition, subtraction, alteration"—is already the norm.[20]

However, even if such a future is as desirable as it seems to me, I don't expect to be dragged there by computers or squads of technological determinists. If the approach to knowledge and culture enabled by wikis is part of this, we need to ensure that our students know the *why* as well as the *how* of the wiki way. The technical knowledge is ultimately irrelevant without this ideological commitment. One of the ways I addressed this issue was to assign Larry Lessig's *Free Culture*. The students seemed captivated by Lessig's arguments and empowered by his rhetoric. They connected their work on the wikibook to Lessig's notion of free culture, where simple motivation, not legal permission, is required to contribute to culture. After a semester spent negotiating and abnegating authority, these students could really appreciate Lessig's passion for his subject. They were ready to go out into the world and tell others what this freedom tastes like.

I would like to finish off this chapter by returning to my earlier theme of service learning and igniting the civic potential of our students. Though there are certainly many legitimate ways one can go about introducing students to the concept of giving back to their community, I think wikis offer something truly special—they combine public service with "shaping" and being active members of that public. Wikis, be they juggernauts like Wikipedia or humbler projects like a free rhetoric and composition wikitext, offer a democratic alternative to the mass society. In her book *Developing Media Literacy in Cyberspace*, Julie Frechette eloquently describes how "the public's vision of the world, society, and self is shaped by words and images projected by the mass media."[21] Wikis turn these mass media on their head. Wikis are truly mass-produced, many-to-many writing spaces whose very design prevents the corporate control structure so prevalent in the "culture industry." They allow the people to participate directly in making meaning. This is a good thing because, as free software guru Richard Stallman explains, "It is demoralizing to live in a house that you cannot rearrange to suit your needs."[22]

No, wikis are not perfect, wikis are not easy, wikis are not secure, and wikis are not authoritative. Unlike Fox News, wikis aren't always fair and balanced. They do not inspire what Jay David Bolter calls "worshipful reading."[23] A distinguished professor can edit them. So can a child. Long live the wiki.

NOTES

The quotation at the beginning of the chapter is from Andrea Lunsford and Lisa Ede, "Collaborative Authorship and the Teaching of Writing," in *The Construction of Authorship: Textual Appropriation in Law and Literature*, ed. Martha Woodmansee and Peter Jaszi (Durham: Duke University Press, 1994), 356.

1. See Larry Sanger, "Why Wikipedia Must Jettison Its Anti-Elitism," http://www.kuro5hin.org/story/2004/12/30/142458/25.

2. Bruce Thyer, *Successful Publishing in Scholarly Journals* (Thousand Oaks, CA: Sage, 1994).

3. Ben H. Bagdikian, *The New Media Monopoly* (Boston: Beacon Press, 2004), 3.

4. Lawrence Lessig, *Free Culture* (New York: Penguin, 2004), 277.

5. Indeed, my page was the only one left untouched by this deplorable miscreant.

6. Paul Parsons, *Getting Published: The Acquisition Process at University Presses* (Knoxville: University of Tennessee Press, 1989), 7.

7. For the "Five Pillars" of Wikipedia, see http://en.wikipedia.org/wiki/Wikipedia:Five_pillars.

8. See http://wikitravel.org/en/Wikitravel:Policies_and_guidelines.

9. Andrew Feenberg, *Transforming Technology: A Critical Theory Revisited* (New York: Oxford University Press, 2002), 15.

10. Ibid., 3.

11. Ibid., 89.

12. Jean-François Lyotard, *The Postmodern Condition: A Report on Knowledge* (Minneapolis: University of Minneapolis Press, 2002), 67.

13. Ibid.

14. Bo Leuf and Ward Cunningham, *The Wiki Way: Quick Collaboration on the Web* (Upper Saddle River, NJ: Addison-Wesley, 2001), 329.

15. Leuf and Cunningham, *The Wiki Way*, 328.

16. See Matthew Barton, "The Future of Rational-Critical Debate in Online Public Spheres," *Computers and Composition* 22, no. 2 (2005): 177–90.

17. See Matthew Barton, "My Brilliant Failure: Wikis in Classrooms," http://kairosnews.org/node/3794.

18. Andrea Lunsford and Lisa Ede, "Collaborative Authorship and the Teaching of Writing," in *The Construction of Authorship: Textual Appropriation in Law and Literature*, ed. Martha Woodmansee and Peter Jaszi (Durham: Duke University Press, 1994), 356.

19. Stanley Chodorow, "Scholarship, Information, and Libraries in the Electronic Age," in *Development of Digital Libraries: An American Perspective*, ed. Deanna B. Marcum (Westport, CT: Greenwood Press, 2001), 6.

20. Ibid., 6.

21. Julie Frechette, *Developing Media Literacy in Cyberspace: Pedagogy and Critical Learning for the Twenty-First-Century Classroom* (Westport, CT: Praeger, 2002), 25.

22. Frechette, *Developing Media Literacy*, 125.

23. Jay David Bolter, *Writing Space: Computers, Hypertext, and the Remediation of Print*, 2d ed. (Mahwah, NJ: Lawrence Erlbaum, 2001), 168.

Writing in the Wikishop: Constructing Knowledge in the Electronic Classroom

Many electronic media that teachers use in the classroom, like discussion boards and blogs, are used either as tools of convenience (to make announcements or continue class discussion) or as an alternative medium for a writing assignment (using blogs as a reading journal or creating a Web site out of an essay). But wikis are difficult to incorporate into traditional writing instruction because they represent a radically different understanding of writing—a text essay can't be transformed into a wiki simply with the addition of an image and some links. Not to say that the wiki as a medium for writing, or as a tool for writing instruction, can't be successfully exploited, as Cathlena Martin, Michael C. Morgan, and others in this volume demonstrate. However, I would like to examine the pedagogical implications of wikis as constantly changing knowledge structures and to conceive of wiki participation as, beyond a potentially useful tool for teaching writing, a means for revealing to the individual student the constructed nature of knowledge. This understanding, even in a partial and underdeveloped state, can promote in students their own active role in learning. As a teacher, my interest is less in using wikis to teach writing skills than in exploring the possibilities of wikis to teach *with* writing and to discover what wikis can tell us *about* writing, particularly the role writing plays in the construction of knowledge. Wikis demonstrate that writing is not only an ongoing process but also a process that is continually modified by many contributors and that ultimately creates knowledge about the world. Contributing to a wiki not only reveals to the student his or her role in an ongoing conversation about a given subject but also reveals his or her contribution to the construction of knowledge about that subject. Wikis are therefore an evocative model of what James Berlin dubbed "social-epistemic rhetoric." This understanding of rhetoric views knowledge as grounded in language and arising from interchanges among the individual, the discourse community, and the material conditions of existence.[1] In plain language, what we know results from ongoing conversations that take place among real people in real situations.

As Brian Lamb notes in his article "Wide Open Spaces: Wikis, Ready or Not," wikis reflect the original vision of Internet pioneer Tim Berners-Lee.[2] In a 1999 talk he gave at MIT's Computer Science and Artificial Intelligence Laboratory, Berners-Lee describes his vision of the World Wide Web as

> an information space through which people can communicate, but communicate in a special way: communicate by sharing their knowledge in a pool. The idea was not just that it should be a big browsing medium. The idea was that everybody would be putting their ideas in, as well as taking them out. This is not supposed to be a glorified television channel.[3]

Berners-Lee sees the Web not simply as a repository of information but as a place where information can be shared and where people, "putting their ideas in, as well as taking them out," work together to share knowledge. But beyond sharing knowledge, the Web allows knowledge to mingle and transform and in effect encourages participants to create new knowledge. The Web in general and wikis in particular are akin to Kenneth Burke's "unending conversation" (a comparison that Stephanie Vie and Jennifer deWinter elaborate on in their essay in this volume).[4] But it is important to note the effect of asynchronous participation in this online "conversation." In participatory media like wikis, conversation can manifest itself as editing. Berners-Lee "wanted the Web to be . . . an interactive space where everybody can edit . . . I started saying 'interactive,' and then I read in the media that the Web was great because it was 'interactive,' meaning you could click. This was not what I meant by interactivity."[5] Rather, he seems to have meant something like an unending, knowledge-producing conversation. Unfortunately, after a long development of the Web as commercial portal and information source, interaction on the level of content remains rare, except in wikis.

Wikis and Knowledge Construction

Most people only think of wikis in relation to the familiar Wikipedia, the vast information repository of problematic academic credibility. Indeed, as Robert E. Cummings notes in the introductory essay to this volume, such cases relating to Wikipedia as Stephen Colbert's provocative satire of "truthiness" and the profligate character assassination of John Seigenthaler linger prominently in the public conception of wikis. However, even at their most problematic, Wikipedia and especially smaller information structures like ElephantStaircase (a wiki of do-it-yourself projects) or This Might Be A Wiki (devoted to the band They Might be Giants) are powerful examples of the social construction of knowledge through writing.[6]

The Teaching Wiki at one time offered an extensive list of possible effects in teaching with wikis. This seventeen-item list, like most information available on a wiki, was created collaboratively over time by an engaged audience. In this essay, I'd like to focus on four features that resonate with the idea of socially constructed knowledge. Wikis

- Introduce the concept of open source software/writing
- (de)Authorize the text
- Create more fluid and dynamic texts. Discourage "product oriented writing"; facilitate "writing as a process"
- Provide real rhetorical circumstances for writing.[7]

These four points operate on the assumption that writing circulates among participants and that these participants create knowledge by means of this circulation. Most wikis demonstrate some or all of these phenomena. Not only do wiki engines tend to be open source, but the philosophy of authorship is similarly based on an ethos of continual modification and improvement by many agents. This mass authorship (of software and text) obviously calls into question the nature of authority—it comes not from an elite position but from consensus. Authority is never permanently established because texts are always in flux, always open to improvement and modification (not to mention vandalism and debasement). Finally, any wiki that is actually used as a shared resource has an obvious and "real" purpose. This last point ultimately entangles the others, since controversies about the authority and usefulness of Wikipedia dominate so much discussion of wikis. Early conceptions of Wikipedia and the wiki model of knowledge creation may have been overly optimistic, but, regardless, the remaking of the arch-authoritarian knowledge source of the encyclopedia into a collaborative, shifting, and socially situated phenomena has profound implications for the classroom.

Wikipedia and Knowledge Construction

Before detailing a classroom environment built around the wiki-based sharing and creation of knowledge, I will more closely examine Wikipedia's challenge to traditional notions of the encyclopedia. The prevalent usage of wikis, seen prominently in Wikipedia but also in smaller-scale wikis, suggests that the wiki form remediates the traditional encyclopedia. Jay David Bolter, from whom I borrow the term *mediation*, notes that any writing space, from the book to the hypertext,

> is a material and visual field, whose properties are determined by a writing technology and the uses to which that technology is put by a culture of readers and writers. A writing space is generated by the interaction of material properties and cultural choices and practices. . . . Each fosters a particular understanding both of the act of writing and of the product.[8]

The significant remediation of our time is from print to hypertext, and of course the encyclopedia and wiki fit into these respective larger categories. It is odd, and worth noting, that one of the most rigid and authoritarian manifestations of print, the encyclopedia, has as its hypertextual counterpart one of the most open and fluid writing spaces conceivable. As a result of this remediation, traditional ideas of who an author is and what a text does change. No longer is the author a single "authority" who gets the last word by writing a permanent text. Instead, authority is shared by whoever wants to participate.

In this volume, Matt Barton outlines the usefulness of the wiki medium for encyclopedic content: "Like any good encyclopedia, wikis excel at making large quantities of expert information accessible to nonexperts; they democratize knowledge." Daniel Pink describes this democratization in Wikipedia as a "One for All" model of an encyclopedia:

Instead of one really smart guy, Wikipedia draws on thousands of fairly smart guys and gals. . . . Instead of clearly delineated lines of authority, Wikipedia depends on radical decentralization and self-organization— open source in its purest form. Most encyclopedias start to fossilize the moment they're printed on a page. But add Wiki software and some helping hands and you get something self-repairing and almost alive. A different production model creates a product that's fluid, fast, fixable, and free.[9]

Pink's description illustrates that the four points highlighted previously (open-source software/writing, problematizing textual authority, process orientation, and real rhetorical circumstances) are all inherent in Wikipedia. Knowledge on Wikipedia is truly "open source" in that anyone can contribute content, edit, clarify, and enrich an entry. Instead of a few select guardians of knowledge dictating what is known about a subject, a large number of readers can become the authors of an article, so the traditional authority of the author is turned over to the readers. Wikipedia's "product" is therefore always under revision and in transition. The creation of knowledge is a never-ending process that everyone with an Internet connection can (and arguably should) participate in.

Wikis in the Writing Classroom

But what does this remediated encyclopedia offer teachers? The idea of students sitting in rows in a writing classroom, composing encyclopedia articles for twelve to fifteen weeks, is more than a little silly. It sounds like a particularly pointless way to run a writing class. Perhaps a student could gain sufficient expertise to draft and revise an article, but such a closed, product-oriented activity would leave the student with (a) limited expertise in some constrained area and (b) an understanding of writing, and knowledge, as segmented and isolated. But working in the context of the remediated encyclopedia, on a wiki, a student could initiate and revise writing relevant to the course material. A writing class could be transformed into a "wikishop" that uses writing to produce knowledge about a subject. I base my term *wikishop* on Gregory Ulmer's idea of the writing classroom as "textshop." Ulmer derives an "experimental humanities" from the sciences, proposing the "textshop" as "a laboratory in which the students attempt to re-produce the experiments of the humanities. . . . In learning science, students not only read about a given idea, they are expected to be able to reproduce the experiments themselves, finally reaching a point when they face a problem without solution (yet)."[10] Richard Smythe elaborates the implications of Ulmer's ideas: "Students come to realize that the texts they read can become a source of instructions or a springboard for an intervention into the textual network to which they, as language users, belong."[11] But rather than modeling writing on scientific experimentation, the wikishop approach borrows its model from its own form, the wiki. A class based on writing a collaborative wiki might become a textual network that produces knowledge through writing.

Such a class would by nature be process oriented, since all writing is continually subject to discussion, reconsideration, and change; egalitarian, since the authority of texts is continually open to negotiation; and network literate, since in wikis relationships are expressed solely through links. All knowledge and all expression are distributed across a network of pages and users. While a wikishop would be an unusual way of teaching a class, it would teach students how a body of knowledge is formed and holds together. Scholarship on teaching and learning forcefully demonstrates that this engaged, participatory environment is conducive to student learning.[12] Among the key practices of learning-centered teaching is the need to share authority and responsibility for learning among teachers and students: Learning is not simply the transmission of facts from a teacher's mouth to students' ears. Rather, learners must actively pursue it, often collaboratively. Dan Gilbert, Helen L. Chen, and Jeremy Sabol's essay in this collection outlines how wikis can become cornerstones to learning communities. In the following, final section of this essay, I will cover similar ground, but with special attention to the framework of the social construction of knowledge.

Setting up the Wikishop

Prior to the ascendancy of Wikipedia, numerous writers noted that users accustomed to most Web sites' hierarchical organization and directed navigation felt lost the first time they visited a wiki, learning how to rely on text searches and "what links here?" lists rather than customary Web hierarchies. While experience with Wikipedia and Web 2.0 information structures such as tags might alleviate some of this confusion, the task implied by a fresh (underpopulated) wiki might be similarly daunting. A wikishop could be confusing for "new users" (students), but the instructors can help clarify by doing a few simple things: commit to the wiki as the main project for the class; limit the subject area of the wiki; and develop a grading system that would account for this nontraditional model of writing.

First, the wiki would have to be the primary writing activity of the class. There are a few practical and pragmatic reasons for this. Not only do the wiki interface and markup take a little getting used to, but the ideas of group authorship and associative organization would challenge students' assumptions about writing. The idea that any user can edit any content flies in the face of the idea that writing is individual property, and the idea that they will need to figure out how all this information fits together would be just as challenging for most. Another reason to commit to the wikishop for an entire course is that, to fully explore the possibilities of networks and revision, a sizable body of content would need to be created, which takes time. To enforce the idea of the wiki as the main course activity, a sizeable portion of class time should be devoted to working on the wiki and discussing new developments on the wiki.

The course would need some unifying topic or theme. Again, to develop enough expertise for meaningful exchange and editing and to create associative pathways, a certain critical mass is necessary. The unifying topic could be most anything: computer culture, Modernist poetry, or any other subject limited enough that students could develop reasonable expertise but wide enough to allow for many contributions. Perhaps the biggest objection a writing teacher would have to the subject-centered, remediated-encyclopedia model is what seems a focus on information rather than rhetorical strategies. From a writing-as-product point of view, generating this kind of content seems little better on a wiki than in the rows of encyclopedists I described earlier. But specific features—like the ease of revision and a dynamically generated discussion forum attached to each page—cause a writer to become aware of and inspect the basis of individual understandings of a given topic. A wiki suggests that knowledge is grounded in language and arises from interchanges among the individual, a wider community, and the specific conditions of the writing. It's difficult to say whether this is more important than refining the persuasive essay, but, regardless, I'm not suggesting that writing a wiki is an appropriate project for an introductory writing course. Rather, a slightly more advanced course could use writing to explore a topic as well as reflect on the nature of writing itself.

Grading collaboratively created work is always difficult. The best solution is to have students make an out-of-wiki argument on the quality of their in-wiki contributions. These contributions are easy for anyone to track, so long as the wiki being used requires a log-in. A complete history of each user's contributions could provide a rich body of work to analyze. A participant in a wikishop could identify patterns in his or her writing and in the nature of changes that others make to their contributions. Such self-awareness would be much easier to track in a documented process like a wiki change log than in a final product like a traditional essay. M. A. Syverson's work on the Learning Record (LR) provides an ideal assessment model for a wikishop participant. The LR, an electronic portfolio system, allows an instructor to keep abreast of individual progress, to foreground course goals, and to base assessment on what students can demonstrate that they have learned. The LR requires students to document and interpret their work and to make arguments about their development and performance. Specific course goals give each LR its strands, or focal points. (For instance, in my first-year composition courses, I often use the strands of rhetorical strategies, writing skills, research, and information technology.) The course strands provide a context for students to understand and assess their own work.[13] Strands for a wikishop class might include the subject of the course (obviously), collaboration, information technology, rhetorical strategies, knowledge creation, or any other relevant topic.

Technical know-how for starting a wikishop, for both student and instructor, would not need to be extensive. The standard markup for wikis is very simple, and some wiki engines have simplified it further. The instructor would have to decide what wiki to use, whether a wiki engine should be installed on a department server for the class to use, whether a new Web-based wiki should be created, or whether an existing wiki should be added to the class. In any case, students would have real circumstances and a real audience for writing, either limited to the class or as broad as a public wiki's community. The regular users of a preexisting wiki might resent the invasion of "noobs," so it is probably better to choose one of the many open-source wiki engines available. MediaWiki, which runs Wikipedia, is the most popular, though the Web-based PBwiki is easily accessible, simple to use, and has been reliable when I've used it for short-term class activities. Whatever wiki an instructor chooses, some experimentation will be necessary to figure out the ins and outs of the particular application. Most wikis have a "sandbox" for just this kind of playing around.

With some technology, allure influences incorporation—a teacher might decide to incorporate podcasts or Web design because, in part at least, these media are current and attractive. On more than one occasion I have retrofitted a rationale for teaching with some "cool" or new technology. Even though wikis can't be called pretty or hip, it might seem that I've done it again: fabricated a pedagogy out of a technology rather than find a technology suited to a pedagogy. But as I look over what I've written, I find many resonances with my teaching philosophy, a philosophy that is something like a wiki—continually under revision and subject not to anonymous users but to many sometimes unexpected influences. As a teacher, I believe that the most effective kind of teaching is what George Hillocks calls "environmental."[14] Therefore, I see the teacher's role as twofold: to design environments in which students face learning challenges and to guide students through these challenges. In a wiki, the teacher must guide students through a knowledge structure of their own creation. This act of guidance in turn will change the wiki environment, for the better.

NOTES

1. James Berlin, *Rhetoric and Reality: Writing Instruction in American Colleges, 1900–1985* (Carbondale: Southern Illinois University Press, 1987), 165–80.

2. Brian Lamb, "Wide Open Spaces: Wikis, Ready or Not." *Educause Review*, September–October 2004, 37–48.

3. Tim Berners-Lee, talk to the Laboratory for Computer Science thirty-fifth anniversary celebrations, Cambridge, MA, April 14, 1999, http://www.w3.org/1999/04/13-tbl.html (accessed February 20, 2007).

4. Kenneth Burke, *The Philosophy of Literary Form: Studies in Symbolic Action*, 3d ed. (Berkeley: University of California Press, 1973), 110–11.

5. Ibid.

6. ElephantStaircase Wiki, http://www.elephantstaircase.com/wiki/index.php?title=Main_Page (accessed December 14, 2006); Scott Redd and Brad Will, "This Might

Be a Wiki: The TMBG Database," http://www.tmbw.net/wiki/index.php/Main_Page (accessed December 14, 2006).

7. Joe Moxley, The Teaching Wiki, University of South Florida, http://teaching wiki.org (accessed December 14, 2006). A number of other items on the list could be achieved by multiple electronic or traditional means: teaching revision, thinking hypertextually, invigorating student writing, and so on. These are worthy goals, but my intent is to map wikis to the social construction of knowledge.

8. Jay David Bolter, *Writing Space: Computers, Hypertext, and the Remediation of Print*, 2d ed. (Mahwah, NJ: Lawrence Erlbaum, 2001), 12.

9. Daniel Pink, "The Book Stops Here," *Wired* 13, no. 3 (March 2005), www.wired.com (accessed February 20, 2007).

10. Gregory L. Ulmer, "Textshop for an Experimental Humanities," in *Reorientations: Critical Theories and Pedagogies*, ed. Bruce Henrickson and Thais E. Morgan (Urbana: University of Illinois Press, 1990), 113–32.

11. Richard Smyth, "Students as Producers: Using the World Wide Web as Publishing House," Horizon, http://horizon.unc.edu/index.html.

12. A particularly useful introduction to this scholarship is Maryellen Weimer, *Learner-Centered Teaching: Five Key Changes to Practice* (San Francisco: Jossey-Bass, 2002).

13. The LR is invaluable for teachers and students alike because it integrates course work, goals, and assessment in one system. Because it captures evidence and analysis in a permanent archive, it provides a wealth of data useful in assessing individual student progress and overall course effectiveness. For more information on the LR, see designer Margaret Syverson's explanatory Web page at http://www.cwrl.utexas.edu/~syverson/olr/contents.html.

14. George Hillocks, *Teaching Writing as Reflective Practice* (New York: Teachers College Press, 1995), 54–57.

Wiki Lore and Politics in the Classroom

"Wiki? Friut, Vegetable or Perhaps a Small Animal from New Zealand"

This was a student's response, spelling error and all, when asked her impression of the class wiki. Her opinion was surprisingly similar to those of the other nineteen students, who ranged from college freshmen to seniors. And she wasn't too far off in her attempt to relate this strange word to another culture either. As readers know by now, *wiki* is Hawaiian for "quick" or "informal," and the exotic origin of the word seeps through into the technology itself even when people don't know what a wiki is. Another student wrote, "I had no clue what a wiki was; my best guess was that it was some kind of tropical themed tavern."[1] While a wiki is like a tavern insofar as it is a communal space to sit and share, no drinks with little umbrellas are served. It is a fully editable Web site, which can be a productive addition to the classroom.

The first half of this chapter details my (Cathlena Martin) virgin voyage, as well as most of my students' first encounters, with setting up and using a wiki in a college classroom. After two semesters of using the wiki, I shared my wiki experiment with another instructor (Lisa Dusenberry); the second half of the chapter recounts and analyzes her use of the wiki in composition courses. Together, we explore the uses and hierarchies of a class wiki through a range of college English courses and attempt to address several questions involving wikis and the classroom such as the following: Does a wiki truly provide a common, collaborative space where students can be creative and address the theoretical concerns of a college classroom? How do students accept and use their public, online writing space? Do wikis provide the same type of online voice as blogs? Is using a wiki for compositional writing seen by students as a subversive or marginal writing space? Does the writing medium of a wiki place an informal, creative bent on academic writing for a college class? Is a wiki only appropriate in a class dealing with popular media? These are a lot of questions for a short chapter on wikis in the composition and communication classroom, and we don't have all of the answers, but with a new media tool such as wikis, we sometimes just need to start with questions. This chapter is largely in the format of two mini case studies involving Cathlena's ENG 1131: Writing through Media and ENG 2300: Film Analysis classes and Lisa's ENG 2210: Technical Writing and ENG 1102: Introduction to Argument and Persuasion classes. Our anecdotal evidence derives from student comments about our respective class wikis and their wiki projects.

Launching into the World of Wikis: Cathlena Martin's Pedagogical Application

In the fall semester of 2005, I decided to add a wiki to my ENG 1131: Writing through Media class at the University of Florida, as a medium for student writing. Because the wiki worked so well in my media class, I subsequently incorporated a wiki into my course for spring 2006, ENG 2300: Film Analysis, to see if this medium could function as successfully in a more widely taught English class.[2] Since this trial run, I have used a wiki in every English literature and composition course because a class wiki provides an ideal online interface with which to address the fissures and overlaps between creative, collaborative, and theoretical work, while also providing students a space they can access and edit. By giving students the means to edit class pages, they are granted more agency in the development of class assignments and can actively contribute in a manner so that other students can view class work and progression.

I want to begin with an example of a physical space that acts like an online wiki. In Gainesville, Florida, a traditional college town, a 1,120-foot stretch of retaining wall located on a major thoroughfare has become a literal, physical wiki space. Each day the wall boasts a new graffiti tag with announcements of bands, endorsements of campus politics, and memorials to fallen

Gators. It is used as a space to post both serious materials like "Stop Geno-
cide" and everyday greetings such as "Happy Birthday." In figure 1, one can
see a girl painting "I love you" on the wall. Her newest paint post covers the
news from yesterday as she edits the wall to include her message. The wall
acts as a wiki in a physical space because of its communal nature and editing
interface. While the analogy will break down eventually, as all analogies do,
this example nevertheless provided my students with an accessible definition
of a wiki. Recently, the University of Florida library has begun archiving images of the Thirty-fourth Street wall into a collection they call "Concrete
Blog: Messages on the Wall." The Web site hails the space as "Gainesville's
most public diary" (http://www.uflib.ufl.edu/digital/collections/wall/). However, they mislabeled the digital collection because the wall does not function
as a blog or diary, where the community can add to and collect moments of
life. The wall functions as a wiki.

The fundamental principles that guide a wiki are quick and informal
means of editing and collaborating content online, which is why I chose a
wiki to use with my classes, particularly for their group work. This basis of
collaboration supposedly levels the playing field by creating an equality of
authorship and collaboration. The main questions I want to focus on have to
do with whether a wiki truly provides a common, collaborative space where
students can be creative and address the theoretical concerns of a college
classroom and, if so, how this occurs. Even after one day of using the wiki,
my students could see the pros and cons. The following quote from one of
my media students is typical of how students responded when asked about
their experience with the class wiki:

> The wiki is a large network of information that is linked to one another.
> Anybody who can use a computer can edit a wiki and share their per-
> sonal knowledge with the world. Wikis have the potential to be used for
> all fields, professions, and by anybody with a computer. Further, a wiki
> can inspire people to be creative and create a community where people
> can share their ideas and personal knowledge with each other. With the
> potential for anybody to edit a wiki, some downfalls of this technology
> are bound to occur. People have the ability to publish misleading infor-
> mation and hurtful words or opinions; which the whole world or com-
> munity are able to see. However, this shortcoming can be easily avoided
> by creating a closed community where anybody can sign up, but their

Fig. 1. Wiki wall. (Photograph courtesy of Cathlena Martin.)

posts are monitored for inappropriate material and they can be kicked out at any time. In all I think that a wiki is a very promising concept and should only get better with time.

Of course, the class setting offers the kind of closed community that this student sees as beneficial. But what about the concept of sharing ideas? Most professors have taught collaborative assignments or had collaborative scenarios, which were either team projects or class presentations by two or more students. But how do students assemble these projects? Sometimes they are each responsible for an individual section, which they proceed to e-mail to one group member who compiles the content. Sometimes they sit around a computer together and have one person type while others brainstorm. Whatever the method, a wiki solidifies and contains this process, archiving the students' projects online and making them available for the rest of the class to see. A wiki provides immediacy and access, as well as a record that is available to a large number of people and that can be easily archived. Also, the wiki has the ability to become a public document online, thus making it possible to share student work with a larger public audience and possibly instill greater authorial responsibility. Google Documents is slowly catching up in capabilities but provides a different writing environment where students rely more heavily on the style of the Microsoft suite rather than the Web site–like PBwiki. A wiki is self-contained, and while one can upload Word documents or images, it doesn't need any outside applications to function.

To introduce my class to the wiki at the beginning of the fall semester, I assigned a wiki grammar team project. Each team of four members was assigned a particular punctuation or grammatical issue that they were responsible for becoming an expert on and presenting to the class. I asked them as a team to put up an overview of their grammar points and a link to their online grammar game(s) or online activity. This way they were preparing themselves to be better writers, conducting research, and using the wiki both in a team capacity and as a presentation tool.

This worked well, and students were surprised by how easy the wiki was to use. Some were afraid that they would have to learn programming codes in order to use the wiki. However, this is not the case with the particular wiki that I used.[3] It does have a few unique commands for formatting, but there is no HTML knowledge involved. The edits are made much the same way they are in a Word document. When searching for a wiki to use with my class, I researched wikis to find one that did not require the administrator to run a PERL script or have a personal server. Some wikis require additional software and extensive installation. In addition to an easy setup, my other stipulation was a user-friendly interface with WYSIWYG page editing. Some wikis charge for their service and do not allow file uploading. But PBwiki, or peanut butter wiki, admirably fulfills its claim to "Make a free, password-protected wiki as easily as a peanut butter sandwich" and provides an easy, student-friendly, teacher-friendly wiki service.

My semicolon grammar team provides a good example of how a wiki can function as a collaborative space. The team set up their own semicolon wiki page apart from the general class grammar wiki page, adding their contact e-mails and AIM addresses so that they could easily contact their group members. For this project, they divided the work and were responsible for presenting different aspects regarding the semicolon. However, with the wiki, they could easily reference what the other group members were doing and how their progress was going. Additionally, this group added a section called "Group Notes" and a section for additional presentation ideas to use as a brainstorming space.

Each group may assign sections to divide the workload for this larger research project, but it should present a cohesive whole by completion, and this raises an issue that is relevant to the editing and the equality of authorship in a wiki: namely, that the person who makes the final edit gets the last word. Yet, even before that final revision, a group member can go into the wiki and reword, edit, delete, and add whatever she wants. A whole essay could be deleted with the click of a button. This is where collaboration, teamwork, and communication come into play. Not only do students have to produce research for this assignment, but they edit their peers' writing and create a cohesive tone for their project. As one of my students wrote about the wiki when asked to evaluate it, "Although there are many benefits to the wiki, I see one drawback: No one's thoughts and entries stay untouched by others. The purity of an initial entry can be completely disturbed by another's desire to make changes. But this can also be a good thing."

Also, a large, underlying hierarchical structure emerges in terms of editing and final revision, not from the students but because of the administrator (Admin) of the wiki. As the Admin, I retain power above the general collaborators on the wiki. So while the wiki takes an important step in decentering the classroom and distributing power to the students, it can't completely comply with this teaching model. And, actually, I have been thankful for that shred of Admin power. For example, I had a situation involving passwords. The Admin holds the ability to change the wiki password. If a general writer tries to change the password, the power and entrance to the communal space, an e-mail goes to the Admin, who can deny or accept the password change. I received just such an e-mail after the first day of class. While I was thrilled that my students wanted to play around with the technology after the first day, I was surprised (although I probably shouldn't have been) that they tried to alter the security and gain control of the wiki.

Additionally, as the Admin and teacher, I monitor the class wiki more closely than the students do and make judgment calls on what posts to leave visible. For example, on the class wiki front page, a student wrote, "Go Gators!! Georgia Sucks!!" While I am all for school spirit, I didn't want "Georgia Sucks" on my class wiki, so I deleted it but left "Go Gators." Students are keenly aware of the teacher/Admin presence, which can create an unexpected benefit. Because the wiki is online, the teacher can constantly check on a project's progress and also have access to which members of the group are contributing. This added extra incentive to one procrastinating student who said: "because I'm a procrastinator, the fact that Cathlena could check my progress on the wiki at any time made me more apt to work on it. That pushed me to work on it sooner than I would have normally."

For both the media and film classes, the final project could have been written as a research paper, but the wiki gave the groups flexibility with collaboration, graphics, layout, and links. Sometimes the online format was a detriment to their prose, but overall the projects succeeded in meeting my learning goals. I was so pleased with the wiki's effect on my courses that I decided to share my experience at the University of Florida English Graduate Organization Conference in October 2005. Lisa Dusenberry attended and, excited by the possibilities that the wiki provides for collaborative writing, decided to integrate the wiki into her composition courses. The rest of the chapter is devoted to her case study in hopes that we can provide some insight into how the wiki functions in different course contexts and with different pedagogical approaches.

Vision and Revision: Composition in Lisa Dusenberry's Collaborative Classroom

After learning about Cathlena's success with the wiki, I implemented a PB-wiki in my ENC 2210: Technical Writing and, later, my ENC 1102: Introduction to Argument and Persuasion classes. My primary goal in using the wiki for my technical writing course was to facilitate the group writing projects that the students were asked to complete, but I also wanted to expose the students to evolving technologies and have them consciously interrogate the nature of writing in a professional context. The use of the wiki invigorated the course and provided an extra layer of written negotiations and decisions for the students to navigate. While the applications of the wiki for a collaboratively heavy writing course like technical writing were apparent, the positive reactions of the students led me to integrate the wiki into my course on argumentation and to interrogate the possibilities of using the wiki for peer response, discussion, and diffusion of some of the hierarchical authority of the classroom.

For my technical writing courses, I had the privilege of teaching in the University of Florida's Networked Writing Environment (NWE). These computerized classrooms allowed students to participate and collaborate on the wiki during class and allowed me to observe the different ways in which my students approached group writing on the wiki. When I first introduced the wiki to my students, their reactions were similar to Cathlena's students. They were nervous about how much technological skill the wiki would require and about how their writing might be affected by the public nature of the wiki. As an instructor, one of my main concerns was establishing a positive tone for the wiki and making sure students felt like it was a safe space to post their ideas. Balancing this need for safety with the desire to make students comfortable enough to make changes to the wiki required constant negotiation between myself and the students and among the students themselves. To set the tone for the collaborative community, I asked them to create a personal page on the wiki where they described themselves, explained their writing experiences, and included any other information they would like the class to know about them. Aside from the practical purpose of getting them used to the wiki's technical workings, this also demonstrated many of the assumptions the students made about audience and formality and created a more intimate relationship between their personal lives and their classroom personas.

These personal pages were graded, which opened up an avenue for us to discuss what kinds of authority are in play with the wiki, their reactions to my commenting on their pages in such a public forum, and the different audiences the students chose to address. Some students formally completed the assignment as if it were a traditional written memo to the instructor, but others wrote more informally, using the common tone and abbreviations of other online forms like instant messaging. The students articulated both their excitement and frustration at continually having a public audience to consider when they created documents: "Sometimes I don't want fellow students editing my own writing."

Not only did I critique their writing, but their peers interacted with their ideas and had control over their writing. Using this individual writing experience as an introduction, I asked the students to complete multiple group assignments using both the pages on our main course wiki and their own group wikis. These group assignments ranged from short in-class exercises to a long-term, multipart project developing, testing, and revising a technical manual on a topic of their choice. In these group writing experiences, both the students and I found the wiki to be very useful, but not without some limitations and frustrations.

Our positioning in the NWE allowed me to observe the protocols each group chose to operate by. I purposefully allowed the students to use the wiki as a tool in their own processes and did not stipulate exactly how they had to collaborate using it. PBwiki allows both students and instructors to see who has altered any particular page, to see when she altered it, and to compare the changes in the page over time. As an instructor, it was an amazing tool for observing which students made changes, the types of revision work they were doing (global, local, editing), and how the group members made themselves accountable to each other. By comparing the changes the students made to their personal pages as they created them, I could see what kinds of decisions they were making about diction and "appropriate" information. Showing these changes in class allowed the students to tangibly examine each other's revision process and to discuss their motivations behind altering their own and each other's writing.

When asked about their impressions of the wiki as a tool for their writing, nearly all of the students commented on the wiki as an archive of course content and their experience developing and navigating it, leaving comments such as: "The in-class-activities page was useful because I could go back and look over things I had forgotten." The students could experience and reexperience our activities in light of the new material we added as we went along. These wiki pages, then, provided us with the ability to model the revision process as a class and dynamically participate in the writing process together—using both their assignments and the actual course itself as inroads to understanding the limitations and instabilities of written language. Students' comments resonated with the way the technology foregrounded revision and organization: "We were able to see the process everyone was making, we could edit each other's work, and we can all have the same format." This ability of the wiki to demonstrate each individual's process and the mechanisms people use to approach their own writing continued to be a valuable asset in teaching argumentation. By observing and participating in different parts of each other's texts, students were able to better understand writing for audiences and the importance of examining their own language and structure.

As for the group wiki projects, some groups would gather around one computer and make the changes together in a more traditional model of group work. For them, the wiki became a means to share and record their collective work, as well as a way for the rest of the class to interact with their ideas. A few groups, however, used the wiki in a more asynchronous way, logging in to the wiki outside of class and completing portions of their project at different times. The groups who went with this model often went through a period of struggle as they tested the medium and tried different ways to work with each other's data. One student reported on the confusion of this initial period, "My least favorite thing about the wiki is that after a while it can get overwhelming. Our group posted so many comments and questions on our page that we all got a little confused after a while." But learning to sort out organizational systems and come to a cohesive document prepares students for the challenges they will meet if they pursue writing in the future. As they negotiate who creates the body of the text and what kinds of changes and corrections their particular group will allow, the students learn more about the intentionality and struggle that produces good writing.

Not only does the wiki underscore the variable nature of writing and revision, but it also brings the visual element of students' writing to the forefront. The layout and accessibility of the wiki impressed students. It required them to help shape the architecture of the course and gave them more of a sense of ownership over the class itself. One student commented that the wiki "feels like my personal page to create what ever I want. I can add graphics, I can add little stars and other symbols which makes indentions or bolds my font. The wiki is cool." But for all of their enthusiasm for the technology and their respect for the collaborative space the wiki provides, students were very resistant to the main purpose of the wiki—editing, sharing, and utilizing each other's work. One student identified the ease of editing as her least favorite feature of the wiki, which is surprising considering that is one of the defining characteristics of the wiki: "My least favorite feature about the wiki is the ability to change content other people posted. I value my writing and ideas; if other people plagiarized or changed my content, I would be upset."

Many students echoed this concern over the ownership they felt for the pages they produced: "Anyone with access can change anything that they want. There is no security and you have to keep checking it if you're paranoid someone will change something you wrote." Contrary to my expectations, most of my students were not comforted by our ability to track changes and revert pages to previous versions. The instability of the technological space made them nervous. They expressed frustration at being unable to identify each others' motivations in making changes and ascertain whose corrections were more valid: "I woke up the morning the technical definitions were due to find that 3 hours of revising and editing had been undone; luckily I saved my work, but nevertheless it was frustrating." As Stephanie Vie and Jennifer deWinter note in their essay in this volume, "Disrupting Intellectual Property: Collaboration and Resistance in Wikis," this destabilization of individual authority conflicts with the historical development and guiding ideologies surrounding intellectual property. Thus, using the wiki in the classroom creates a complex interaction between accessibility, authorship, hierarchies of power, negotiations of community values, and (social) anxiety.

Part of the paranoia comes from the use of the wiki for graded assignments and the imposition of the instructor's authority. Students are very aware of the (imagined) ramifications of other students changing their writing for the worse. The wiki also places them in a potentially competitive space, despite the technology's collaborative and communal functions. The evaluative demands of the classroom conflict with the decentered, nonhierarchical structure of the wiki. Since the students' writing is available for each other to view, they feel pressured to protect their ideas from each other to make sure they get appropriate grade-related credit. This tension can be productive and force the student to create more polished writing, but it often manifests itself in the common refrain of "everybody can steal your ideas."

The wiki is a tool I will continue to use in the classroom not only because it is an effective system for course management but because of the ways it foregrounds the constructed nature of language and writing. It encourages students to think about process and provides tangible ways to envision revision. Students engage with the digital medium because it reflects their use of social media, chat programs, and the Web. Several of my students commented that they wanted to create wikis to use for projects outside of my class. Using the technology in the classroom not only benefits their writing but also asks them to think consciously about the visual design of their documents. These skills will enhance their ability to express themselves digitally. To students, the wiki is a medium of expression that engages with their established experience with social media; to instructors, the wiki is a simple course management tool[4] with complex pedagogical implications. In the future, I plan on more fully integrating the wiki into the course, asking students to write in the medium and to peer edit using its archival and asynchronous features to the best of their ability. For now, however, I am satisfied with getting other instructors excited about using wikis in the classroom as Cathlena did for me.

As instructors successfully using wikis in our classrooms, we hope to work toward sharing our experiences, recruiting more wiki users, and articulating the pedagogical and theoretical implications of using the wiki in the classroom. The wiki has enhanced our courses considerably, and students have responded enthusiastically. But don't just take our word for it. Please peruse our class wikis and student-generated wiki projects, start your own class wiki, and share the wiki tool with a colleague. And who knows? With time, a class wiki may be as standard as a no. 2 pencil.

NOTES

1. All student identities have been deliberately kept anonymous in this essay.

2. Four class wikis are addressed in this article: Writing Thru Media class wiki, http://writingthrumedia.pbwiki.com/; Film Analysis class wiki: http://uffilmanaly sis.pbwiki.com/; Technical Writing class wiki: http://ENC2210sample.pbwiki.com; and Intro to Argument and Persuasion class wiki: http://lisadusenberry.pbwiki.com/. Additionally, sample student wiki projects on media can be found at http://writingthru mediatwo.pbwiki.com/ and http://writingthrumediathree.pbwiki.com/; sample student wikis on film can be found at http://uffilmanalysisone.pbwiki.com/ and http://uffilmanalysistwo.pbwiki.com/; sample student projects for technical writing can be found at http://enc2210gp1.pbwiki.com/ and http://enc2210gp2.pbwiki.com/Fi nalDefinition.

3. PBwiki, http://pbwiki.com/ (accessed December 13, 2006).

4. Recently, PBwiki has moved to a WYSIWYG editor that works like Google Documents or Microsoft Word and no longer requires users to use PBwiki code or HTML, making it even easier for both students and instructors to use the technology.

GlossaTechnologia: Anatomy of a
Wiki-Based Annotated Bibliography

We academics love our books. As the centuries-old vessels for containing and disseminating knowledge in various disciplines, books truly are the coin of the realm. We love our books so much, in fact, that we even create special types of books that do little more than catalog and comment upon other, more "real" books—metabooks, if you will, or what we more commonly call reference books. Among the various types of reference books, perhaps the most useful is the annotated bibliography, that peculiar metabook that not only lists citations to scholarly monographs, articles, and documents on a particular topic of inquiry but also includes a brief descriptive or evaluative paragraph for each entry that gives readers some inkling of its relevance or quality. Indeed, annotated bibliographies can be valuable tools for the wide-eyed academic venturing forth into a new project because they neatly encapsulate and comment upon a broad range of texts germane to a particular field or subfield. Library science guru James L. Harner describes the best models of this genre as "intelligent, accurate, thorough, efficiently organized works that foster scholarship by guiding readers through accumulated studies as well as implicitly or explicitly isolating scholarly concerns, identifying topics that have been overworked, and suggesting needed research."[1] Annotated bibliographies do have their drawbacks, however. For instance, because of the technological constraints of print, they are static documents (until a publisher deems a new edition necessary), usually offer the qualitative assessment of only one reviewer, and (if your topic deals with new technologies, let's say) can suffer a rather short shelf life.

But what if we weren't bound by those constraints of medium or form or generic habit? What would become of that venerated metabook if we were to take the sine qua non of the annotated bibliography and place it into a new medium in order that it might take on a new look and feel and, in the process, a new functionality? Wikis can potentially allow us to overcome the constraints of the printed page by creating an open-access, real-time environment where scholars with a common interest can participate in the shared task of building a useful academic resource. This chapter chronicles the travails involved in using wiki software to establish GlossaTechnologia, an open, expanding annotated bibliography of texts on the topic of digital technology in rhetoric and composition studies.[2] Specifically, I will address two main issues behind the implementation of GlossaTechnologia. In addition to positing a theoretical rationale for using wiki-based technology to construct a dynamic annotated bibliography based upon social networking and infrastructural theories, I will also discuss the pragmatic and technical dimensions of establishing and maintaining the wiki, including issues related to site vandalism and content vetting. Such problems aside, GlossaTechnologia demonstrates how wikis can be used to effectively harness the collective intelligence of a group of scholars to extend the knowledge base of a specific topic of interest and, by extension, their shared discipline. Further, it also functions as a site that increases the degree of interactivity between its collaborators, strengthening the sense of community in the field.

WikiWhy? A Theoretical Rationale
for GlossaTechnologia

I'd first like to retrace the thinking that initially led to the creation of this particular wiki-based project, the type of project that Mark Phillipson in this volume would categorize as a resource wiki, because its primary function involves "the assemblage of a collaborative knowledge base."[3] As stated earlier, GlossaTechnologia is a hybrid wiki/annotated bibliography of scholarly works relevant to the intersection of digital technology and rhetoric and composition studies. A collection of such works is, in its own right, a valuable resource, but it also seems especially fitting that the medium should in some way reflect the content of the message—otherwise, the irony of a print publication dealing with digital technology would be lost on no one. In this context, a Web-based bibliography made sense, although at first the question of what form—static Web site, blog, discussion board—was still very much up in the air. The name of the project, not incidentally, is derived from the *Glossa Ordinaria*, a famous book from the late Middle Ages that the classicist-cum-technologist James O'Donnell describes as "the common and widely disseminated medieval Bible commentary whose origins are still shrouded in mystery and which continued to grow and be relevant for centuries."[4] Although admittedly less ambitious than the centuries-old *Ordinaria*, the more modest GlossaTechnologia bears at least a conceptual resemblance to its forebear as a multiauthored, collaborative scholarly compendium.

Of course, annotated bibliographies can already be found online. *The Bedford Bibliography for Teachers of Writing* and *The Bedford Bibliography for Teachers of Basic Writing* are two examples from my academic field, both of them Web-based versions of print editions.[5] The fact that the online bibliographies are relatively faithful translations of their print-bound counterparts is precisely what makes them problematic in my mind. Aside from the benefit of increased access to the texts, there's no real payoff to bringing them online in this static form because the constraints posed by the medium of print—the inability to manipulate content, the lack of growth, the impermeable wall separating the readers from the writers—are still very much in play. By contrast, I wanted to adapt the annotated bibliography to this new medium in such a way that it extended its overall reach and utility by being updatable, dynamic, and dialogical. In short, I wanted the text to benefit from the multiple perspectives of its reader-contributors, and the wiki format struck me as a perfect way to meet that particular goal.

Although the wiki has been around since the mid-1990s, when Ward Cunningham's WikiWikiWeb first appeared, it has only recently become popular.[6] In fact, searching the LexisNexus database for *wiki* and related terms shows a dramatic uptick in popular media coverage in the last few years (2004–present), with a comparable dearth of coverage prior to 2000. Contemporary Web culture increasingly supports the social networking paradigm, and this bodes well for the wiki platform in general. This shift to social networking epitomizes the comparatively democratic read-write Web originally envisioned by the World Wide Web's creator, Tim Berners-Lee. Popular sites such as del.icio.us, Flickr, and Digg, where participants share, rate, construct folksonomies for, comment on, or tag content, have created a more hospitable climate that has enabled the wiki to flourish.[7] The benefit of such a paradigm is the potential to transcend individual intelligences via the phenomenon Steven Johnson calls "emergence." In his book of the same name, Johnson describes the effect that often occurs in networked systems, a "whole is smarter than its constituent parts" argument. According to Johnson, networked systems solve problems by drawing on masses of relatively stupid elements rather than a single, intelligent "executive branch." They are bottom-up systems, not top-down. They get their smarts from below. In a more technical language, they are complex adaptive systems that display emergent behavior. In these systems, agents residing on one scale start producing behavior that lies one scale above them: ants create colonies; urbanites create neighborhoods; simple pattern-recognition software learns how to recommend new books.[8] Add to Johnson's list the wiki-based annotated bibliography. When multiple contributors append annotation to annotation to annotation, patterns eventually develop that scale beyond the individual contributions, and an emergent type of consensus begins to form. In cases such as this, the more cooks in the kitchen, the better the broth.

WikiHow? A Pragmatics for GlossaTechnologia

Although pondering the theoretical contours of this project can be somewhat gratifying, it does not do much in the way of getting the site actually built. As a result, I'm going to shift my focus to the pragmatics of Glossa-Technologia and the logistical and technical details my development team and I worked out as we moved toward implementation.

Perhaps the most important initial decision we had to make was the choice of wiki platform. While there are a number of Web-based wiki products to choose from (among them PBwiki, TiddlyWiki, and Seed Wiki), in the end we chose to install MediaWiki on our own server account, the software engine behind the Wikipedia behemoth.[9] In our case, installing MediaWiki was somewhat involved because it was not an application supported by Fantastico, an automatic installer program we use on our server space. Thus, we needed to install it manually, but in the end the process was hardly complicated, especially since the MediaWiki site has fairly thorough documentation outlining the various steps involved as well as troubleshooting advice. There were a couple of reasons we selected MediaWiki over its Web-based counterparts. Although the setup is inherently more difficult, it is by far the most flexible and full-featured engine, allowing easier access to manipulate template files, style sheets, and the like. We also felt it was more capable of handling issues of scale—we wanted to be able to redesign or recategorize content easily if the organizational structure were to grow out of control. Additionally, MediaWiki's own flavor of wiki formatting tags is more familiar because of Wikipedia, WikiQuote, and other popular, high-profile wikis. Because wiki tags can be a bit arcane to new users, we wanted to use a platform that is positioned to become the lingua franca for wiki coding.

Aside from the technical issues, there are other factors to consider with respect to handling the creation and organization of content. Perhaps the most important issue deals with content vetting. How are we to ensure that the additions to GlossaTechnologia are in keeping with the site's scope and level of quality? To a large degree, this is the strength of a wiki: contributors determine community standards dynamically. And certainly at this early moment in the site's existence, our community is small and of a single mind-set as to what GlossaTechnologia should be. As a result, contributions and emendations have mostly been expected and appropriate to the site's mission. As the enterprise grows, however, so grows the risk of feature creep, and the need for as-yet-unaccounted-for functions, categories, and organizational structures will become apparent. Thus, developing strategies to maintain site cohesion will likely become more pressing in the near future. As one measure of curtailing such creep, we are currently in the midst of drafting a help document for the wiki that defines style, annotation length, and other best practices, with the acknowledgment that these attributes may well evolve as the site grows.

Of course, more than unintentional errors or irrelevant content, the problem of intentional site vandalism by spammers, trolls, and other malfeasants is one that inherently plagues wikis, or so the mainstream media would have us believe. Site vandalism can certainly be a real problem for wikis with higher traffic flows than ours, with Wikipedia perhaps the biggest target, but so far it has not been a big dilemma for GlossaTechnologia. For the immediate future, the development team is comfortable handling any needed fixes on the fly; anticipating a potential increase in vandalism in the future, we agree, will require revisiting this ad hoc policy, and we will perhaps consider locking certain portions of the site such as the pages peripheral to the bibliography itself (i.e., help documentation, contributors lists, the site's mission statement, etc.). At any rate, whether intentional or not, inappropriate content is to some extent a necessary part of building a sense of solidarity among a wiki community, a principle shared by the technorati. In fact, in a recent column for *Wired* magazine, noted technologist Joi Ito addressed just this issue when he was asked if Wikipedia was too vulnerable to the marks of vandals. Ito was particularly vociferous in his defense of Wikipedia:

> I have never seen a mainstream media article about Wikipedia that didn't itself contain errors. What's the retraction time for those errors? Wikipedia works because it's dynamic and alive and doesn't require the same structures as old-fashioned, slow media. Every time I make a change online, I notice it being checked and elaborated on in minutes. I wish people would stop comparing a living organism to deadwood.[10]

WikiWhen? Thoughts about the Project's Growth and Future

Chaos often breeds life, when order breeds habit.[11]

Any project developer worth his or her salt will tell you that, while it is important to mind the store of the present, it is perhaps even more important to anticipate the vicissitudes of the future. GlossaTechnologia is no exception in that regard. Already at this preliminary stage—what we might call our "alpha build"—we are seeing evidence of the aforementioned spammers on the wiki. In fact, an overzealous pharmaceutical representative recently hijacked our front page, enticing visitors to try certain body-altering drugs rather than contribute to our modest enterprise. Fixing the intrusion was easy enough, as we simply reverted the page to a previous iteration and locked the page to unauthorized edits, but the incident illustrates the attention needed to maintain a cohesive and clutter-free site.

Additionally, we quickly realized the need to devote some of our attention to developing a cleaner interface for contributors. For instance, rather than have contributors manually create them, we would rather have a front-page, one-click solution for easily adding new bibliographic entries. We are also looking into automated categorization for the entries as well, where users supplying new entries can check various boxes designating certain categories (media theory, digital literacy, etc.) rather than input them manually. Such streamlining measures will hopefully ensure that the site remains sticky for new and returning contributors alike.

Creating a sticky site, one that users want to continue to visit and build onto, is about more than just technical refinements—it also requires cultivating a network of human resources. Unlike the other wiki-based projects detailed in the "Wikis and the Higher Education Classroom" section of this volume, this one assumes a markedly different audience of readers and contributors. The motives and motivations for participating on the wiki are different when the audience is a group of loosely affiliated scholars from a range of institutions, ranks, and cultural contexts rather than a comparatively tightly knit group of students persuaded to participate in an instructor's assignment. Therefore, building and sustaining a community around this project, especially at this preliminary stage, will require some behind-the-scenes politicking, entreaties to colleagues for contributions, done in pyramid-scheme fashion, where each of the core team of developers reaches out to a handful of colleagues in the field and so on—in other words, some type of social fire stoking that will eventually result in a more or less self-sustaining community. We hope that after an initial period of somewhat artificial social networking the wiki will begin to take on a community dynamic of its own, precisely the kind of community evolution described by Gilbert, Chen, and Sabol in their chapter "Building Learning Communities with Wikis," included in this volume:

In the best-case scenario, a wiki becomes part of a thriving and sustainable learning community. In such a community, learners must move from just adopting the practices to adapting the tools. In this stage, the community moves from a centralized top-down structure to an organic structure where all contributors feel ownership over the intellectual framework, the site navigation, and wiki content. As a community, learners and the instructor collaboratively decide what information or media to include and how it should be organized. As the needs of the students evolve, they feel empowered to modify the tool to meet those needs. The community is also in a position to speculate what it might need for future work and can change the tools and work practices to support expected needs.[12]

Even in its most idealized form, GlossaTechnologia can't help but be a little rough around the edges; such is the simultaneous curse and blessing of the wiki structure. Still, a certain segment of potential readership may appreciate or even prefer a vetted, edited version of the site, not unlike Wikipedia's recently released Version 1.0, which is an offline version of the wiki available on DVD or in printed form issued by the editorial staff of Wikipedia. While on its face, such a static incarnation doesn't seem to embody the spirit of the wiki ethos, the option may actually be beneficial to the long-term viability of the project in a couple of respects. The self-serving rationale suggests that such products might lure otherwise unlikely readers to the site to see additional content not contained in the static version (in other words, the wiki is a value-added alternative). Moreover, a print edition may entice some readers to become contributors themselves, perhaps leading to subsequent editions. As for a more altruistic argument, a wider dissemination of the resource in multiple formats/media would help propagate a valuable resource so that it might aid those scholars just beginning to inquire into the topic.

Once it begins to realize its full potential, GlossaTechnologia stands to embody Harner's definition of what an annotated bibliography should be: a work containing the "determination, meticulousness, energy, time, critical acumen, and literary detective skills that one associates with the best scholarship of any kind."[13] Harner's claims, written well before the advent of the World Wide Web, outline a metric that the wiki format is well positioned to meet or even surpass, given its evolving, dynamic, self-correcting nature. Because this project is still in its gestational stages—fresh out of planning and into implementation—I hope to return to the ideas put forth in this chapter to assess whether my theoretical rationale is borne out by a more battle- hardened, mature GlossaTechnologia. To those ends, I not only invite feedback on the project but also encourage readers of this present volume to submit to the GlossaTechnologia project themselves by visiting http://www.rhetoricalcommons.org/gt/ and adding their own voices to the fray.[14]

NOTES

1. James L. Harner, *On Compiling an Annotated Bibliography* (New York: Modern Language Association, 1985), 1.

2. GlossaTechnologia, http://www.rhetoricalcommons.org/gt/ (accessed February 15, 2006).

3. Mark Phillipson, "Wikis in the Classroom: A Taxonomy," this volume.

4. James J. O'Donnell, *Avatars of the Word: From Papyrus to Cyberspace* (Cambridge, MA: Harvard University Press, 1998), 63. For more information on *Glossa Ordinaria*, see "Glossator," in Wikipedia, the Free Encyclopedia, http://en.wikipedia.org/wiki/Glossator.

5. Nedra Reynolds, Bruce Herzberg, and Patricia Bizzell, *The Bedford Bibliography for Teachers of Writing*, 6th ed. (Boston: Bedford St. Martin's Press, 2003), http://www.bedfordstmartins.com/bb/ (accessed February 17, 2006); Linda Adler-Kassner and Gregory R. Lau, *The Bedford Bibliography for Teachers of Basic Writing*, 2d ed. (Boston: Bedford St. Martin's Press, 2005), http://www.bedfordstmartins.com/basicbib (accessed February 17, 2006).

6. Ward Cunningham, WikiWikiWeb, Cunningham and Cunningham, Inc., http://c2.com/cgi/wiki (accessed February 15, 2006).

7. del.icio.us, Yahoo! Inc., http://del.icio.us/ (accessed February 14, 2006); Flickr, Yahoo! Inc., http://flickr.com (accessed February 15, 2006); Digg, http://www.digg.com/ (accessed February 15, 2006).

8. Steven Johnson, *Emergence: The Connected Lives of Ants, Brains, Cities, and Software* (New York: Scribner, 2001), 18.

9. PBwiki, http://pbwiki.com; TiddlyWiki, http://tiddlywiki.com; Seed Wiki, http://www.seedwiki.com; and MediaWiki, http://www.mediawiki.org/wiki/MediaWiki.

10. Joi Ito, "Ping: Is Wikipedia Too Vulnerable to Pranks and Errors?" *Wired*, March 28, 2006.

11. Henry Adams, *The Education of Henry Adams* (New York: Penguin, 1995), chap. 13.

12. Dan Gilbert, Helen L. Chen, and Jeremy Sabol, "Building Learning Communities with Wikis," this volume.

13. Harner, *On Compiling an Annotated Bibliography*, 32.

14. I would like to thank my development team, which includes Jason Palmeri (Ohio State University), J. Chambley (Ohio State University), and Scott Banville (Georgia Tech), for their help thus far in generating content for the wiki. I would also like to acknowledge our Web master, Ashley Miller, for her tireless contributions to the design and overall technical maintenance of the site.

An (Old) First-Timer's Learning Curve:
Curiosity, Trial, Resistance, and Accommodation

Come 'n listen to a story 'bout a man named Bob
A Boomer rhetorician, tried to open up his job,
He thought wiki-space was the place he oughtta be,
So he loaded up his server, tried some virtuality.
(Tried, that is. Multimedia; collaboration.)

This is a story about feeling excited, feeling old, feeling new, and feeling nervous. And I suspect that it's a story that many people who use new digital technologies, especially Web technologies, can identify with, especially when they use them for the first time.

First, the statutory confession: I am still a wiki novice. Or perhaps a wiki wannabe.

I know how wikis work; I know what they are capable of doing. I have used them; I have taught in, through, and with them. But I have yet to make use of them in the ways that they can, and perhaps should, be used. The reasons for this apparent resistance lie completely within myself—my own praxis of the last twenty years, governed by generational "terministic screens,"[1] and institutional stances growing out of the fluid nature of textual and personal privacy in the early twenty-first century. However, my experiences with wikis in my classes, as well as my reflections on this praxis, are pushing me toward more openness in my teaching structures and away from some of the remaining vestiges of current-traditional pedagogy in my teaching.

The Story

In spring 2004 and summer 2005, I decided to jump into the wiki stream and see how the water felt. I'd been impressed by a presentation on wikis at the Conference on College Composition and Communication, as well as discussions of wikis in Techrhet, an electronic mailing list for (mostly) writing teachers who use digital computer technology in their pedagogy and/or who study the effects of these technologies on writing and communication. But what really wowed me about wikis—and wows me now—was their front-end simplicity, instant editability, and the clear implication from their structurability that writing works in multiple planes and in multiple media. Who, I thought, would not want a system that allowed students to engage the multiple literacies digital technology provides? Who would not want a system that was nice looking; consistently formatted; and instantly changeable without having to mess with a hosting site log-in, independent of a complex authoring system, or even, for that matter, having to navigate to a virtual drive on one's computer? This, I thought, was cool, and I wanted to use a wiki because it was cool and because it represented what writing and its teaching are becoming. There is an irresistible pull of "coolness" for me, a forty-something admitted technophile. Indeed, I believe firmly that "cool" has a very appealing pull to over-forties in the techno-teaching biz, probably because it represents to us an opening up of the same old thing that many of us have done for longer than we may care to admit. (But more on this anon.)

So I went "a-huntin fer a wiki." This was not as easy as it might seem. I teach at an almost entirely Microsoft-dominated campus. Most wikis, though, don't provide the "slip a CD in and click the Install button" functionality of most Windows programs. This is not particularly odd, since interactive wikis tend to run on servers, for the most part, and many servers run on Unix or Linux. But for a writing teacher who also co-runs his Windows-based departmental Web server, this fact wasn't a big help.

I looked for a Windows-compatible, easily installable wiki application. Not easy; not impossible. Searching through several sources, asking colleagues and e-mail list correspondents, and Googling for wikis led me to a bewildering array of wikis, but few for Windows. I eventually settled on CourseForum, a commercially available wiki from CourseForum Technologies, designed specifically for education. I chose it because it contained, in a point-and-click installation package, all of the features of wikis that make them unique: Web presence, group or individual modifiability, ability to include multimedia elements, and relative ease of use. In structure and application, it is a "classic" wiki, providing the opportunity for students (or whomever, really) to work collaboratively on documents and add (albeit in a more limited fashion than a Web authoring program) graphics and links to resources either within the wiki or external to it.

Here's what I did: I created two different wiki spaces for two different sections of first-year composition. In spring 2004, I created a wikispace for a final project of an online first-year composition class; I envisioned it as an easy-to use Web authoring space for students who might otherwise have had to master a stand-alone authoring tool. Students could either create their own Web page from scratch and have me load it on the department server, or they could create it on CourseForum themselves in a password-protected space I made for them and have it right there, on the Web, as soon as they created it. This was an end-of-term project, and the opportunity extended only to the Web page project. In summer 2005, I created a course suite for an online first-year composition class. For this class, the wiki was used essentially as a course management system (CMS). I created separate, passworded spaces for each student, in which the students could post their papers, either written on the wiki space or attached as a Word document. They drafted; I read and commented; they revised; I graded.

Of course, you know what is wrong from reading these descriptions: I didn't really need a wiki to do what I had done. I didn't use the wiki as a wiki; I was, essentially, using the wiki the same way I would have used Blackboard or another CMS. To coin a phrase, I wasn't exploiting the wikiness of the wiki that had attracted me in the first place; to put it another way, I wasn't being true to the wiki's essence.

The Problem

I felt, and still feel, a pretty serious irony here, because for many years I've espoused the "transformative" model of writing class curricula in my publications and teaching. Simply put, writing is changing from static text to something that lives, breathes, and moves and from something that had length to something with length and breadth. If, therefore, we as writing teachers are going to teach writing, we might as well teach the kind of writing that is changing rather than simply teach traditional text production with tools that allow, if not suggest, other possible options. The profound irony, of course, is that I did not take advantage of the possibilities of the wiki. I fell back into the safe, the usual, the predictable, the easy. Did I "do the same old thing"? Sadly, yes.

True, a wiki can perfectly well be a CMS; the wiki does storage, retrieval, and (arguably) multimediation and hypertextuality as well as many other CMSs and even better than some (you can't link from page to page in Blackboard, for example, and uploading files can, depending on the wiki, take a lot less effort and fewer clicks). But the fact of using a wiki to do the same things as other tools bugged, and still bugs, me; I used the wiki for purposes that could have been replicated by other software tools. In addition, by assigning passwords to students' individual wiki spaces, I kept student work separate and unitary, reinforcing the idea that writing is a completely solitary act and preventing even the possibility of collaboration.

The Reasons

Reason 1. The twenty-first-century writing teacher who grew up anytime before, say, 1990 is a curious, polypolar creature. She or he has feet firmly in two rhetorical traditions (actually not traditions—it would be better to call them two completely different planets). This teacher's praxis is often an exquisite tug-of-war between the desire and strongly felt need, not to mention the theoretical and experiential certainty, to employ truly transformational technopedagogy—such as a wiki, or multimediation, or visual rhetoric, or online learning, or any one or more of a number of technoliteracies that are shaping our profession—on the one hand, and the very difficult to discard traditions and patterns of earlier-learned and hard-to-break, even primary, rhetorical literacies. So many of us came of rhetorical age, so to speak, in what I call the "Age of Rhetorical Linearity" that the movement into hyper-mediation, and toward substantial extratextual mediation, is a profound and career-changing, if not indeed life-changing, experience.

Let's take my own praxis as an example. My first teacher training was almost literally a firm handshake and a copy of a Sheridan Baker rhetoric (*The Complete Handbook and Stylist*, 2d ed.). Keyhole diagrams, march! I went to college in the late 1970s and to grad school in the early 1980s. Linearity ruled. I typed most of my college and MA-level papers on a manual typewriter. In my PhD program, I taught in a computer lab, but the focus of the lab was to enable people to use the IBM PCs as, essentially, typewriters that allowed easy revision. Papers were papers, not multimedia projects; they were still the black-and-white constructions that college students had been writing since the mid-1800s or earlier. What did I write from undergraduate through graduate school, from 1975 to 1990? Papers. My only "interactive space" was the department lounge, or the bar my friends and I went to on Friday evenings, or perhaps the telephone, but it wasn't the Web, and any meaning I made in these spaces was probably not academic.

Like Jed Clampett, from the *Beverly Hillbillies* TV show of the 1960s, I am treading between two worlds. And therefore when I hear Rich Rice note (for example), "writing teachers are not highly visually literate" and are "not skilled visual readers,"[2] I jump up and raise my hand to testify, because he's talking about me. I yearn for openness and a wiki-enabled community of writers, eagerly and freely collaborating on meaning. But—and this is a really significant but—like Betsy, the old horse drawing the milk delivery wagon in the classic film *Meet Me in St. Louis*, I tend to gravitate to older paths, older patterns; like Betsy, who stops at a house even though its occupants have moved away, I and others tend to move in the same places, and I lean me in the direction of "papers," teacher-to-reader dyads, and things like "thesis statements," while still wanting to "move away" toward contemporarily effective teaching.

Reason 2. We live in a culture of openness and security, of knowledge expansion and knowledge hiding. Google freely gives us all the information we could ask for, yet there are some things we must keep secret, for practical reasons—such as our Social Security numbers—or for our own personal reasons. We spread our lives upon the Internet, yet we may also retreat when others spread their lives too close to ours in venues such as Facebook, My-

Space, or Friendster. In an atmosphere in which we are still navigating the "rules" of publicity and privacy, the old saw of "information wants to be free" doesn't make us feel all that much better, and while we find ourselves marveling at the cheek, the moxie, the boldness of those who put on the Web what we see with wonder and amazement, we are at once attracted and repelled. We log on to Facebook and marvel at the aptitude of our students in forming communities of interest and affinity, yet we are startled at the nature of the photos that, after repeated warnings, they still place online.

We're on a playing field in which the things we can do are fast outstripping the concepts we've long held of what we should do. Therefore, in such an inchoate environment we and our administrative systems find ourselves constructing boundaries—safe boundaries, appropriate boundaries, and legal boundaries. In my case, institutional policy had a part in my decision; the administrative culture where I work values the safety and privacy of student work. For example, we've been encouraged to make student blog comments anonymous when we use Blogger, whose blogs are, technically, open to the Web (and cannot currently be limited via password to the blog's members). Other discussions on Techrhet, as well as mandates at my own institution, have raised the issue of how private student work must remain. For example, can a student be required to do group work on a wiki—or elsewhere? If work is publicly available on the Web, what information may/must/ought to be concealed? What are the policies, assumptions, or requirements of the university, college, department, or program? The ability of a wiki to be password protected (or not) relatively easily adds to the security of student work; it also works against the "communal rhetoric" or "public rhetoric" nature of wikis that make them so inviting to teachers in the first place.

In this context, then, I have stuggled—and continue to struggle—with the issue of collaboration. Although I have in theory always desired to promote collaborative projects among my students, I have also found it difficult to put this goal into practice, in part because I can't stop thinking, as many of us doubtless do, that the student paper is the student's paper. Brian Lamb echoes this sense of absolute ownership—and the subsequent fear of collaboration or community—when he notes a common resistance thread: "[Newcomers often say] 'If anybody can edit my text, then anybody can ruin my text.' Human nature being what it is, to allow free access to hard earned content is to indulge open-source utopianism beyond reason."[3]

What Next?

Earlier I noted that I had not been true to the wiki. This sounds a little odd, perhaps, because it seems as if the software is driving the class. I was, and am, crucially aware of the oft-repeated injunction not to let the technology drive the class. Notre Dame's Barbara Walvoord enjoins us, for example, to let the outcomes of the course determine the technology and not the other way around.[4] And, quite honestly, "not being true to the wiki" does, admittedly, make the wiki sound either like a soon-to-be disappointed deity or a HAL 2000–like, omnipresent intelligence—"Bob? What are you doing, Bob? Why are you separating and password protecting all the student papers, Bob?"—or perhaps some kind of 1960s self-actualizing guru.

But if we take a look at the wiki as a technology that enables a certain praxis; and if we take a closer look at the polyrhetorical nature of a twenty-first-century writing class; and, finally, if we accept collaborative creation as a value, a good, that we must promulgate in our classes, we can see ways in which the technology can drive the class—indeed, ways that it must drive the class. If we accept that one of the purposes of a twenty-first-century writing class is to navigate literacies beyond the textual and to "pay attention," as Cynthia Selfe urges, to the technologies we use to make literate artifacts, then the choice of technology can determine the outcome rather than the other way around, because the technology, rather than being adjunct to the enterprise of teaching the subject, is in significant and consistent ways the subject itself of the teaching.[5]

Handholds for Wiki Novices

First, realize that a wiki can be a lot of things, one of which is a wiki. You can use a wiki as a CMS, or as a paper dump, or as a collaborative work space wherein you can track changes and encourage a sense of collaborative exploration. The Office of Learning Technology at the University of British Columbia puts it this way:

> There is no quicker way to get text online. Anyone can post from any machine and there are no permissions required or passwords to remember. This makes wikis ideal for keeping an ongoing list of resources, posting meeting agendas and notes, or creating a space for collaborative brainstorming and composition. . . . [U]sers . . . are using wikis to support group work, for project planning, as bulletin boards, to author content for WebCT courses, to complement conferences and events, and to support course experiments in hypertext composition.[6]

But Brian Lamb states: "Indeed, an instructor could structure and regulate interaction to such an extent that the wiki is effectively transformed to a stripped-down course management system. But doing so risks diluting the special qualities that make wikis worth using in the first place."[7] You choose; you're the teacher. I will only say that if you aren't aware of what wikis can do and enable, you may find yourself feeling like you're driving the Ferrari at twenty miles an hour because you don't know how to get out of first gear.

Take a good look at yourself. (Or, in the best traditions of academic jargon, "interrogate your praxis.") Ask yourself, "What do I want to do? Where do I want my students to end up? What do I want them to know/believe/comprehend/be at the end of the term?" The most important thing any teacher can do with any kind of digital technology—or, really, any technology—is to consider her or his own teaching style, the outcomes that she or he has thoughtfully decided on for the course and students, and the possible technologies that can be employed to best achieve those outcomes. A wiki may not be where you want to go—though as flexible as they are, you might want to give one a look.

Take some time to jump in and test the water. Have fun. You'll need to. Wikis are not spur of the moment things. If you are the kind of writer and teacher who values linearity, then you should put in a goodly bit of time before you "go live" with the wiki on a class of real, human students. One very good reason for doing so is that while you can impose linearity on the texts you put in a wiki, wikis themselves resist linearity—indeed, they flout it. They can and do go all over the place.

Wikis invite creative messiness. They are ideally places where writers can get in there and wallow around in an (almost) totally textual environment. If you can't handle messiness, or the potential for such, or if you need to give it some time, then do just that—give it some time. Look around. Push the buttons, ring the bells, blow the whistles—shoot, you might even read the documentation. Get on others' wikis and play in the spaces that are there just for that purpose. We live and teach in a world wherein new venues, ideas, descriptions of writing, rhetorical expressivities, and rhetorics are springing up almost daily. The opportunity to try things out and see what will happen is absolutely necessary. Wikis—like all innovative, nontraditional pedagogies and technologies—deserve a chance. (And I've got to say that one of the great features of wikis—that they "save copies of successively edited versions" so that "work that has been deleted or defaced with a couple of clicks of the mouse" can be retrieved—is worth its weight in gold, for I accidentally deleted this entire chapter the evening it was due; five minutes later, I had retrieved a slightly earlier version and was typing away.)

Be a pioneer. Even though there may be a plethora of prepackaged systems, in a box or online, available for teachers, wikis are still, to some extent, in a grassroots stage. If you want a wiki, you'll likely have to ask for one, and you may well have to explain what a wiki is and why you want to use it (especially if you want to host it on your school's Web server).[8]

Do your homework. Look at several wiki packages. Ask around at your school to see if anyone is using wikis; ask your IT division if they can host a wiki on a school server. You may be the only one at your school who wants to do this. This is not necessarily a bad thing, but you need to be aware that you'll likely have to figure out how it works yourself. Though there are many resources for wiki novices, wikispace and its navigation are still, I believe, at least partially in the "Hmm, let's see how this works" stage.

Help the people who will help you. Sitting down and thinking for a minute about how to pitch a wiki installation will reap benefits in the end. Be ready to explain why you want the wiki. Since you'll have played around with one and will know what it can do, you'll be able to call one up on the Web and show what it can do. Instructional technology offices, in my experience, are often looking for ways to engage faculty with learning technology—that is, after all, their job—and they may be quite receptive to a faculty member wanting to try something new.

Model wikispace for your students. If there is anything I learned from my summer's nonevent with my students, it was that, if I wasn't there, they wouldn't be there either. Wikis are not a matter of "If you build it, they will come." Though they may be profoundly technology-savvy, wikis may be unfamiliar to them. Build your own pages; ask them to edit, modify, and repurpose them. Show them Wikipedia; choose an article that needs editing and edit it for them on the screen. Explain the concept of wikispace; then encourage student buy-in by having them create small, informal group pages that others can add to and edit. Modeled guidance in wikispace can lead to an understanding of collaborative ethics and group rhetoric and can avoid free-for-all anarchy.

Loosen up. This, of course, is the hardest thing for me to learn, after having been "in power" for more than twenty years. But Joe Moxley, M. C. Morgan, Matt Barton, and Donna Hanak state it best: in a wiki, "Textual authority is dialogical. Revision is privileged in the wiki. Each new reader can suddenly become a writer. The draft that matters is the last draft. Power and authority are given to the community rather than an individual or official staff."⁹ Start now, then, to see how you will be able to let texts be altered on a daily, if not hourly, basis. Think of how you can encourage a kind of freedom to write, to tinker, to experiment.

Would I do it again? You bet. Indeed, I am doing it again. This summer I am teaching the same online class but building it much differently. Students will still have separate places for some short assignments, but they will also have open spaces in which they will place and edit their papers. I'm working on a collaborative project to which they will all contribute, and, perhaps most important, we'll start the term with a discussion—in the wiki, of course—of collaboration, collaborative ethics, and the nature of the wiki space. Will it work? I don't know. The most important lesson that I find I will have to teach myself, though, is to remind myself constantly what I am doing and why I chose the technology in the first place. As I allow the technology to help me drive the pedagogy, it's more important than ever for me to pay attention to the technology. I am, however, much more confident now than I was a year ago. I've faced my praxis—perhaps the most difficult step—I've come to an accommodation on the issues of privacy (students will need to log on to the wiki but will have few other restrictions), and I'm (almost) ready to go. Like Jed Clampett, once I've gotten used to the issues and people in this new world, I hope to be a lot better able to navigate in it.

NOTES

1. James Berlin, *Rhetoric and Reality: Writing Instruction in American Colleges, 1900–1985* (Carbondale: Southern Illinois University Press, 1987), 17. Berlin discusses "terministic screens" as those elements of one's background and composition that inevitably affect and color one's point of view, absolute neutral objectivity being, according to Berlin (who refers to Kenneth Burke, Hayden White, Michel Foucault, and others), impossible.

2. Rich Rice and Cheryl Ball, "Reading the Text; Remediating the Text," *Kairos* 10, no. 2 (spring 2006), http://english.ttu.edu/kairos/10.2/binder2.html?coverweb/rice ball/index.html (accessed May 8, 2006).

3. Brian Lamb, "Wide Open Spaces: Wikis, Ready or Not," *Educause Review*, September–October 2004, 37–48 (quote is from p. 40), http://connect.educause.edu/Li brary/EDUCAUSE+Review/WideOpenSpacesWikisReadyo/40498.

4. Barbara Walvoord, workshop presentation at Creighton University, spring 2000.

5. Cynthia Selfe, *Technology and Literacy in the Twenty-First Century: The Importance of Paying Attention* (Carbondale: Southern Illinois University Press, 1999).

6. Office of Learning Technology, Weblogs and Wikis, University of British Columbia, http://www.olt.ubc.ca/projects_home/pp.html (accessed May 9, 2006).

7. Lamb, "Wide Open Spaces," 45.

8. You don't have to host it on your school's server, of course; wikis can be hosted on any of a number of commercial Web hosts; some hosts have setups that allow one to automatically install a wiki in one's space on their server.

9. Joe Moxley, M. C. Morgan, Matt Barton, and Donna Hanak, "For Teachers New to Wikis," http://writingwiki.org/default.aspx/ Writingwiki/For%20 Teachers %20New %20to%20wikis.html (accessed March 20, 2006).

Bibliography

Adams, Henry. *The Education of Henry Adams.* New York: Penguin, 1995.

Adler-Kassner, Linda, and Gregory R. Lau. *The Bedford Bibliography for Teachers of Basic Writing.* 2d ed. Boston: Bedford St. Martin's Press, 2005. http://www.bedfordst martins.com/basicbib.

Aguiar, Ademar, and Gabriel David. "WikiWiki Weaving Heterogeneous Software Artifacts." Paper presented at the 2005 International Symposium on Wikis. http://www.wikisym.org/ws2005/proceedings/paper-07.pdf.

Alexander, Christopher. *A Pattern Language: Towns, Buildings, Construction.* New York: Oxford University Press, 1977.

Bagdikian, Ben H. *The New Media Monopoly.* Boston: Beacon Press, 2004.

Barton, Matthew. "The Future of Rational-Critical Debate in Online Public Spheres." *Computers and Composition* 22, no. 2 (2005): 177–90.

Benkler, Yochai. *The Wealth of Networks: How Social Production Transforms Markets and Freedom.* New Haven: Yale University Press, 2006.

Berlin, James. *Rhetoric and Reality: Writing Instruction in American Colleges, 1900–1985.* Carbondale: Southern Illinois University Press, 1987.

Berlin, James. *Rhetorics, Poetics, and Cultures: Refiguring College English Studies.* West Lafayette, IN: Parlor Press, 2003.

Berners-Lee, Tim. Talk presented at the MIT Laboratory of Computer Science thirty-fifth anniversary celebration. Cambridge MA, April 14, 1999. http://www.w3.org/1999/04/13-tbl.html.

Berthoff, Ann E. "A Curious Triangle and the Double-Entry Notebook." In *The Making of Meaning: Metaphors, Models, and Maxims for Writing Teachers,* 41–47. Montclair, NJ: Boynton Cook, 1981.

Berthoff, Ann E., and James Stephens. *Forming, Thinking, Writing.* 2d ed. Portsmouth, NH: Boynton Cook, 1988.

Blogs and Wikis Contributors. "BlogsAndWikis: TheCollectiveNotebook." Bemidji State University. http://ferret.bemidjistate.edu/~morgan/WeblogsAndWikis/wikka.php?wakka=TheCollectiveNotebook.

Blom, Phillipp. *Enlightening the World: Encyclopédie, the Book That Changed the Course of History.* New York: Palgrave Macmillan, 2005.

Bolter, Jay David. *Writing Space: Computers, Hypertext, and the Remediation of Print.* 2d ed. Mahwah, NJ: Lawrence Erlbaum Associates, 2001.

Bowdoin College. Romantic Audience Project. http://ssad.bowdoin.edu:8668/space/snipsnap-index;jsessionid=16rfhc650fb6.

Bowdoin College. Romantic Audience Project 2. http://ssad.bowdoin.edu:9780/snipsnap/eng242-s05/space/start.

Bowen, Matthew R. "WriteHere.net." http://web.archive.org/web/20060310114550/http://www.writehear.net/moin.cgi/FrontPage.

Breton, André. *Les Manifestes du Surréalisme: Suivis de Prolégomènes à un Troisième Manifeste du Surréalisme ou Non*. Paris: Sagittaire, 1946.

Breton, André. *Second Manifesto*. 1930. Quoted in Alastair Brotchie, compiler, *Surrealist Games*. London: Redstone Press, 1991.

Bruffee, Kenneth A. "Collaborative Learning and the 'Conversation of Mankind.'" *College English* 46, no. 7 (November 1984): 635–52.

Burke, Kenneth. *The Philosophy of Literary Form: Studies in Symbolic Action*. 3d ed. Berkeley: University of California Press, 1973.

Burrow, Andrew Lincoln. "Negotiating Access within Wiki: A System to Construct and Maintain a Taxonomy of Access Rules." Paper presented at the ACM Conference on Hypertext and Hypermedia, Santa Cruz, CA. http://portal.acm.org/citation.cfm?id=1012831.

Bush, Vannevar. "As We May Think." *Atlantic Monthly*, July 1945, 101–8.

Cadello, James P. "Fears and Questions Concerning Technology." In *Technology, Morality, and Social Policy*, ed. Eager Hudson, 1–14. Lewiston, NY: Edwin Mellen Press, 1997.

Castells, Manuel. *The Rise of the Network Society*. Vol. 1 of *The Information Age: Economy, Society, and Culture*. Cambridge, MA: Blackwell, 1996.

Center for History and New Media. "Hurricane Digital Memory Bank." George Mason University et al. http://www.hurricanearchive.org.

"Chancellor Davis Keynotes Fall Conference Meeting." *The Georgia Conference: AAUP Summary* 24, no. 2 (fall 2006). http://www2.gsu.edu/%7Ehishdh/AAUP%20Fall%202006.pdf.

Chazalette, Jean-Christophe. "Wikipen." http://en.wikipen.org/wiki/Main_Page.

Chen, Helen L., David Cannon, Jonathan Gabrio, Larry Leifer, George Toye, and Tori Bailey. "Using Wikis and Weblogs to Support Reflective Learning in an Introductory Engineering Design Course." In *Human Behavior in Design '05*, ed. J. S. Gero and U. Lindemann, 95–105. Sydney: University of Sydney, Key Centre of Design Computing and Cognition, 2005.

Chen, Helen L., Dan Gilbert, and Jeremy Sabol. "Using Wikis to Build Learning Communities: Successes, Failures, and Next Steps." Poster presented at the annual meeting for the Educause Learning Initiative, San Diego, CA, January 29–31, 2006.

Chodorow, Stanley. "Scholarship, Information, and Libraries in the Electronic Age." In *Development of Digital Libraries: An American Perspective*, ed. Deanna B. Marcum. Westport, CT: Greenwood Press, 2001.

The Colbert Report. Comedy Central, Production No. 101. Originally aired October 17, 2005.

The Colbert Report. Comedy Central, Production No. 2096. Originally aired July 31, 2006.

Columbia University. SacredGotham. http://sacredgotham.ccnmtl.columbia.edu.

Columbia University. "Social Justice Movements: About." http://socialjustice.ccnmtl.columbia.edu/index.php/About. 2006.

Coover, Robert. "The End of Books." *New York Times*, June 21, 1992, 11, 23–25.

Cunningham, Ward. "ConvertThreadModeToDocumentMode." Cunningham and Cunningham, Inc. http://c2.com/cgi/wiki?ConvertThreadModeToDocumentMode.

Cunningham, Ward. "DoTheSimplestThingThatCouldPossiblyWork." Cunningham and Cunningham, Inc. http://c2.com/xp/DoTheSimplestThingThatCouldPossibly Work.html.

Cunningham, Ward. "DoubleLines." Cunningham and Cunningham, Inc. http://www.c2.com/cgi/wiki?DoubleLines.

Cunningham, Ward. "Informal History of Programming Ideas." Cunningham and Cunningham, Inc. http://c2.com/cgi/wiki?InformalHistoryofProgramingIdeas.

Cunningham, Ward. "RefactorTowardsTheCenterOfThePage." Cunningham and Cunningham, Inc. http://c2.com/cgi/wiki?RefactorTowardsTheCenterOfThePage.

Cunningham, Ward. "ThereforeBut." Cunningham and Cunningham, Inc. http://www.c2.com/cgi/wiki?ThereforeBut.

Cunningham, Ward. "ThreadMess." Cunningham and Cunningham, Inc. http://c2.com/cgi/wiki?ThreadMess.

Cunningham, Ward. "WhyWikiWorks." Cunningham and Cunningham, Inc. http://c2.com/cgi/wiki?WhyWikiWorks.

Cunningham, Ward. "Wiki History." Cunningham and Cunningham, Inc. http://c2.com/cgi/wiki?InvitationToThePatternsList.

Cunningham, Ward. WikiWikiWeb, Cunningham and Cunningham, Inc., http://c2.com/cgiwiki.

Cushman, Ellen. *The Struggle and the Tools: Oral and Literate Strategies in an Inner City Community.* Albany: State University of New York Press, 1998.

Davies, Jonathan. "Wiki Brainstorming and Problems with Wiki Based Collaboration." University of York, 2004. http://www-users.cs.york.ac.uk/~kimble/teaching/students/Jonathan_Davies/wiki_collaboration_and_brainst orming.pdf.

del.icio.us. Yahoo! Inc. http://del.icio.us.

Désilets, Alain. Sébastien Paquet, and Norman G. Vinson. "Are Wikis Usable?" In *Wikisym 2005: Proceedings of the 2005 International Symposium on Wikis,* 3–15. New York: Association for Computing Machinery, 2005.

Digg. http://www.digg.com.

Dunbar, Robin. "Neocortex Size as a Constraint on Group Size in Primates." *Journal of Human Evolution* 20 (1992): 462–93.

edwiki.org. "Design Patterns for EduWikis—IncubatorWiki." http://edwiki.org/mw/index.php/Design_Patterns_for_EduWikis.

Elbow, Peter. *Writing without Teachers.* New York: Oxford University Press, 1973.

ElephantStaircase Wiki. http://www.elephantstaircase.com/wiki/index.php?title=Main_Page.

Encyclopædia Britannica, Inc. "Fatally Flawed: Refuting the Recent Study on Encyclopedic Accuracy by the Journal Nature." March 2006. http://corporate.britannica.com/britannica_nature_response.pdf.

Ess, Charles, ed. *Philosophical Perspectives on Computer-Mediated Communication.* Albany: State University of New York Press, 1996.

Feenberg, Andrew. *Critical Theory of Technology.* New York: Oxford University Press, 1991.

Feenberg, Andrew. *Transforming Technology: A Critical Theory Revisited.* New York: Oxford University Press, 2002.

Ferguson, Alfred R., ed. *The Collected Works of Ralph Waldo Emerson.* Vol. 1. Cambridge, MA: Harvard University Press, 1971.

Flannery, Kathryn T. "Composing and the Question of Agency." Review of *Writing as Social Action,* by Marilyn Cooper and Michael Holzman; *Reclaiming Pedagogy: The Rhetoric* of the Classroom, by Patricia Donahue and Ellen Quandahl, eds.; Rescuing the Subject: A Critical Introduction to Rhetoric and the Writer, by Susan Miller; Expecting the Unexpected: Teaching Myself—and Others—to Read and Write, by Donald M. Murray; and The Presence of Thought: Introspective Accounts of Reading and Writing, by Marilyn S. Sternglass. College English 53, no. 6 (October 1991): 701–13.

Flickr. Yahoo! Inc. http://flickr.com.

Foucault, Michel. "What Is an Author?" Partisan Review 42 (1975): 603–14.

Frechette, Julie. Developing Media Literacy in Cyberspace: Pedagogy and Critical Learning for the Twenty-First-Century Classroom. Westport, CT: Praeger, 2002.

Freire, Paulo. Pedagogy of the Oppressed. Trans. Myra Bergman Ramos. New York: Continuum, 1993.

Garza, Susan Loudermilk, and Tommy Hern. "Collaborative Writing Tools: Something Wiki This Way Comes—Or Not!" Kairos 10, no. 1 (2005). http://english.ttu.edu/kairos/10.1/binder2.html?http://falcon.tamucc.edu/wiki/WikiArticle/Home.

Giles, Jim. "Special Report: Internet Encyclopedias Go Head to Head." Nature, March 28, 2006. http://www.nature.com/nature/journal/v438/n7070/full/438900a.html.

GlossaTechnologia. http://www.rhetoricalcommons.org/gt/.

Goldman-Segall, Rick. "Configuration Validity: A Proposal for Analyzing Multimedia Ethnographic Narratives." Journal for Educational Multimedia and Hypermedia 4, no. 2 (1995): 163–82.

Goldman-Segall, Rick. "Gender and Digital Media in the Context of a Middle School Science Project." Meridian, an Online Journal on Middle School Education 1, no. 1 (1948), http://www.ncsu.edu/meridian.

Goldman-Segall, Ricki. "Learning Constellations: A Multimedia Ethnographic Research Environment Using Video Technology to Explore Children's Thinking." PhD diss., MIT, 1990.

Guzdial, Mark. "Information Ecology of Collaborations in Educational Settings: Influence of Tool." In Proceedings of Computer-Supported Collaborative Learning 1997. Toronto, ON, 1997. http://www.oise.utoronto.ca/cscl/papers/guzdial.pdf.

Guzdial, Mark, Pete Ludovice, Matthew Realff, Tom Morley, and Karen Carroll. "When Collaboration Doesn't Work." Georgia Institute of Technology, 2002. http://coweb.cc.gatech.edu:8888/csl/uploads/24/CMCI-ICLS-final.pdf.

Guzdial, Mark, Jochen Rick, and Colleen Kehoe. "Beyond Adoption to Invention: Teacher-Created Collaborative Activities in Higher Education." Journal of the Learning Sciences 10, no. 3 (2002): 265–79.

Harner, James L. On Compiling an Annotated Bibliography. New York: MLA, 1985.

Harvard University. "Biotechnology: Academic, Government & Industry Interactions and Tensions 2006." http://web.archive.org/web/20070827140819/http://www.hcs.harvard.edu/~cyberlaw/wiki/index. php/Biotech.

Hawisher, Gail, and Cynthia Selfe. "The Rhetoric of Technology and the Electronic Writing Class." College Composition and Communication 42 (1991): 55–65. Reprinted in The Writing Teacher's Sourcebook, 4th ed., ed. Edward P. J. Corbett, Nancy Myers, and Gary Tate. New York: Oxford University Press, 2000.

Heim, Michael H. "Heidegger and McLuhan and the Essence of Virtual Reality." In Philosophy of Technology: The Technological Condition: An Anthology, ed. Robert C. Scharff and Val Dusek, 539–55. Malden, MA: Blackwell, 2003.

Higdon, Jude. "Teaching, Learning, and Other Uses for Wikis in Academia." *Campus Technology.* http://www.campustechnology.com/articles/40629.

Hillocks, George. *Teaching Writing as Reflective Practice.* New York: Teachers College Press, 1995.

Hillside.net. "Hillside History." 2003. http://hillside.net/history.html.

Hillside.net. "A History of Patterns." 2003. http://www.c2.com/cgi/wiki?HistoryOfPatterns.

Hine, Christine. *Virtual Ethnography.* London: Sage Publications, 2000.

Hof, Robert D. "Something Wiki This Way Comes." *Business Week,* June 7, 2004, 128.

Horner, Bruce, and Min-Zhan Lu. *Representing the "Other": Basic Writers and the Teaching of Basic Writing.* Urbana, IL: NCTE, 1999.

Howard, Rebecca Moore. *Standing in the Shadow of Giants: Plagiarists, Authors, Collaborators.* Stamford, CT: Ablex, 1999.

"if:book." Institute for the Future of the Book. http://www.futureofthebook.org/blog/2006/02/the_value_of_voice.html.

Ito, Joi. "Ping: Is Wikipedia Too Vulnerable to Pranks and Errors?" *Wired,* March 28, 2006.

James, Heather. "My Brilliant Failure: Wikis in Classrooms." *Kairosnews.* http://kairosnews.org/node/3794.

Johnson-Eilola, Johndan. *Nostalgic Angels: Rearticulating Hypertext Writing.* Norwood, NJ: Ablex, 1997.

Johnson-Eilola, Johndan, and Amy Kimme Hea. "After Hypertext: Other Ideas." *Computers and Composition* 20 (2003): 425.

Johnson, Steven. *Emergence: The Connected Lives of Ants, Brains, Cities, and Software.* New York: Scribner, 2001.

Kaiser Family Foundation. "Generation M: Media in the Lives of 8–18 Year-Olds." Kaiser Family Foundation. March 9, 2005. http://www.kff.org/entmedia/entmedia030905pkg.cfm.

Koschmann, Timothy. *DCSCL: Theory and Practice of an Emerging Paradigm (Computers, Cognition, and Work).* Mahwah, NJ: Lawrence Erlbaum, 1996.

Kozlovsky, Roy. "The Junk Playground: Creative Destruction as Antidote to Delinquency." Paper presented at the Threat and Youth Conference, Teachers College, Columbia University, April 1, 2006. http://threatnyouth.pbwiki.com/f/Junk%20Playgrounds-Roy%20Kozlovsky.pdf.

Kress, Gunther. *Literacy in the New Media Age.* London: Routledge, 2003.

Lamb, Brian. "Wide Open Spaces: Wikis, Ready or Not." *Educause Review,* September–October 2004, 37–48. http://connect.educause.edu/Library/EDUCAUSE+Review/WideOpenSpacesWikisReadyo/40498.

Landow, George P. *Hypertext 2.0: The Convergence of Contemporary Critical Theory and Technology.* Baltimore: Johns Hopkins University Press, 1997.

Landow, George P., ed. *Hyper/Text/Theory.* Baltimore: Johns Hopkins University Press, 1994.

Lanham, Richard A. *Analyzing Prose.* 2d ed. New York: Continuum, 2003.

Lashinsky, Adam. "Cashing in on Wiki-ness." *Entrepreneurs* 154, no. 5 (2006): 34.

Lessig, Lawrence. *Free Culture.* New York: Penguin Press, 2004.

Leuf, Bo, and Ward Cunningham. *The Wiki Way*. Boston: Addison-Wesley, 2001. http://www.wiki.org.

Lih, Andrew. "Wikipedia as Participatory Journalism: Reliable Sources? Metrics for Evaluating Collaborative Media as a News Source." *Proceedings of the Fifth International Symposium on Online Journalism*, Austin, TX, 2004.

Lunsford, Andrea, and Lisa Ede. "Collaborative Authorship and the Teaching of Writing." In *The Construction of Authorship: Textual Appropriation in Law and Literature*, ed. Martha Woodmansee and Peter Jaszi, 417–38. Durham, NC: Duke University Press, 1994.

Lynch, Clifford. "Authenticity and Integrity in the Digital Environment: An Exploratory Analysis of the Central Role of Trust." In *Authenticity in a Digital Environment*. Washington, DC: Council on Library and Information Resources, 2000.

Lyotard, Jean-François. *The Postmodern Condition: A Report on Knowledge*. Minneapolis: University of Minnesota Press, 2002.

Manovich, Lev. *The Language of New Media*. Cambridge, MA: MIT Press, 2001.

McDowell, Dan. "Children of the Holocaust: A Webquest for 10th Grade World History and Humanities." http://www.guhsd.net/mcdowell/wq/children.

McDowell, Dan. "Holocaust Wiki Project." http://www.ahistoryteacher.com/holocaust/tiki-index.php.

McDowell, Dan. "Holocaust Wiki Project Evaluation." http://www.ahistoryteacher.com/holocaustproject/holocaust-rubric.html.

McGill University. "339–2005 Speed of Soundsome—McGill University Physics Department Technical Services Wiki." 2006. http://www.ugrad.physics.mcgill.ca/wiki/index.php/339-2005_Speed_of_Soundsome.

McGill University. "PHYS-339 Measurements Lab—McGill University Physics Department Technical Services Wiki." http://www.ugrad.physics.mcgill.ca/wiki/index.php/PHYS-339.

McHenry, Robert. "The Faith-Based Encyclopedia." Tech Central Station. http://www.techcentralstation.com/111504A.html.

McLuhan, Marshall. *Understanding Media: The Extension of Man*. New York: Signet Books, 1964.

MeatballWiki. http://www.usemod.com/cgi-bin/mb.pl.

MediaWiki. Wikimedia Foundation. http://www.mediawiki.org/wiki/MediaWiki.

Meltzer, Françoise. *Hot Property: The Stakes and Claims of Literary Originality*. Chicago: University of Chicago Press, 1994.

Miller, Susan. "The Student's Reader Is Always Fiction." *Journal of Advanced Composition* 5 (1984): 15–29.

Morgan, M. C. "BlogsAndWikis: HomePage." Bemidji State University. http://ferret.bemidjistate.edu/~morgan/WeblogsAndWikis.

Morgan, M. C., and Blogs and Wikis Contributors. "BlogsAndWikis: StyleGuide." Bemidji State University. http://ferret.bemidjistate.edu/~morgan/WeblogsAndWikis/wikka.php?wakka=StyleGuide.

Moulthrop, Stuart. "You Say You Want a Revolution? Hypertext and the Laws of Media." *Postmodern Culture* 1, no. 3, http://www.uv.es/~fores/programa/moulthrop_yousay.html.

Moxley, Joe. "The Teaching Wiki." University of South Florida. http://teachingwiki.org.

Moxley, Joe, M. C. Morgan, Matt Barton, and Donna Hanak. "For Teachers New to

Wikis." WritingWiki.org. http://writingwiki.org/default.aspx/Writingwiki/ For%20 Teachers%20New%20to%20wikis.html.

Murray, Donald M. *Learning by Teaching: Selected Articles on Writing and Teaching.* Portsmouth, NH: Heinemann/Boyton-Cook, 1982.

Nature. "Internet Encyclopaedias Go Head to Head." *Nature,* December 22, 2005, 438, 900–901. Online access to the *Nature* study begins at http://www.nature.com/nature/journal/v438/n7070/full/438900a.html.

Nelson, Theodor. *Literary Machines: The Report On, and of, Project Xanadu Concerning Word Processing, Electronic Publishing, Hypertext, Thinkertoys, Tomorrow's Iintellectual . . . Including Knowledge, Education and Freedom.* Sausalito, CA: Mindful Press, 1981.

Norman, Donald. *The Design of Everyday Things.* New York: Basic Books, 1988.

Nunan, David. *Collaborative Language Learning and Teaching.* New York: Cambridge University Press, 1992.

O'Donnell, James J. *Avatars of the Word: From Papyrus to Cyberspace.* Cambridge, MA: Harvard University Press, 1998.

Ong, Walter. *Orality and Literacy: The Technologizing of the Word.* London: Methuen, 1982.

Page, Susan. "Author of False Wikipedia Biography Apologizes." *USA Today,* December 12, 2005, final ed.

Parsons, Paul. *Getting Published: The Acquisition Process at University Presses.* Knoxville: University of Tennessee Press, 1989.

PBwiki. http://pbwiki.com.

Pennsylvania State University. Epoche Wiki. http://epochewiki.pbwiki.com/.

Pennsylvania State University. Epoche Wiki:RhetoricAndComposition. http://wikiped agogy.schtuff.com/english_15_pedagogy_602_teachers_practicum 2006.

Phillipson, Mark. "Wide Open: Implementing a Class Wiki." Paper presented at the Columbia University Seminar on New Media Teaching and Learning, New York City, October 27, 2005.

Phillipson, Mark, and David Hamilton. "The Romantic Audience Project: A Wiki Experiment." Romantic Circles: Romantic Pedagogies Commons. http://www.rc.umd .edu/pedagogies/commons/innovations/rap/index.htm.

Pink, Daniel. "The Book Stops Here." *Wired* 13, no. 3 (March 2005). www.wired.com.

Plato. *Statesman.* Ed. and trans. C. J. Rowe. Warminster, UK: Aris and Phillips, 1995.

Poster, Mark. "Cyberdemocracy: The Internet and the Public Sphere." In *Virtual Politics: Identity and Community in Cyberspace,* ed. David Holmes, 212–28. Thousand Oaks, CA: Sage, 1997.

Poster, Mark. *The Mode of Information: Poststructuralism and Social Context.* Chicago: University of Chicago Press, 1990.

Poster, Mark. *The Second Media Age.* Cambridge: Polity, 1995.

Poster, Mark. *What's the Matter with the Internet?* Minneapolis: University of Minnesota Press, 2001.

Redd, Scott, and Brad Will. "this might be a wiki: The TMBG Database." http://www .tmbw.net/wiki/index.php/Main_Page.

Reynolds, Nedra, Bruce Herzberg, and Patricia Bizzell. *The Bedford Bibliography for Teachers of Writing,* 6th ed. Boston: Bedford St. Martin's Press, 2003. http://www.bedford stmartins.com/bb.

Rheingold, Howard. "Rheingold's Rants." July 4, 1998. http://www.rheingold.com/ rants/.

Rice, Rich, and Cheryl Ball. "Reading the Text; Remediating the Text." *Kairos* 10, no. 2 (spring 2006). http://english.ttu.edu/kairos/10.2/binder2.html?coverweb/riceball/index.html.

Rupley, Sebastian. "What's a Wiki? Even as Blogs—Web Logs Posted by Individuals—Proliferate, a Complementary Form of Online Collaborative Communication Is Taking Off: Wikis." *PC Magazine*, June 20, 2003, 23.

San Diego State University. "EdGamesF03." http://www.edwiki.org/edgames/pmwiki.php?n=EdGames.EdGamesF03.

Sanger, Larry. "Why Wikipedia Must Jettison Its Anti-Elitism." http://www.kuro5hin.org/story/2004/12/30/142458/25.

Scardamalia, Marlene. "CSILE/Knowledge Forum®." In *Education and Technology: An Encyclopedia*, 183–92. Santa Barbara: ABC-CLIO, 2004. http://ikit.org/fulltext/CSILE_KF.pdf.

Scardamali, Marelene, and Carl Bereiter. "Computer Support for Knowledge-Building Communities." *Journal of the Learning Sciences* 3, no. 3 (1994): 265–83. http://carbon.cudenver.edu/~bwilson/building.html.

Scardamali, Marelene, and Carl Bereiter. "Higher Levels of Agency for Children in Knowledge Building: A Challenge for the Design of New Knowledge Media." *Journal of the Learning Sciences* 1, no. 1 (1991): 37–68.

Seed Wiki. 8th Fold Consulting. http://www.seedwiki.com.

Seigenthaler, John. "A False Wikipedia 'Biography.'" *USA Today*, November 30, 2005, final ed.

Selfe, Cynthia. *Technology and Literacy in the Twenty-First Century: The Importance of Paying Attention.* Carbondale: Southern Illinois University Press, 1999.

Skidmore College. "Delta: Final Thoughts—SkidmoreGreekTragedy." http://academics.skidmore.edu/wikis/Greek_Tragedy/index.php/Delta:_Final_Thoughts.

Skidmore College. "NorthWoods." http://academics.skidmore.edu/wikis/NorthWoods/index.php/Main_Page.

Skidmore College. "SaratogaCensus." http://academics.skidmore.edu/saratoga_census/wiki/index.php/Main_Page.

Skidmore College. "SkidmoreGreekTragedy." http://academics.skidmore.edu/wikis/Greek_Tragedy/index.php/Main_Page.

Smyth, Richard. "Students as Producers: Using the World Wide Web as Publishing House." Horizon. http://horizon.unc.edu/index.html.

Spolsky, Joel. "It's Not Just Usability." Joel on Software. September 6, 2004. http://www.joelonsoftware.com/articles/NotJustUsability.html.

Stanford University. "Digital Journalism In-Class Wiki Page." http://traumwerk.stanford.edu:3455/Rheingold/117.

Stone, Brad. "It's Like a Blog, But It's a Wiki." *Newsweek*, November 1, 2004, 34.

Stvilia, Besiki, Michael B. Twindale, Les Gasser, and Linda C. Smith. "Information Quality Discussions in Wikipedia." Technical Report. ISRN University of Illinois at Urbana-Champaign Information Sciences—2005/2+CSCW, 2005. http://mailer.fsu.edu/~bstvilia/papers/qualWiki.pdf.

Taylor, Chris, and Coco Masters. "It's a Wiki, Wiki World." *Time*, June 6, 2005, 40.

Thyer, Bruce. *Successful Publishing in Scholarly Journals.* Thousand Oaks, CA: Sage, 1994.

TiddlyWiki. UnaMesa Association. http://tiddlywiki.com.

Trimbur, John. "Consensus and Difference in Collaborative Learning." *College English* 51, no. 6 (1989).

Tufte, Edward R. *The Cognitive Style of Power Point: Pitching Out Corrupts Within.* 2d ed. Cheshire, CT: Graphics Press, 2006.

Tyler, Stephen A. "Post-Modern Ethnography: From Document of the Occult to Occult Document." In *Writing Culture: The Poetics and Politics of Ethnography*, ed. James Clifford and George E. Marcus, 122–40. Berkeley and Los Angeles: University of California Press, 1986.

Ulmer, Gregory L. "Textshop for an Experimental Humanities." In *Reorientations: Critical Theories and Pedagogies*, ed. Bruce Henrickson and Thais E. Morgan, 113–32. Urbana: University of Illinois Press, 1990.

University of British Columbia. "Teaching English Language Arts." http://wiki.elearn ing.ubc.ca/tela/HomePage.

University of British Columbia Office of Learning Technology. "Weblogs and Wikis." University of British Columbia. http://www.olt.ubc.ca/projects_home/pp.html.

University of Maryland, Baltimore County. "BIOL414/614 at UMBC—Projects." http://www.umbc.edu/bioclass/biol414/wiki/index.php?page=Projects.

University of Maryland, Baltimore County. "Eukaryotic Genetics and Molecular Biology." http://www.umbc.edu/bioclass/biol414/wiki/index.php?page=Home.

University System of Georgia. *Board of Regents Policy Manual.* http://www.usg.edu/re gents/policymanual/policyman.pdf.

Vasseur, Catherine. *L'Image sans mémoire.* Notebooks of the National Museum of Modern Art, spring 1996, 71–91.

Venners, Bill. "Exploring with Wiki: A Conversation with Ward Cunningham, Part I." *Artima Developer.* http://www.artima.com/intv/wiki.html.

Wales, Jimmy. "Letter from the Founder." Wikimedia Foundation, April 2005. http://wikimediafoundation.org/wiki/Founder_letter.

Walvoord, Barbara. Workshop presentation. Creighton University, spring 2000.

Weimer, Maryellen. *Learner-Centered Teaching: Five Key Changes to Practice.* San Francisco: Jossey-Bass, 2002.

Wenger, Etienne. *Communities of Practice: Learning, Meaning, and Identity.* Cambridge: Cambridge University Press, 1999.

Wenger, Etienne. "Communities of Practice: Learning as a Social System." *Systems Thinker*, June 1998. http://www.co-i-l.com/coil/knowledge-garden/cop/lss.shtml.

WikiFish Contributors. "Wiki Good Style." WikiFish. http://www.seedwiki.com/wiki/ wikifish/wiki_good_style?wpid=77845.

Wikipedia Contributors. "Five Pillars of *Wikipedia*." Wikipedia, the Free Encyclopedia. http://en.wikipedia.org/wiki/Wikipedia:Five_pillars.

Wikipedia Contributors. "Glossator." Wikipedia, the Free Encyclopedia. http://en.wikipedia.org/wiki/Glossator.

Wikipedia Contributors. "History of Wikipedia." Wikipedia, the Free Encyclopedia. http://en.wikipedia.org/wiki/History_of_Wikipedia.

Wikipedia Contributors. "List of Wiki Software." *Wikipedia: The Free Encyclopedia.* http://en.wikipedia.org/wiki/List_of_wiki_software.

Wikipedia Contributors. "Neutral Point of View." Wikipedia, the Free Encyclopedia. http://en.wikipedia.org/wiki/Wikipedia:Neutral_point_of_view.

Wikipedia Contributors. "Nupedia." Wikipedia, the Free Encyclopedia. http://en
    .wikipedia.org/wiki/Nupedia.
Wikipedia Contributors. "Refactoring." Wikipedia, the Free Encyclopedia.
    http://en.wikipedia.org/wiki/Refactoring.
Wikipedia Contributors. "Refactoring Talk Pages." Wikipedia, the Free Encyclopedia.
    http://en.wikipedia.org/wiki/Wikipedia:Refactoring_talk_pages.
Wikipedia Contributors. "Talk:Bosniaks." Wikipedia, the Free Encyclopedia.
    http://en.wikipedia.org/wiki/Talk:Bosniaks.
Wikipedia Contributors. "User: Nikola Smolenski." Wikipedia, the Free Encyclopedia.
    http://en.wikipedia.org/wiki/User:Nikola_Smolenski.
Wikipedia Contributors. "Wiki." Wikipedia, the Free Encyclopedia. http://en
    .wikipedia.org/wiki/Wiki.
Wikipedia Contributors. "Wikipedia Signpost 2006–06–05 Oversight." Wikipedia, the
    Free Encyclopedia. http://en.wikipedia.org/wiki/Wikipedia:Wikipedia_Signpost/
    2006–06–05/Oversight.
Wikitravel Contributors. "Policies and Guidelines." Wikitravel. http://wikitravel.org/
    en/Wikitravel:Policies_and_guidelines.
Winchester, Simon. *The Meaning of Everything: The Story of the Oxford English Dictionary.*
    New York: Oxford University Press, 2003.
Young, Jeffrey R. "Wikipedia Founder Discourages Academic Use of His Creation."
    Chronicle of Higher Education, June 12, 2006. http://chronicle.com/wiredcampus/arti
    cle/1328/wikipedia-founder-discourages-academic-use-of-his-creation.

Contributors

Matt Barton is an assistant professor of English at St. Cloud State University in St. Cloud, Minnesota, where he teaches undergraduate and graduate courses in composition, rhetoric, technology, and professional writing. He has published scholarly articles and book chapters on wikis, content management systems, blogs, video games, and virtual workplaces. He is the author of *Dungeons & Desktops*, a monograph on the history of computer role-playing games published by A. K. Peters Press.

Jonah Bossewitch is a PhD student in communications at Columbia's School of Journalism and is also a full-time technology architect at the Columbia Center for New Media Teaching and Learning. He has over a decade of experience as a professional software architect, designer, and developer. He is an active open source contributor whose technical interests include Linux, Python, content management, and social software. He graduated from Princeton University with a BA in philosophy and has an MA in communication and education from Teachers College, Columbia University.

D. A. Caeton is pursuing a PhD in the Cultural Studies Graduate Group at the University of California, Davis. His work is situated at the nexus between disability studies and technocultural studies, with an emphasis on the technologies of the body. Currently, his research explores the convergences of tactile information technologies with digital information technologies, as well as the ways by which bodies are choreographed through somanormative modes of discourse. Prior to his work at UCD, D. A. Caeton taught introductory composition courses at California State University, Fresno, and at Fresno City College.

Helen L. Chen is a research scientist at the Stanford Center for Innovations in Learning and a founding member of Electronic Portfolio Action and Communication International (EPAC), a community of practice focusing on pedagogical and technological issues related to electronic learning portfolios. Her current research focuses on the evaluation of ePortfolios and other social software tools to facilitate teaching, learning, and assessment for students, faculty, departments, and institutions.

Robert E. Cummings teaches writing at Columbus State University in Columbus, Georgia, as an assistant professor of English. In addition to coediting *Wiki Writing*, he will soon complete *Lazy Virtues: Teaching Writing in the Age of Wikipedia* (Vanderbilt University Press, 2008). Beyond researching electronic writing platforms, he works as CSU's director of first-year composition and serves as the program specialist of its Quality Enhancement Plan, a five-year Writing Across the Curriculum/Writing in the Disciplines effort to revitalize writing in the college's classrooms.

Jennifer deWinter is a PhD candidate in rhetoric, composition, and the teaching of English at the University of Arizona. She studies the global circulation of new media and the rhetorics of media convergence. Her pedagogical interests focus on the power relationships that computerized technologies introduce into the writing classroom, from computer games to wikis. She works closely with the Learning Games Initiative, a research consortium at the University of Arizona, to theorize the cultural and pedagogical impact of computer games.

Lisa Dusenberry is a PhD student in English at the University of Florida and an IT specialist for UF's Networked Writing Environment. Aside from teaching composition and technical writing, she helps instructors develop and implement pedagogies for networked classrooms. Her research focuses on the intersections between developing digital forms and children's literatures and cultures. She is especially interested in the play of power within texts and how it is reflected in their historical and material changes.

David Elfving is pursuing an MA from the University of Illinois at Chicago. His research focuses on social interactions through collaborative software. When not thinking about wikis, he works as a user experience designer in San Francisco, California.

Michael Felczak is a PhD student in the School of Communication at Simon Fraser University and the online editor at the *Canadian Journal of Communication*. He is also a researcher for the Public Knowledge Project, Centre for Policy Research on Science and Technology, and the Applied Communication Technology Lab at SFU. His research interests intersect technology with its social, political, and economic contexts and include Internet development and policy, free/open source software, and new media.

John Frankfurt is a project manager at the Columbia Center for New Media Teaching and Learning. He has worked with faculty at Columbia to implement wikis in classes ranging from architecture, political science, and creative writing to sustainable development. He is also an adjunct assistant professor at Columbia's School of the Arts and Hunter College's Department of Film and Media.

Dan Gilbert is an academic technology specialist at the Stanford Center for Innovations in Learning and a lecturer in the Stanford School of Education. He works on designing learning spaces and exploring the intersection of physical and virtual spaces.

Robin D. G. Kelley is a professor of history and American studies and ethnicity at the University of Southern California. His recent publications include *A Disjointed Search for the Will to Live* (2003); *Freedom Dreams: The Black Radical Imagination* (2002); *White Architects of Black Education: Ideology and Power in America, 1865–1954* (2001); *Ellen Gallagher: Preserve* (2001); and *Discourse on Colonialism* (2000).

Will Lakeman is an independent scholar living in England.

Cathlena Martin, a PhD candidate at the University of Florida, teaches professional communication at the University of Florida and communication arts at Samford University. She researches children's culture through literature, comics, film, and new media. Her dissertation work focuses on the intertextual nature of children's literature and culture in a digital age.

John W. Maxwell is a faculty member of the Master of Publishing Program at Simon Fraser University, where his focus is on the impact of digital technologies in the Canadian book and magazine industries. His PhD work (curriculum and instruction) focuses on the cultural trajectory of personal computing over the past three decades. John has worked in new media since the early 1990s, in Web design, content management, electronic publishing, learning technologies, and virtual community building. His current research interests include the history of computing and new media and contemporary myth making in the face of digital media.

Ben McCorkle is an assistant professor of English in the Rhetoric, Composition, and Literacy program at Ohio State University's Marion campus. His research interests involve the historical interplay between writing technologies and the rhetorical canon of delivery, and he is the founding editor of the wiki-based bibliography GlossaTechnologia.

Ericka Menchen-Trevino is a PhD student in the Media, Technology, and Society program in the School of Communication at Northwestern University. Her research interests include perceptions of privacy and the social aspects of information seeking on the Web.

Michael C. Morgan is a professor of English at Bemidji State University in Minnesota. He teaches courses in digital rhetoric, Web content writing, technical writing, and Weblogs and wikis.

Thomas J. Nelson is an assistant professor in the University College of Virginia Commonwealth University. He has written on technology and learning and twentieth-century American poetry.

Mark Phillipson is a senior program specialist at the Columbia Center for New Media Teaching and Learning and an adjunct assistant professor in the Department of English and Comparative Literature at Columbia. Previously, he taught at the University of California, Berkeley, where he earned a PhD in English, and at Bowdoin College. He also holds an MS from the Graduate School of Library and Information Science at Simmons College.

Jeremy Sabol is an academic technology specialist at Stanford's Center for Teaching and Learning and a lecturer in the Structured Liberal Education program. His work at the Center for Teaching and Learning centers around helping faculty and graduate student teaching assistants integrate technology into their teaching.

Alexander Sherman consults to the nonprofit sector, focusing on urban life and culture. With environmental, educational, and arts organizations, his consulting practice has included governance, fund-raising, finance, marketing, exhibit and experience design, and entrepreneurial initiatives. Applying collaborative and analytical methods, he has helped leading U.S. and U.K. organizations enhance the impact of their missions and improve the world.

Stephanie Vie is an assistant professor of composition and rhetoric in the Writing Program at Fort Lewis College, Durango, Colorado. Her current research focuses on the uses of online social networking spaces such as MySpace and Facebook in composition pedagogy.

Bob Whipple holds the A. F. Jacobson Chair in Communication at Creighton University. He writes on cognitive and administrative issues in multimediated composition and teaches literacy and technology, workplace writing, and first-year writing.

Index